CLASS, STATE, AND INDUSTRIAL STRUCTURE

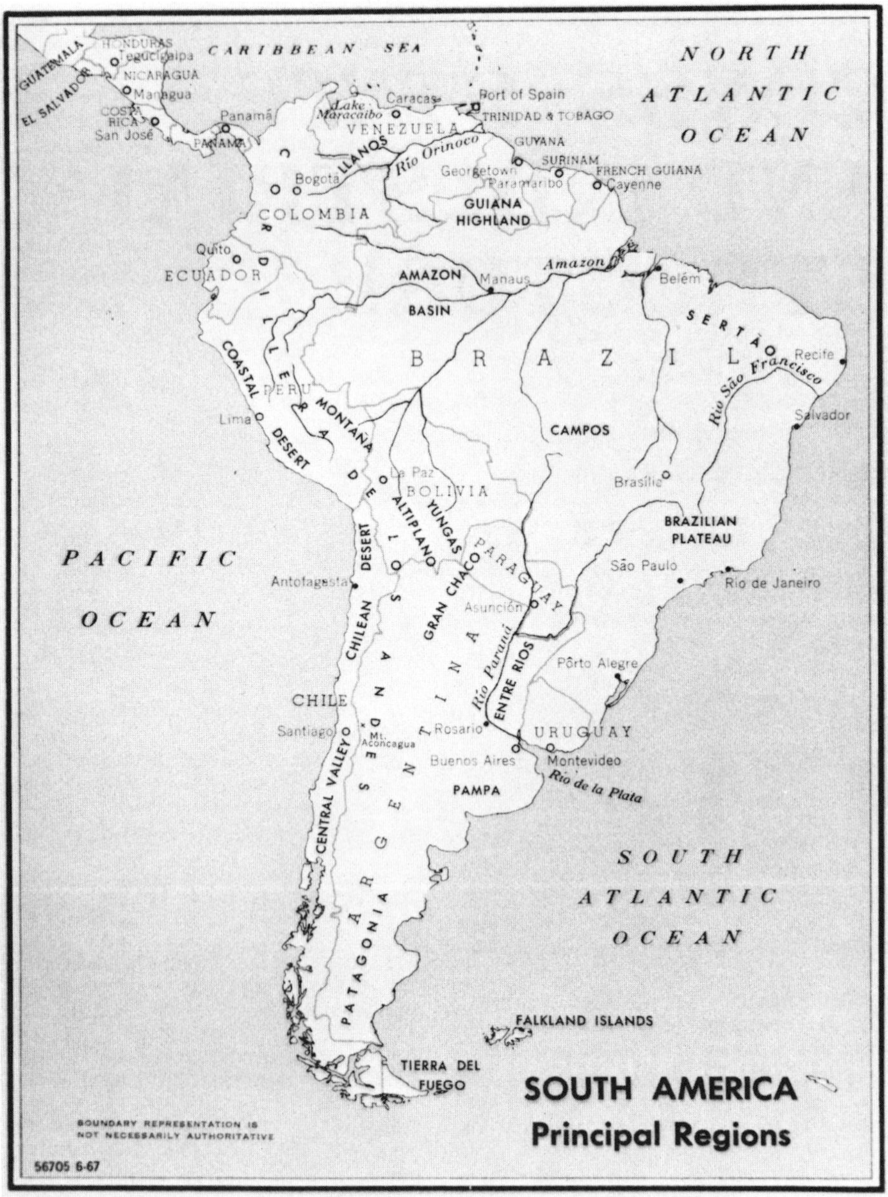

CARIBBEAN SEA
NORTH ATLANTIC OCEAN
GUATEMALA
HONDURAS
Tegucigalpa
EL SALVADOR
NICARAGUA
Managua
COSTA RICA
San José
PANAMA
Panamá
Lake Maracaibo
Caracas
Port of Spain
TRINIDAD & TOBAGO
VENEZUELA
LLANOS
Río Orinoco
GUYANA
SURINAM
FRENCH GUIANA
Georgetown
Paramaribo
Cayenne
Bogotá
COLOMBIA
GUIANA HIGHLAND
Quito
ECUADOR
AMAZON
BASIN
Manaus
Amazon
Belém
SERTÃO
Recife
BRAZIL
Río São Francisco
Salvador
CORDILLERA DE LOS ANDES
COASTAL DESERT
PERU
Lima
MONTAÑA
CAMPOS
La Paz
BOLIVIA
Brasília
ALTIPLANO
YUNGAS
BRAZILIAN PLATEAU
PACIFIC OCEAN
Antofagasta
DESERT
GRAN CHACO
PARAGUAY
São Paulo
Rio de Janeiro
Asunción
CHILEAN
ARGENTINA
Río Paraná
ENTRE RIOS
Pôrto Alegre
CHILE
Santiago
Mt. Aconcagua
Rosario
URUGUAY
Buenos Aires
Montevideo
CENTRAL VALLEY
PAMPA
Río de la Plata
SOUTH ATLANTIC OCEAN
PATAGONIA
FALKLAND ISLANDS
TIERRA DEL FUEGO
SOUTH AMERICA
Principal Regions
BOUNDARY REPRESENTATION IS NOT NECESSARILY AUTHORITATIVE
56705 6-67

CLASS, STATE, AND INDUSTRIAL STRUCTURE

The Historical Process of South American Industrial Growth

FREDERICK STIRTON WEAVER

Contributions in Economics and Economic History, Number 32

GREENWOOD PRESS
WESTPORT, CONNECTICUT • LONDON, ENGLAND

Library of Congress Cataloging in Publication Data

Weaver, Frederick Stirton.
Class, state, and industrial structure.

(Contributions in economics and economic history; no. 32 ISSN 0084-9235)
Bibliography: p.
Includes index.
1. South America–Industries–History. 2. South America–Economic conditions. 3. South America–Commerce–History. I. Title.
HC165.W35 338'.098 79-6571
ISBN 0-313-22114-6 lib. bdg.

Library of Congress Catalog Card Number: 79-6571
ISBN: 0-313-22114-6
ISSN: 0084-9235

First published in 1980

Greenwood Press
A division of Congressional Information Service, Inc.
88 Post Road West, Westport, Connecticut 06881

Printed in the United States of America

10 9 8 7 6 5 4 3 2 1

To my parents

CONTENTS

ILLUSTRATIONS

TABLES

PREFACE

The major purposes of this book are to explore the processes of economic change and stagnation in South America and to demonstrate how comparative history is a necessary analytical tool for understanding the character of and prospects for future economic growth. All too often in North American colleges and universities, history and economic development are still considered to be very distinct fields, taught in specialized courses by people in different academic departments. The history courses tend to teach the "facts," connected for the most part by the clock and calendar, while courses on economic development stress "analysis," represented as universalistic, value-free principles independent of time and place. In practice, of course, the historical facts are selected from a virtually infinite array according to what is deemed important, reflecting the criteria of some prior (but implicit) conceptual framework. On the other hand, economic analysis is in large part the historical product of English and North American capitalist development, and by generalizing from these experiences, it contains a definite ideological conception of what economic development is all about.

I am not purporting to write objective history, but I deliberately present my argument about the most productive connections between history and analysis in ways I hope will be conducive to the reader's appreciating its premises and its differences from predominant traditions in liberal and Marxist scholarship. Also with the reader in mind, I have attempted as much as possible to cite English-language works generally available in North American libraries. The citations suggest further reading on particular points as well as give corroboration, and I have chosen a form which intrudes least on the presentation.

Among the large numbers of colleagues, students, and other friends whose good advice, criticisms, and ideas have helped make this a better book, I am particularly grateful to Julia Coan Allen, Carollee Bengelsdorf, Ronald Berg, Robert Brenner, Herbert Gintis, Frank Holmquist, Miriam Slater, Stanley Warner, and especially Walter Goldfrank, Roberto Márquez, and Serena Arpenè Weaver. Articles which I have published in the *Journal of Inter-American Studies and World Affairs*, *Latin American Perspectives,* Occasional Paper Series of the University of Massachusetts Program of Latin American Studies, *Politics & Society, Science and Society,* and *Studies in Comparative International Development* over the last dozen years have also been an important means for me to develop my thinking about several of the issues dealt with in the book. Bobbie Belliveau, Susan Ingersoll, Rosalyn Reiser, and most importantly, Bette White were incredibly patient, cheerful, and efficient in typing and retyping the manuscript, and faculty grants from the University of California, Santa Cruz, and Hampshire College helped in tangible ways.

This book is part of an extensive debate on capitalist development, and I look forward to refining my ideas and questioning my conclusions as I continue to participate in that debate. As you read the book, therefore, I would very much appreciate your actively reflecting on the arguments and sending me any comments, questions, suggestions, and criticisms.

CLASS, STATE, AND INDUSTRIAL STRUCTURE

1

INTRODUCTION: MODELS, METHODS, AND HISTORICAL STUDY

The purpose of this book is to present an analytical, historical background for the study of contemporary problems of industrial growth in the major nations of South America. Drawing from their histories as well as from the histories of the more completely industrialized nations of Western Europe and North America, my intention is to show that the conditions and patterns of partial industrialization in South America are such that general models of economic growth are of only limited usefulness. To find the roots of current economic conditions in the nations, one must appreciate their particular historical experiences with industrial growth and place them in the context of worldwide capitalist development.[1]

In such an endeavor there is a variety of historiographical methods from which one may choose. The clearly ascendant, albeit still controversial, approach to economic history in the United States at present is the so-called new economic history or cliometrics. The defining characteristic of this method is the rigorous application of economic theory and modern statistical techniques to historical data, and its practitioners have made important contributions to a reinterpretation of United States economic history.[2] The success of the new economic history in studying United States economic growth, however, reflects the rather special circumstances of this nation's history, particularly that economic expansion occurred within a relatively stable set of liberal capitalist institutions that were "givens" in the history of the northern states as well as other nonslave societies founded by England, societies that were, in de Tocqueville's words, "born free" of a feudal heritage. These special circumstances of U.S. growth are vital for understanding the limited usefulness of the method of the new economic history as well as for appreciating its practioners' scorning of the importance of social and political change for industrial development.

Dimensions of social life beyond what is narrowly economic simply lie outside the analytical scope of new economic history, an incompleteness that corresponds to the limitations basic to orthodox economic theory on which it is based. In both the neoclassical (micro) theory of price formation and resource allocation and the Keynesian (macro) theory of aggregate economic performance, ignoring non-economic phenomena is appropriate for discussing commodity and exchange relationships. This body of theory, as a legitimate product of capitalist development, has obvious elements of capitalist ideology, but these are rather obvious and lie more in the structure of the theory's abstractions (that is, in what it chooses not to explain) than in the way in which the selected variables are related. In general, I believe that conventional economic theory offers logically rigorous prescriptions for efficiency in allocating productive resources and empirically validated descriptions of capitalist commodity and exchange relations.[3] The usefulness of central concepts from neoclassical economic theory for planning in the so-called socialist countries and the postwar employment of economics and economists by public and private institutions in the U.S. to sustain and manipulate capitalist relations are two examples of applications of conventional economics which, although strongly ideological (in the sense of Benton, 1977, pp. 170-199) are still useful in concrete ways.

Nevertheless, it must be recognized that economic theory's narrow focus, while necessary for its elegant precision, seriously constricts its scope of explanation. To understand the nature of economic growth in which wide-ranging social change is required to create a materially progressive economy, one must go more deeply than commodity and exchange relations. When economic theory is used as the central intellectual construct guiding such a study (for example, North and Thomas, 1971), its explanatory limits are conspicuous. To formulate a theory of historical and contemporary economic development from the few variables that conventional theory includes necessarily entails using, explicitly or not, one of the following types of assumptions about the institutions and culture in which economic aspects of social life are embedded: (1) the social structure that goes with liberal capitalism or else a powerful state insulated from social pressures (as in the case of the developmental planning literature) already exists, or (2) economic change will easily and automatically lead to accommodating changes in the social order. The first assumption is defensible in addressing U.S. or Soviet growth; the second might be valid for limited studies of British industrialization. But when applied to contemporary underdevelopment in South America, the theory's incompleteness is dangerously misleading.

In studying South America, North American economists have responded in different ways to the conceptual limits of orthodox theory. Development economists who respect the confines of conventional theory are limited to considering appropriately narrow problems like inflation and balance-of-payments deficits, or to construct increasingly sophisticated planning models, ignoring the social base of politics. On the other hand, a large number of economists recognize the need for a broader conception of the development process. But all too often their attempts to use conventional theory to relate national institutions and behavior patterns that do not correspond to nineteenth-century Britain or the contemporary U.S. to economic variables result in lists of "obstacles to development" and a serious loss of rigor and general applicability.[4] Although a large amount of important taxonomic, empirical, and planning material has been generated by these efforts, the inability to view more of other aspects of society from within the economy in a systematic manner jeopardizes conclusions about the relations between even purely economic variables. But further, it impedes judgment of the importance of a particular set of relations to the entire process of development, with the consequence that comprehensive treatment of such questions as the differences between and interdependence of contemporary and historical development and the origin and structural importance of the "obstacles" is made impossible. It is revealing that some of the more interesting attempts to open up the scope of economic theory for the purpose of studying economic development hark back to the old-time political economy of Adam Smith and David Ricardo, theorists who were grappling with contemporary processes of social and economic change in their own nation (for example, Lewis, 1954; Myint, 1958).

To return more specifically to economic history, probably the strongest tradition of organizing history for seeing underdevelopment and development in a unified historical framework has been that of defining successive stages through which all developing nations pass. The criteria for defining and distinguishing stages have varied: predominant economic sectors (List, Clark); length of exchange routes (Bücher); medium of exchange (Hildebrand); consumer goods/capital goods output proportions (Hoffman); and so on.[5] In spite of the specifically economic character of the indices, stage theorists have not found it difficult to include a large number of social and cultural variables in their work, whether they regard noneconomic factors as determining or determined by strictly economic phenomena. Leaving aside the well-documented empirical and interpretive flaws of particular writers' use of this approach, stage theorizing itself has important shortcomings as an organizing device for using history to understand Latin American underdevelopment. Inadequate theories of historical motion underlie most stage theories, frequently reducing the stages to a series of static categories related only by chronology and deductive logic. More important, general stage theories, like conventional economic theory, abstract in order to identify in developmental processes characteristics applicable to all times and places, and they consider any differences they observe among industrialization processes to be attributable to individual particularities of each nation's culture and history. This quality is inherent in the stages-of-growth method; the historical experience of the developed countries is the material from which the general propositions are distilled, thus precluding an understanding of contemporary underdevelopment as a distinct but interdependent historical process. Scholars in this tradition regard underdevelopment as simply a peculiar hanging on to non-European (frequently non-English) customs and institutions which again form a collection of "obstacles to development," obstacles essentially similar to those overcome by European and

North American economies. Stage theories thereby necessarily underemphasize the interdependence of national histories, in particular the strong influence of European and North American development on South America, and impede exploration of aspects that are important to understanding current problems.[6]

These difficulties in new economic history and stage theories have led me to draw from the fundamentals of Marxian theory for studying the processes of economic development, in spite of the fact that some of Marx's general pronouncements resemble those of a stage theorist. "In broad outlines, Asiatic, ancient, feudal and modern bourgeois modes of production can be distinguished as progressive [i.e., successive] epochs in the economic formation of society" (Marx, 1859, p. 329). That this was more than a mere division into periods is indicated by the often-quoted statement, "The country that is more developed industrially only shows, to the less developed, the image of its own future" (Marx, 1867, pp. 8-9). In spite of the seemingly mechanical rigidity of these statements, Marx's own historical work was not confined by these categories (see, for example, Marx, 1848; 1852; and 1857-1858). Nevertheless, even if one were to consider Marx to be a stage theorist in the same manner as Bücher and Hildebrand, there is a vital difference: Marx's criteria for defining particular stages flow directly from a theory of historical change designed to explain the movements from one stage to another. I consider this theory, freed from the concept of stages of growth, to be the useful element of Marx's work.

As a background to Marx's theory of social change, it is important to describe three fundamental principles of Marxian method. The first is that important elements social life cannot be isolated for analytical purposes from the whole without causing major distortion. The economy, social structure, politics, and ideology, for example, do not have any meaningful existence independent from each other. Only the continuous interrelations among them give definition to any one of these aspects of social life.[7] The second crucial feature of Marxian method that distinguishes it from liberal analysis is its conception that society is *made,* not given. Not only is it made, but it is constantly being remade by human action. There is thus little point to lengthy discourses on social statics and states of equilibrium. The appropriate analytical approach is to identify through historical study the major forces in society as processes, not "facts." The third general tenet is that technical and social relations of production are the major sources of economic and social change, and they must be regarded as being prior to any consideration of market exchange and commodity relations. These social relationships are themselves processes; they are continually constructed and reconstructed through the struggle between those who benefit from current patterns of hierarchy, authority, status, and privilege, and others less favorably situated.

These three principles are extremely general, and more specific theoretical guides are necessary for studying social change. The principal interwoven components of Marxian theory at the more specific level are historical materialism, the labor theory of value, and dialectical reasoning. Historical materialism is based on the idea that, fundamental to any capitalist society, workers own nothing but their capacity to labor. In order to live at even subsistence levels, they must sell that capacity to work (labor power) to capitalists who, as a class, monopolize the ownership of the means of production (buildings, machines, land, and so on). The resulting antagonistic relationship in production pervades all other dimensions of social life and sets limits on the range of feasible changes in such social structures as family organization, political institutions, and ideology. This historical materialism must not be confused with the ahistorical assumption about individual motivation which underlies orthodox economic theory, that is, "rationality"—the striving of individuals to maximize their material returns.[8] Nor should historical materialism be regarded as a mechanistic scheme of "base" determining "superstructure"; the connections among different spheres of social life are considerably more complex and interesting.

The unequal power relations between the working class and possessing class enable the latter to receive a generous portion of what workers produce merely through their ownership of property. This exploitive feature of capitalist organization is emphasized by defining as "value" the amount of human effort involved in producing useful commodities, including the portion of that effort that is embodied in machinery and scientific and technical skills. "Surplus value" is the amount of value extracted from the production process and accruing to propertied classes and the state through the exercise of coercion; hence, receiving surplus value does not imply a functionally valuable role in the production process but rather the wielding of power. This power relation among classes is the primary focus of the Marxian labor theory of value. Marx's value theory, therefore, must be clearly distinguished from a theory of prices. His use of value theory was consistent with Ricardo's in that he saw it as a way to delineate, in a society with considerable division of labor, the allocation of that principal productive resource—human labor power—but he went beyond Ricardo in employing it as a means to deal systematically with class relations, especially in regard to the creation, form, and use of surplus value (Desai, 1974). This application becomes difficult when studying any modern society, for clearly a simple two-class division is insufficiently refined to identify the major social forces or to understand the significant extent of differentiation and conflict within each class.

These problems will be discussed as they arise in later chapters, but the category of surplus value is still crucial at least as a starting point for such a study. The predominant means by which surplus value is appropriated from workers (for example, profits vs. taxes) is critically important for understanding the dynamics of a society. Even if virtually all surplus value is realized in private profits, we still need to know whether it is appropriated by large corporate bureaucracies dealing with a stable, organized work force or by entrepreneurs in small firms dealing with an atomized group of workers who have recently come to the city from the countryside. Moreover, surplus value represents the principal source of enlarging the society's productive capacities. While a certain amount of surplus value must always be used for social control (that is, keeping workers working for employers by means of police, army, and propaganda), if all of it is utilized for this purpose and for luxury consumption by the wealthy, the society will not progress materially no matter how much surplus value is appropriated. Marx believed that capitalism, as opposed to earlier modes of production (for example, feudalism), was inherently progressive in material terms, because market competition among those who appropriated surplus value forced them to use the bulk of it for expanding productive capacity and increasing the productivity of labor simply to maintain their advantageous economic and social positions. This activity was potentially beneficial to the working classes, for it increased the chances for higher wages if workers could exert sufficient pressure on employers. But even more important, Marx saw inherent contradictions in this process, contradictions which would lead to the destruction of the capitalist order and enable the establishment of a more humane social system. But capitalism no longer appears to be a necessarily progressive mode of production, and certainly Marx's expectations about the form of its demise have not been borne out. Subsequent chapters will show how Marx's method can be used to understand the historically changing character of capitalist development.

Apart from specific predictions, however, this well-known example of Marx's reasoning illustrates another important aspect of the Marxian method: dialectical thinking. The dialectical conception of social change insists that the mainspring of social change lies in conflicts and contradictions that are inherent in social organizations and that long-run stability demands explanation—equilibrium is not a natural condition. Institutions and relationships which may at one time have strengthened and sustained a social system continue to develop and change in ways that not only reduce their functional support of a social order but even become inimical to its continued existence. When joined to historical materialism (dialectical materialism), the principal sources of this undermining and negating process are changes in the social relations of production which become incompatible with other features of capitalist society. The dialectic need not have metaphysical nuances (Swingewood, 1975, pp. 11-32, passim); as a concrete conception of the form of social change, it stands in the same relationship to social theory as an "ideal of Natural Order" does to natural science theory (Toulmin, 1961, pp. 44-82).

Unlike the general principles of holism, historical process, and materialism in general, the more specific propositions of historical materialism, labor theory of value, and dialectical mechanisms can be considered methodologically as abstractions, or in the parlance of economic theory, as assumptions. Like the use of abstraction in conventional economic theory, they simplify reality in order to isolate the phenomena of particular interest. As such, of course, they are empirically vulnerable, but they should be judged according to whether or not they so seriously distort reality that conclusions based on them are not reliable.[9] The important difference of these propositions from conventional economic theory lies in the analytical purpose of such abstraction. Marx abstracted precisely in order to relate the economy to other dimensions of social life. The result is particularly appropriate for development economics because it enables a theory of social change to be incorporated into a theory of economic growth, thus establishing broader context and criteria for comparing different paths of national development. In that this side of Marx's work treats commodity and exchange relations only in a general, qualitative manner, it is a complement to orthodox theory, and a means for systematically grounding commodity and exchange relations in the broader systems of social relations. This is the point that was missed by an earlier generation of economic development textbooks which, unlike more recent ones, included a summary of Marxian theory within a brief intellectual history of growth-and-development theories. Invariably the authors emphasized Marx's "laws of motion" of advanced capitalism, such as the determination of factor shares and employment, business cycles, and eventual breakdown (see, for example, Adelman, 1961; Baldwin, 1966, pp. 29-33; Furtado, 1967, pp. 11-35; Higgins, 1968, pp. 76-87; and Okun and Richardson, 1961, pp. 70-83). To focus on the parts of his work that most resemble modern economic theory, as these textbooks do, is to miss the portions with the greatest potential contribution to development economics. Economic development for Marx was not the working out of the logic of capitalist relationships, but the very rise of capitalism in England, transforming a slowly growing, agricultural society into one in which rapid material progress flowed from liberal institutions.

To clarify further the use of Marxian theory in designing research about the process of industrialization, it is probably better to regard materialism, the labor theory of value, and the dialectic as *questions* central to understanding and comparing the operation of different societies rather than as component abstractions of a universalistic theory about how the world works.[10] This increases the method's flexibility; addressing these questions to different industrialization experiences, even with a variety of answers, becomes a vehicle for organizing diversity within a unified analytical framework focused on economic change and development, thus generating the basis for comparison and generalization. The Marxian method can thereby be wrested from the particular stages derived from its application to Western Europe, stages which have taken on a supra-historical life of their own and which still haunt the works of some students of Latin American affairs ("Is it feudal or is it capitalist?"), merely obscuring social and economic reality in that area.

These remarks on method, as brief as they are, still point in different directions from prominent trends in scholarship on Latin America by historians and especially by economists. They strongly indicate that class is the appropriate unit of analysis, and although I will apply it flexibly and with qualification, neither the individual nor the nation-state is a particularly useful unit for the purposes of this book. Closely related to this choice, the principal focus will be on internal social dynamics. In the nineteenth and twentieth centuries, foreign influences have continually and profoundly conditioned internal social and economic processes within the nations of South America, sometimes to the point that distinguishing external from internal is difficult. Nonetheless, the nineteenth- and twentieth-century histories of the South American nations are not merely passive and malleable with respect to foreign penetration. This book criticizes the propensity of much recent scholarship, especially that identified generally with "dependency theory" (see chapter 4), to underestimate the integrity and vitality of the national histories of South American nations by attributing a peculiar potency to international political and economic relations. These external influences are often represented as determinants of domestic patterns rather than as important elements of the context in which domestic social forces developed. To go back to the question concerning unit of analysis, these external effects do not bear on nations in some general sense, but on particular classes, groups, and sectors within nations. In the same vein, I do not personify nations ("Chile wanted . . ."; "Argentina needed . . ."); this device is an illusory identification of dominant classes' desires and requirements with that of society as a whole, thereby eliminating consideration of internal conflict and sources of social change.

The aim of this book is to interpret patterns of industrial growth in South America, and the most fruitful approach for understanding those patterns lies in focusing on class relations. As such, the book is not a treatise on technical economics of either the orthodox or Marxian tradition. Nor, in spite of the presence of several tables, is it an empirical study, because the fundamental problems in understanding South American industrial growth lie not in the quality and sufficiency of data but in the questions and categories applied to the data. Nevertheless, there are some technical aspects of industrial growth, especially the economic interdependencies within and among sectors, which must be explored, and input-output analysis is ideal for this purpose. Although input-output analysis is in essence no more than a special arrangement of economic data, that arrangement highlights the pattern of interrelatedness among productive units in a manner that other methods do not, and its identification of distinctive types of economic activity allows the easy integration of commodity relationships with broader analyses that emphasize technical and social relations of production.

Table 1.1 is a simplified version of the 1967 input-output table for the United States. Input-output data for 1967 are available for 367 product groups, but the summary table is sufficient for our purposes. In Table 1.1, all national economic activity is divided into nine product groups and arrayed along both the top and left side of the table. Before beginning a description of the input-output relations, however, the list of product groups in Table 1.1 offers a good opportunity to clarify the use of some key terms. Product groups 4 through 7 are of manufacturing, the essential core of the industrial sector which usually includes mining, construction, and transportation as well. Industrial growth refers principally to an expansion of manufacturing output, which historically has demonstrated a capacity for self-reinforcing growth of a type that has activated other economic activities in ways not apparent in mining, construction, and transportation. This does not mean that mining, construction, and transportation production will be ignored any more than agriculture and service activities will be, but they are not the center of attention. Terms such as "industrialized" and "industrially developed" are used interchangeably, and these expressions mean the purely quantitative phenomenon of industrial growth (principally propelled by manufacturing) having occurred to the extent that the sector is producing somewhere between 30 and 40 percent of total national output.[11] I eschew more multifaceted and qualitative definitions of industrialization, because other aspects of industrial development have changed in important ways over the last two hundred years. A very narrow definition of industrialization allows freer discussion of associated changes in the other realms of social and political life.

To begin exploring the properties of the input-output table, take as an example product group 4 (Food, textiles, wood, and miscellaneous manufacturers) on the left side of Table 1.1. Moving to the right along that row, we see that firms in this group sold \$4.1 billion of their output (for example, cloth grain bags) to agricultural firms for use as inputs in producing agricultural products. Moving on along the same row, the table shows that \$0.1 billion of group 4's output, including things like cloth air filters and safety belts, was sold as inputs to mining enterprises, \$6.3 billion of lumber and other products became inputs to construction firms, \$40.7 billion became inputs to manufacturing firms producing foods, textiles, wood, and miscellaneous manufactures (for example, cloth to shirtmakers), and so on through the nine product groups. The sum of group 4's output sold to other firms to be used as inputs (that is, intermediate products used for further production) was \$75.2 billion, shown as the subtotal. Just beyond the subtotal, the table shows that \$96.7 billion of group 4's output was sold directly to consumers (mostly processed food and apparel); \$5.9 billion was purchased by business firms as investment (or capital) goods, which refers to produced means of production that are inputs to further production but are not used up in a year (in the example of product group 4, a wooden chair to a barber shop, but more significantly, factory buildings from group 3 and dynamos and drill presses from group 7); \$4.7 billion sold abroad as exports; and \$4.5 billion bought by local, state, and federal governments. The last number in this row, \$187.3 billion, is the total output of product group 4.

Because the rows show the distribution of sales of intermediate products from firms in each product group to firms in other product groups and of "final" goods to final users, the columns are also interesting. Again using product group 4 as an example, but this time at the top of the table, the first nine numbers in the column under Foods, Textiles, Wood, and Miscellaneous Manufacturers represent product group 4's *purchases* of inputs from each product group. Below the nine product groups, we see that this group also purchased \$5.5 billion of imported intermediate goods, and in transforming its inputs into different kinds of products, this group's productive activity generated \$61.2 billion in income (value added). Most

TABLE 1.1
Input-Output Table for the United States, 1967
(billions of $ U.S.)

	Intermediate Markets										*Final Markets*				
	Product Groups														
	1	2	3	4	5	6	7	8	9	Sub-total	Consumption	Gross Private Domestic Investment	Net Exports	Govt. Purchases	Total Output
Product group 1	18.5	0.0	0.3	31.2	0.0	0.1	0.0	0.2	3.4	53.7	6.2	1.2	3.3	−1.3	63.1
Product group 2	0.1	1.2	0.9	0.1	15.0	5.8	0.1	0.0	0.4	23.4	0.1	0.5	0.8	0.1	24.9
Product group 3	0.6	0.6	0.0	0.6	1.5	1.2	0.5	1.8	9.0	17.8	0.0	54.3	0.0	31.2	103.3
Product group 4	4.1	0.1	6.3	40.7	0.1	4.1	5.2	3.5	10.8	75.2	96.7	6.2	4.7	4.5	187.3
Product group 5	1.4	0.7	2.1	1.6	9.5	6.3	1.5	6.2	6.3	35.6	24.1	0.5	0.8	3.3	64.3

Product group 6	3.1	1.2	25.0	49.5	1.4	24.9	33.4	16.4	18.3	173.8	31.3	4.2	6.3	5.7	211.3
Product group 7	0.4	0.8	0.7	1.9	10.5	6.4	44.5	2.3	5.7	68.0	26.7	46.2	11.5	30.8	183.2
Product group 8	4.1	0.7	10.8	10.3	2.5	11.9	7.2	11.4	15.8	74.7	120.8	8.1	6.5	6.1	216.2
Product group 9	5.2	3.8	7.8	11.2	8.4	17.9	11.6	34.0	56.5	156.4	182.2	0.1	2.3	13.9	354.9
Imports	1.1	2.2	0.1	5.5	1.2	7.2	3.8	2.3	3.2		9.9	0.6	−39.0	4.0	....
Value added	24.2	13.5	45.6	61.2	24.6	85.7	75.2	149.3	227.0		4.7	−1.8	4.5	81.7	795.4

SOURCE: U.S. Bureau of the Census, *Historical Statistics of the United States, Colonial Times to 1970* (Washington, D.C.: Government Printing Office, 1975), pp. 272-273.

NOTE: Product group 1: Agriculture, forestry, fishing
2: Mining
3: Construction
4: Food, tobacco, textile, wood, and miscellaneous manufactures
5: Petroleum and coal products; electricity, gas, and sanitary services

Product group 6: Paper, printing, publishing; chemical, rubber, plastics, leather, stone, clay, glass products; primary and fabricated metals
7: Machinery, equipment, and ordnance
8: Transportation and trade
9: Other services

of this income was distributed in the form of wages and salaries paid to employees in group 4 firms, but profits to owners and taxes to the state are other important components of value added.

When national economic activity is portrayed in this manner, it is clear that firms operate simultaneously in three markets: product markets, in which they sell their output to other firms, consumers, and so on; input markets, in which they buy goods and services from other firms; and labor markets. And through these different markets, the variety of ways in which different types of firms or groups of firms are connected to other productive activity can be gauged, although one must respect the limitations of the data and of the assumptions built into the table's design. The range of this variety can be shown even within the manufacturing product groups (4 through 7), which are connected to each other and to other sectors in significantly different ways. As an example from their product markets, over one half of the output of product group 4 was sold to domestic consumers, while over 80 percent of the sales of product group 6 were intermediate products used by other firms in their production. Manufacturing firms also draw their inputs differently, and a substantial increase in output from one group of firms will stimulate very different patterns of supplier responses, depending on the character of the product whose output originally expanded. Stimulating the production of inputs, known as "backward linkages," has several layers to it. For instance, looking at the column of inputs for product group 7 (Machinery and equipment), it might appear that the production of machinery and equipment was independent of agricultural inputs. But looking on down the column of necessary inputs for product group 7, then down the columns for each of those input-producing groups (particularly the columns of product groups 4 and 9, which sold \$5.2 billion and \$3.8 billion of their respective outputs to firms in group 7), we see that agricultural inputs did indeed play an indirect part, albeit a rather small one, in machinery and equipment production. This process of finding inputs can keep on being pushed backwards (although matrix algebra offers significant shortcuts in computation), and a table of direct and indirect requirements could be derived from the transaction figures of Table 1.1.

The major contribution of input-output analyses for a study of industrial growth, then, is to show how changes in one type of economic activity reverberate throughout the economy.[12] Even though actual input-output tables and techniques will be used very little in later chapters, they will provide a central framework for thinking about the implications of alternative compositions of industrial production.

Related to the manner in which various branches of industrial production demonstrate distinct patterns of interrelatedness, their production processes involve different technologies, amounts and proportions of productive factors, and enterprise scales. Without confronting the chicken-and-egg question about which governs the other—the technical conditions or the social relations of production—it is clear that one highly industrialized economy in which cotton textile production was predominant in the manufacturing sector would be a very different society from a second economy equally industrialized, in which steel, machinery, and chemicals predominated. These examples are not casually selected, for they illustrate the historically changing character of industrial development. This proposition, as has been intimated earlier, is the major organizing theme of the book: the character of capitalist industrial development has changed profoundly over the last two hundred years. Qualitative changes are evident in the product lines and production processes which have led industrial growth, in the social, political, and economic conditions necessary for materially successful industrialization, and in the very mechanisms of that growth. Thereby, the effect of industrial development on the social life of an industrializing nation also has significantly altered. While it is clear that there are some basic similarities in capitalist industrialization (for example, creation of a wage working class, urbanization, and so on), and that preindustrial social formations do significantly affect the process, I argue throughout, with some obvious debt to Leon Trotsky's idea of combined development (Trotsky, 1932, pp. 3-15, 463-470), that the technical and social conditions of capitalist industrial production have changed significantly over time and that these changes have meant that the political and ideological conditions required for sustained industrial growth accordingly have been different at different times. Moreover, changes in the social dynamics of industrialization have been of a regular, historically cumulative nature, and their recognition is crucial for a historical understanding of such processes. Thus, by looking at (1) the evolving character of preindustrial societies in conjunction with (2) the changing requirements and tensions of industrial development at different times (dual historical movements—two sets of moving targets, as it were), we can go beyond Trotsky and comprehend more systematically the sources for uneven patterns of material success and failure of nineteenth-century industrial growth throughout the world and use historical experiences more fruitfully for understanding current industrial growth in South America.

I see three principal phases in capitalist industrial development: the first beginning in the third quarter of the eighteenth century and lasting through the 1860s or 1870s; the second from the third quarter of the nineteenth century to roughly World War I, and the third from the 1920s to the present. These phases are not stages of industrial development through which some nations purportedly have passed and all others must yet pass to become industrialized; they are successive phases in the evolution of capitalist industrial production within already industrialized nations, an evolution which has continued to alter and redefine the character of industrial development for those nations that are currently *becoming* industrialized.

In line with a long tradition of scholarship on the evolution of capitalist production within industrialized nations, I will call these three chronological phases competitive, finance, and monopoly capitalism, respectively. While the labels and periods are consistent with those of Hilferding, Lenin, and more recent authors (for example, Baran and Sweezy, 1966; Levine, 1975), the content of my categories is somewhat different. Both competitive and monopoly capitalism explicitly refer to the organization of product markets, and finance capitalism stresses the role of banks in the circulation sphere. In contrast, the most important distinctions among the phases reside in the technical and social conditions of industrial production and in the industrial product mix which underlies them. The degree to which firms influence the markets in which they buy and sell commodities as well as institutional arrangements for financing production and distributing equity income (profits, interest, and rent) are definitely components of each phase, but I do not consider them to be the defining characteristics as have most scholars who have used them. Furthermore, my chief interest in these phases is the manner in which they conditioned the paths by which nations become or are becoming industrialized, rather than changes in already industrialized nations.

Nevertheless, these successive phases of industrial production must first be identified, and United States history illustrates them very well. As mentioned in the discussion of new economic history, the U.S. has had unusually flexible social and political institutions and an adaptable culture, and these qualities together with more than a century of materially successful industrial growth have meant that northern and western sections of the United States can be used as an archetype of capitalist industrialization. A consequence of this exceptional status, however, is that only very limited generalizations from U.S. history are warranted, and accordingly this excursion into U.S. history is merely descriptive, used to establish some key economic components of the periodization of industrial development.

THE PERIODIZATION OF CAPITALIST INDUSTRIAL GROWTH: THE UNITED STATES

In the first half of the nineteenth century, most products of U.S. factories were wage goods (goods that wage earners buy) for working-class families, a large proportion of which were linked to an unusually progressive agricultural sector. In the 1840s and 1850s, the beginning of large-scale immigration and use of mechanical power in production as well as in transportation (where it lowered transport costs and integrated regional and national markets), were major conditions leading to the expansion of industry. The production of such industrial commodities as cotton and wool textiles, shoes and other leather goods, processed foods and beverages, cast-iron stoves and utensils, and furniture were increasingly drawn into factories employing workers who were paid money wages and organized in interdependent divisions of labor, and utilizing power-assisted machinery. A few factories produced capital goods, and some consumer goods firms (for example, breweries) were large, but by the standards of even fifty years later, mid-nineteenth-century manufacturing produced predominantly wage goods in many small firms which bought and sold in competitive markets, used rudimentary, labor-intensive technologies and simple organizational forms, and made rather low-quality products. These are defining characteristics of competitive industrial capitalism. Most products for well-to-do consumers continued to be made under artisanal conditions (whether located in the United States or abroad) in which machinery and specialization of labor tasks were relatively unimportant.

Significant structural changes in manufacturing occurred in fifty years after the Civil War. Table 1.2 shows that the growth of consumer goods production lagged far behind that of producer goods (that is, intermediate and capital goods) such as steel (replacing iron), rubber, chemicals, glass, and machinery. In 1869 manufactured food, textiles, lumber and wood articles, and leather products (including shoes) still comprised almost half of total manufacturing output, but thirty years later, the output of these goods was only a little more than one fourth of total manufacturing value added. Intermediate and capital goods were not only displacing consumer goods as the quantitatively most important industrial commodities, but they were also undisputedly the leaders in technological and organizational innovation. Although quantitatively a small proportion of the producer goods branch of manufacturing, machine-tool firms (producing metal-working machines) were a key source of technological innovation. The machine-tool firms were small, and their high degree of custom production meant that their own production processes were rather labor-intensive and resembled those of crafts. But these firms were dependent on and contributed to the large-scale, machine-using production processes of other industrial branches (for example, steel and agricultural equipment). In general, especially compared to consumer goods firms, intermediate and capital goods production occurred in large, highly capitalized plants where by the beginning of the twentieth century, work tasks were carefully organized, specialized, and assisted by machinery. The figures in Table 1.2 show that primary power-producing capacity and capitalization among industrial product groups changed considerably more than the composition of output, indicating substantial differences in the way production was organized in intermediate and capital goods firms.[13]

These changes in the technical and social conditions of industrial production help to explain some key social and economic features of the late nineteenth and early twentieth centuries. The magnitude of the financial investment needed for establishing and operating, say, a steel mill on an economically feasible scale encouraged the growth of large investment banks and the use of corporate forms of business organization, thus making finance capitalism an appropriate designation for this phase. Increased scale and complexity of production and marketing led to greater divisions of labor and to the growth of bureaucratic hierarchies for managing and coordinating production and marketing. The emergence of large intermediate and capital goods forms directly increased the centralization of capital in the industrial sector, but the indirect centralizing effects for the economy as a whole were probably at least as important. The shift in the composition of industrial production stimulated backward-linked, large-scale mining and refining enterprises, furthered the development of nationwide transportation and financial systems, and both required and permitted the pervasiveness of complex business bureaucracies capable of managing many diverse operations. All these changes en-

TABLE 1.2
Changes in the Composition of U.S. Manufacturing
(% distributions)

	Value Added in Manufacturing		*Total Primary Power Capacity in Manufacturing (incl. purchases of electricity)*		*Total Capital Invested in Manufacturing*	
	1859	1899	1869	1919	1880	1919
Food, textiles, wood, leather, and associated products (excluding furniture)	46.9	28.6	73.3	34.2	52.4	33.7
Tobacco, apparel, and furniture	11.7	17.6	2.0	1.9	11.1	7.0
Subtotal	58.6	46.2	75.3	36.1	63.5	40.7
Paper, printing and publishing, chemicals, rubber, petroleum, stone-clay-glass, and primary metals	21.1	28.3	16.0	44.9	21.1	32.7
Fabricated metals, machinery, transport equipment, and instruments	16.6	21.5	7.6	18.4	13.5	24.6
Miscellaneous	3.7	3.9	(a)	(a)	1.7	1.7
Subtotal	41.4	53.7	23.6[b]	63.3[b]	36.5	59.0
Total	100.0	100.0	100.0	100.0	100.0	100.0

SOURCES: Value Added: Albert W. Niemi, "Structural and Labor Productivity Patterns in United States Manufacturing, 1838-1919," *Business History Review* 46 (Spring 1972): 71.
Power: Allen H. Fenichel, "Growth and Diffusion of Power in Manufacturing, 1838-1919," in Conference on Research in Income and Wealth, *Output, Employment, and Productivity in United States After 1800* (New York: National Bureau of Economic Research, 1966), pp. 472, 477-478.
Capital: Daniel Creamer, *Capital and Output Trends in Manufacturing Industries, 1880-1948*, NBER Occasional Paper no. 4 (New York: National Bureau of Economic Research, 1954), pp. 36-39.

NOTES: [a]Included in "Fabricated metals, etc."
[b]In the two years, Waterpower comprised 48.2% and 6.0%, respectively, of total power.

couraged mergers and centralization. The gathering of large numbers of industrial, mining, and transport workers together at one working site contributed to the formation of coherent and aggressive labor organizations which, together with some unions in crafts and in geographically concentrated or ethnically homogeneous work forces (for example, apparel) helped to offset, even if only in a slight degree and for a narrow stratum of workers, the tendency for the distribution of income to become skewed toward the capital-owning class. Moreover, the significant proportion of total industrial output in intermediate and capital goods which, relative to consumer goods, are subject to more volatile changes in demand, heightened the vulnerability of the industrial sector and the economy as a whole to cyclical fluctuations. The exercise of centralized economic power in key areas of the economy led to the demand by business groups and others for political intervention and regulation, and economic instability and capital-labor conflicts also paved the way for the growth of the central state in size and authority (Kolko, 1967; U.S. Department of Commerce, 1976, pp. 1102-1108).

Through these mechanisms, then, change in the composition of industrial production in the late nineteenth century contributed to (and was necessary for) new arrangements in social, political, and economic life. By the 1920s, however, another phase of capitalist industrial growth was emerging, a phase which in the context of the United States development appeared to be merely an extension of the technical and social conditions of producing intermediate and capital goods into the production of consumer goods. As such, the new phase—monopoly capitalism—was a matter of degree in U.S. history, but as chapter 7 will show, it has considerable importance in studying the comparative history of capitalist industrialization in general and the post-World War II patterns of South American industrial growth in particular.

Machine tool and chemical firms were the sources of innovations which radically altered the technical conditions of production in such consumer goods as processed foods (including milling and meat packing), cigarettes, shoes, pharmaceuticals, and cosmetics, and large, machine-using firms became predominant in these lines. Even more striking examples of the changes in the character of consumer goods production, however, were in new consumer goods, such as rayon, nylon, and plastic products, the whole range of electrical appliances and, of course, that symbol of United States consumer civilization, the automobile. For convenience and for the lack of a better name, I will include both the new consumer goods and the older ones in which production processes were transformed in a single category called modern consumer goods; these modern consumer goods were the most dynamic product lines of the mid-twentieth century, and their plant scale, organization of work, and market organization resemble more closely that of intermediate and capital goods firms in 1900 than of the leading consumer goods firms of the mid-nineteenth century. This argument, therefore, goes beyond that of the conventional "consumer durables revolution" of the twentieth century (as criticized by Vatter, 1967); the emphasis on the manner in which goods are produced means that the category of modern consumer goods includes not only consumer durables (for example, automobiles and household appliances) but also complementary goods like tires and fuels as well as nylon clothing, pharmaceuticals, and the whole range of previously mentioned articles that are produced in similar ways.

Table 1.3 shows these changes in the composition of consumer goods production. The first group of commodities is, roughly, technologically untransformed consumer goods, and the second group is modern consumer goods, as defined earlier. Table 1.3 understates the extent to which the production mix has changed, because items like nylon textiles, cigarettes, and plastic toys are included in the first consumer goods category even though the manner by which they are produced means that they should be in the second category. Added to the 1967 consumer goods totals are figures for governmental purchases broken down by the same categories (SAM missiles and the like are definitely modern consumer goods) in order to recognize more fully the changed composition of production and the importance of the state in supporting it.

The centrality of modern consumer goods to the economy as a whole is further underscored by looking more closely at the 1967 input-output table. For one important example, firms producing modern consumer goods (per Table 1.3) accounted for two thirds of the demand for primary metals and metal products ("direct and indirect requirements") in that year, and a casual perusal of the input-output table will show that significant proportions of virtually all sectors' production are derivative from consumers' and governments' demand for these types of goods (*Survey,* 1974, pp. 38-43, 50-55).

Modern consumer goods are the leading branches of twentieth-century industrial production, and together with the capital and intermediate goods which are closely linked to them, they constitute the most progressive and prosperous areas of industrial production. Transportation and communications, mining, and finance are other economic sectors in which prosperity is directly correlated with the similarity of their productive organization to that of modern consumer goods and with the closeness of their market ties. Government employment and some professions are also high-income occupations, and their fortunes are also dependent on the leading industrial branches, whether through tax revenues or derived demand linkages (increased demand for services brought on by higher incomes). In contrast, there are important branches of economic activity in which both employers and workers are considerably less well-off. Older types of consumer goods in which production processes have not been transformed (for example, cotton textiles), a large proportion of agricultural output, and many services are produced by small firms earning low rates of return on capital and employing (relative to value added) large numbers of low-paid workers. The capital intensity and technological progressiveness of the leading industrial firms sharply reduce their capacity to create new jobs, and the state and the passive low-wage private sectors are the major sources of new employment opportunities. The state actively promotes leading firms' profitability by making direct purchases and providing a range of services and subsidies in order to encourage general economic growth, and it engages in widespread welfare-type programs for those whom work does not adequately support. This second type of state activity expands market demand for modern consumer goods while it contributes to social peace (Averitt, 1962; Baumol, 1967; Braverman, 1974; Edwards, 1979; Gordon, 1972; O'Connor, 1973).

From U.S. history, then, these are the three phases of capitalist industrial growth whose identification is crucial to studying the manner in which nations become industrialized. This argument has yet to be made, however, and this is the role of chapter 2 which, using English, German, and Russian history, develops the social and political significance of the competitive and finance capitalist phases, a significance not easily discernable from U.S. history but germane for South America.

The third chapter shows how the social conditions of production (that is, how people were organized in production and how they related to each other) in colonial Latin America were regionally differentiated according to the predominant type of economic activity—mines, haciendas, plantations, ranches, and urban crafts—and how this affected the course of the Wars of Independence and subse-

TABLE 1.3
Industrial Consumer-Type Goods
(% value of final goods)

	1899	*1929*	*1967*			
			Consumer Purchases	Government Purchases		
				Federal	**State & Local**	**Total**
Group I goods[a]	68.2	53.2	42.6	0.6	0.4	43.6
Group II goods[b]	6.3	19.3	19.9	13.2	1.0	34.1

SOURCES: 1899 and 1929 from William H. Shaw, *Value of Commodity Output Since 1869* (New York: NBER, 1947), pp. 13-27, 30, 66, 213-234, 290, and U.S. Bureau of the Census, *Historical Statistics of the United States, Colonial Times to 1970,* pt. 2 (Washington, D.C.: Government Printing Office, 1975), pp. 699-702; 1967 from "The Input-Output Structure of the U.S. Economy: 1967," *Survey of Current Business* 54, no. 2 (February 1974): 34-43.

NOTES: [a]Manufactured food, tobacco, dry goods, clothing, footwear, household furnishings (including crockery, cutlery, draperies, etc.), jewelry, clocks and watches: these are Shaw's commodity categories no. 320, 322, 329-331, 335, 339, 340, and 342; input-output commodity categories no. 14-19, 22, 23, 34-42, and 64.

[b]Heating and cooking apparatuses, passenger and recreational vehicles (including accessories, tires, and manufactured fuel), electrical household appliances (including radios, phonographs, and televisions), pharmaceuticals, recreational and photographic equipment: Shaw's commodity categories no. 323, 325, 332, 333, 336-338, 345, 346, 348, and 349; input-output commodity categories no. 13, 27-29, 31, 32, 40, 53-56, 59, and 60-63.

quent political reconstruction. The framework developed in chapter 2 helps explain the lack of significant competitive industrial growth in early nineteenth-century Latin America. The fourth and fifth chapters consider the economic and political changes which occurred during the late nineteenth and early twentieth centuries. Chapter 4, dealing with the impact of foreign trade and investment in late nineteenth-century Latin America, argues that both liberal and quasi-Marxian scholarship have emphasized exchange relations and have thus been unable to offer satisfactory explanations for the diverse experiences of different nations within the international economy. This chapter amplifies the categories of backward, forward, and income-multiplier linkages by which the production of different commodities is related, in order to comprehend the character of the resulting social formations. Chapter 5 focuses specifically on the competitive capitalist forms of industrial growth derived from the most successful export economies. The influence that the technical and social conditions of production exerted on social and political processes and the inter-industry linkages among different production units continue to be the basic analytical tools in the last two chapters to explain the particular patterns of monopolistic capitalistic industrial growth in South America since 1930. Of particular importance in these chapters is the discussion of how and why South American industrial growth could proceed so far, especially in Argentina, Brazil, Chile, Colombia, and Uruguay, without generating the dynamism one would expect from reading both liberal and classical Marxist theories of capitalism. The eighth and last chapter is a short summary and amplification of some of the general issues of analysis raised in this first chapter.

NOTES

1. Supple (1963, pp. 24-48) and Kemp (1978) are reasonable discussions of the usefulness of economic history in studying economic development, although in the first, as in most such discussions, there is no mention of contemporary underdeveloped nations' histories. Cortes Conde and Stein (1977) is an excellent source for Latin American economic history.

2. Redlich (1965) and Stone (1977) are balanced views of the new economic history, McCloskey (1978) and North (1978) are recent surveys by insiders of the accomplishments and unfinished work in new economic history, and Fogel and Engerman (1975) has sparked some excellent critiques of that methodology. A common consequence of that methodology is organizing historical works along the lines of capital, labor, entrepreneurship, and the like. That is, new economic historians have a penchant for cutting the historical analysis and narrative into individual histories of the so-called factors of production, rather than focusing on their interactions. Davis, *et al.* (1972) and the most recent volume of *The Cambridge Economic History of Europe* (Vol. 7, 1978) are examples of this approach, for which Solow and Temin (1978) supply the rationale.

3. "The categories of bourgeois economy . . . are forms of thought expressing with social validity the conditions and relations of a definite, historically deter-

mined mode of production, viz., the production of commodities" (Marx, 1867, p. 76). He goes on to declare that the categories are, however, unsuited for historical study. Along the same lines, see Marx and Engels (1846, pp. 39-43) and Engels (1878, p. 134). But there are real dangers. The neoclassical theory of income distribution, for instance, is principally ideological, and even its internal consistency is doubtful. For a clear statement of its problems, centering around the role of capital (produced means of production), see Nell (1972 and 1972a). Harcourt (1972) is a meticulous survey of the debate for the initiated.

4. Hirschman (1965) offers cogent, historically based criticisms of the "obstacles to development" literature.

5. Hoselitz (1960) is a good survey of some of the most important stage theories. Rostow (1960) should also be mentioned for his influence on the language of development economics. Similar to stage theories in their insistence on similarities in industrial development are the cross-sectional studies—a form of instant history. Chenery and Syrquin (1975) is an example.

6. Bendix (1967) and Tipps (1973) make similar criticism of modernization theory, the sociological counterpart to stages of economic growth. Frank (1969) is a provocative, wide-ranging criticism of development sociology.

7. This is parallel to the status of the individual in Marxian theory. Liberal theory characteristically begins with the individual, and society is understood as simply a conglomeration of independent individuals. Contract theory in politics and consumer demand theory in economics are particularly good examples. Marxian theory, while preserving an important place for individual action, insists that individuals cannot be intelligently defined for purposes of social analysis without a prior understanding of society. For clear discussions of Marxian method and its differences from liberal approaches, see McMurty (1978) and Swingewood (1975).

8. Rostow (1960, pp. 148-149) and Meier (1964, pp. 23-24; and 1970, pp. 92-93) make the egregious error of misinterpreting historical materialism in this manner. Dobb (1955) and Ashcraft (1972) are excellent discussions of historical materialism.

9. Sweezy (1964, pp. 11-19) and Swingewood (1975) intelligently discuss Marx's use of abstraction. I am not advocating a predictionist standard for selecting theories and testing assumptions as Friedman (1966) does; Toulmin (1961, pp. 18-43) demonstrates the serious problems underlying the predictionist approach.

10. Engels clearly supported this approach when he wrote, "The materialist conception of history has a lot of them ["dangerous friends"] nowadays, to whom it serves as an excuse for *not* studying history. . . . But our conception of history is above all a guide to study, not a lever of construction. . . . All history must be studied afresh" (Engels, 1890, pp. 486-487). Genovese (1968) is a scathing criticism of mechanical uses of historical materialism, and Marcuse (1967, particularly pp. 220-257) is a good example of using the dialectic as a guide rather than as a substitute for social analysis.

11. Sutcliffe (1971) surveys these definitional and classification problems. His book is one of the most complete and useful textbooks on the economics of Third World industrial development.

12. Miernyk (1965) and Yan (1969) are introductory textbooks on input-out-

put economics. Hirschman (1978) and Yotopoulos and Nugent (1976) incorporate input-output analysis into their studies of economic development.

13. The shift in the composition of industrial production, along with some of its implications, is described in virtually all U.S. economic history textbooks. For perhaps the most respected (*not* for pedagogical reasons), see the one written by Lance Davis and an all-star cast of new economic historians (Davis, *et al.,* 1972, pp. 419-453). Chandler (1977, pp. 240-376; and 1978) are far richer in scope and detail, relating changes in industrial output to changes in technique, firm organization, and market power. Wolman (1924, pp. 110-118) shows that the pattern of union growth in the late nineteenth century is consistent with the pattern I mention in the text, and Nutter and Einhorn (1969, p. 132) present useful data on industrial organization around the turn of the twentieth century. North (1965), Dowd (1974), Vatter (1978), Ames and Rosenberg (1965), Rosenberg (1963 and 1963a) are also good on various aspects of the economic changes in late nineteenth-century United States.

2

THE DYNAMICS OF CAPITALIST INDUSTRIAL DEVELOPMENT, 1750-1914

Nineteenth-century industrial growth in England, Germany, and Russia illustrates the significant differences between competitive and finance capitalist development and the manner in which their respective pre-industrial societies affected the prospects of large-scale industrialization. This is the principal reason for a chapter on European economic history in a book on South America, but there are two other, closely related reasons. It is necessary to understand the ways in which the changing nature of economic growth in Europe affected those economies' need to draw support from what became the peripheral areas—peripheral to the European core of a world economy whose basis was laid in the sixteenth century. That is, the extent and quality of European, and, later, U.S. economic penetration of Latin America reflected the degree to which their domestic forces of production were developed, and thus the range of external influences on Latin America must be set in this type of historical perspective to be comprehended.

The second reason for including a substantial chapter on European economic history is that our conceptions of the industrialization processes are rooted in these past achievements, and it is therefore helpful to survey the processes of European industrialization in order to determine how much and in what ways the abstract analytical frameworks distilled from these historical experiences can contribute to a study of South American industrial growth.

ENGLAND: COMPETITIVE CAPITALIST INDUSTRIALIZATION

The place of England in the seventeenth- and eighteenth-century world economic system was without doubt one of the necessary conditions for subsequent industrial growth. But the primary contribution of English colonialism and international commerce was not that the resulting profits financed industrial development nor that these international economic and political arrangements were a major determinant of the domestic conditions underlying the first industrial revolution. By the early eighteenth century, the English had established a complex web of multilateral trade relations in which the West Indian slave plantations played a major role. Phyllis Deane (1967, p. 53) describes the eighteenth-century trade patterns—the "triangular trade"—as follows:

> Weapons, hardware, spirits from Britain and calicos from India were shipped to West Africa and exchanged for slaves, ivory, and gold. The slaves were sold in the West Indies for sugar, dye stuffs, mahogany, log wood, tobacco, and raw cotton. The gold and ivory was shipped to the East and Near East for teas, silks, calicos, coffee, and spices. The tropical goods were sold in Europe for Baltic timber, hemp, pitch, and tar (all essential naval stores), and Swedish and Russian iron.

The availability of the northern European raw materials through sales of tropical produce was especially important, because the decline of export markets for English woolens threatened the ability to finance these needed imports. Another multilateral trade system was through the English North American colonies which sold food, lumber, and horses to the Caribbean, raw materials (including cotton and tobacco) to England, and with the proceeds bought a whole range of English manufactured goods, particularly iron products. In both trading networks, the slave-produced tropical goods of the Caribbean were an essential link, and together with the legal and illegal trade with Spanish and Portuguese colonies in the Americas, they were the basis of substantial mercantile fortunes and stimulated the growth of British shipbuilding and auxiliary industries (Davis, 1973). From the list of commodities entering this trade, however, it is clear that by the eighteenth century England had already developed beyond "pure mercantilism," in which foreign trade and colonialism were chiefly a means to earn commercial profits for merchants and fiscal revenues for monarchs. English exports by this time were becoming increasingly important markets for growing English industries and sources of financing imports vital for these productive activities.

The secondary role played by financial returns from colonies in general English industrial growth is underscored by contrasting English, Spanish, and Dutch experiences. In terms of net monetary receipts, English public and private income receivers probably garnered only a small proportion of what the Spanish did from their own colonies, but Spain demonstrated little progressive economic change in consequence. In fact, the specie flowing from the New World into the royal treasury probably retarded the internal social changes necessary for the emergence of capitalist relations and economic growth at this time. The fiscal revenues derived from the New World mines neither created new domestic classes nor strengthened existing ones in Spain, but they did strengthen the Spanish central state to the point where it could not be successfully challenged by any domestic forces. Even the powerful Spanish sheep interests and merchant guilds relied on royal support and franchise. This political position enabled the Spanish king to use large portions of the revenues from the New World to sustain a rigid aristocratic system and to finance the defense of Catholic Europe from the Ottomans in the east and, less successfully, from the Protestant Reformation in the north. These activities were not conducive to the rise of a vigorous industrial capitalism, and this lack of internal economic dynamism accounts for the indifference by Spanish authorities to New World markets for Spanish industrial products and to New World sources of raw materials for domestic industry.

The point here is that Spanish experience demonstrates that monetary wealth derived from colonies, in and of itself, is totally insufficient for explaining English industrial growth. Beyond this, the example of Holland shows that even when the returns from an empire were realized in the form of mercantile profits, as opposed to fiscal (government) revenues, the emergence of industrial capitalism requires a deeper understanding of the process than is available through an emphasis on monetary resources derived from colonial trade (Wilson, 1967).

This perspective does not dismiss the roles of commerce and mercantile wealth in helping to dissolve precapitalist social relations, or of colonial trade in making the acquisition of vital raw materials possible, but rather it insists that changing social relations of production within England occupy the center of the analysis. This means focusing on such factors as the relative openness of pre-industrial English society, the opoortunities for social and occupational mobility, the technical and organizational changes in English agriculture leading to enclosures in the eighteenth century, and the predominance of wage labor in agriculture.[1] It was these internal social processes which most sharply distinguished seventeenth- and eighteenth-century England from other areas and should be the center of attention; England's possession of lucrative colonies and the consequent amassing of mercantile fortunes would, in the absence of appropriate social conditions, have stimulated little in the way of economic dynamism. The relative weakness of feudal bonds and central political controls restricting individual mobility was of critical importance to England's becoming the world's first industrial economy, because the process of competitive capitalist industrial development depended on private individual initiative and included large proportions of the population in widely varying capacities.

In sharp contrast to later types of industrializations, English competitive industrial capitalism emanated in large part from the countryside. Changes in the organization and productivity of English agriculture were vital to the initiation of industrial growth and the support of its continuation. Beginning about 1700, a series of new agricultural methods was introduced (principally from the intensive agriculture of Flanders), and these new cultivation methods profoundly affected English agricultural production and rural life. Among the most prominent of these innovations were new crops and new implements (for example, turnips and the scythe), reducing the amount of land in fallow. Also, new land was brought into cultivation by draining marshes. The consequent increase in agricultural yields (per acre) and productivity (per unit of labor time) is best illustrated by the fact that English agricultural exports grew rapidly through the first half of the eighteenth century, offsetting the declining capacity of West Indian sugar to earn the foreign exchange needed to purchase imports of such materials as iron and raw cotton. Cereal exports in the seventeenth century were insignificant, but by 1750, cereal exports from England were around 200,000 tons—about 13 percent of domestic consumption—with no decline in per capita domestic consumption by a growing population and no reduction—indeed frequent increases—in output of other crops. This increased agricultural production both encouraged and required organizational changes.

Although the English Civil War in the seventeenth century neutralized monarchical opposition to the political consequences of capitalist agriculture, it has been estimated that about one half of the arable land was still being cultivated in the open-field system in 1700. The open-field lands had survived two hundred years of encroachments by large landowners and of disintegration into small properties held and worked by individual families, but the eighteenth-century enclosures rapidly changed social organization in the countryside. The nominal intent of these enclosures, frequently effected by acts of Parliament, was the consolidation of scattered landholdings into more coherent and economically efficient plots with formal titles of ownership, but consistently they resulted in redistribution of land into larger holdings at the expense of the small-holding yeomen. The frequency with which small holders' possession was based on tradition rather than legal title, the costs of required hedging and ditching, the loss of common pastures and woods for grazing, gathering fuel, and hunting, and outright cheating by surveyors in reparceling plots by their size and quality left most small holders with insufficient land even for subsistence. Whether or not the number of small freeholders declined drastically in the late eighteenth century, there was no doubt that by the 1820s and 1830s, the English yeomanry had virtually disappeared, and the English countryside was characterized by large landholdings worked by landless wage laborers.

The point to emphasize in studying enclosures is the transformation of land into private property and agricultural labor into "free" wage labor. As succinctly described by Marx (1857-1858, p. 507), the enclosures made workers

> free in a double sense, free from the old relationships of clientship, bondage and servitude, and secondly free of all belongings and possessions, and of every objective material form of being, *free of all property;* dependent on the sale of its labor capacity or on begging, vagabondage and robbery as its only source of income. It is a matter of historic record that they tried the latter first, but were driven off this road by the gallows, stocks and whippings, onto the narrow path to the labor market. [Italics in original]

The exchange aspects of this freedom are emphasized by celebrants of the process, who, by ignoring the unequal property basis of the wage-labor system, misrepresent its fundamentally coercive character.

But contrary to earlier opinions, this reduction of rural laborers to wage labor did not in itself drive people from the countryside. It appears now that the heightened agricultural activity actually increased employment opportunities in the countryside (although not necessarily at higher levels of material welfare), and the absolute numbers of people employed in English agriculture did not decline until the second half of the nineteenth century. Nonetheless, the vigorous growth of English population that began in the third and fourth decades of the eighteenth century, in the context of heightened occupational and geographical mobility engendered by the wage-labor system, supplied the labor power used by merchants who, to avoid the power of urban guilds, turned increasingly to rural workers. The cottage industries, or putting-out system, that developed was an arrangement by which merchants supplied raw materials to workers who, for example, spun or wove them in their own homes. The major problem of this system from the viewpoint of the merchants, however, was the extremely indirect control that they were able to exercise over the workers. The response to this was to bring cottage workers together into sheds where they could be more closely supervised and their ability to buy the raw materials and sell the product independent of the merchant was sharply reduced. These rude sheds were the forerunners of the nineteenth-century mills and factories; although the factory form had appeared much earlier in some specialized production (for example, cannons, munitions, and shipbuilding), eighteenth-century textile production led the general development of this organizational device. In these early carding, spinning, and weaving mills, there was little division of labor or integration of coordinated work tasks, and for the most part, people simply worked alongside each other under the eye of a foreman, and neither their organization of work nor their tools were much different from what they had been in their cottages. As a consequence, the increased technical efficiency of these early factory arrangements was doubtful, and their advantage to the merchant/entrepreneur was simply the increased control over, and dependence of, the laborers. This organization of production was soon confirmed by the development of water-powered machines and equipment which, through the division of jobs, facilitated supervision, increased worker dependence, made feasible the employment of children in more tasks, and, at some point, even raised labor productivity. By the time the steam engine enabled these rural factories to move away from the streams which had supplied their power, the surplus population followed them to the cities where, together with the Irish, ruined artisans, and the urban poor, they supplied the massive urban proletariat required for accelerated competitive capitalist industrial expansion (Deane and Cole, 1969, pp. 108-109).

These labor-supply conditions in the last quarter of the eighteenth century enabled industrial employment to proceed with little upward pressure on wages, temporary bottlenecks aside. There has been a continuing controversy over late eighteenth- and early nineteenth-century urban workers' standard of living, and the narrow terms of this controversy have tended to obscure the central fact that the pressures of numbers of workers on the supply side held down real wages (for example, Hobsbawm and Hartwell, 1963); whether the real income of the working class between 1780 and 1830 declined slightly, increased slightly, or held constant, it is probably more accurate to regard industrial capitalism as a product rather than the cause of the human misery of the period.

The merchants' effort to preserve and extend their control over industrial production through centralizing production in nascent factories was a failure; although the factory form of industrial production with its attendant hierarchical organization of the process of production did prevail, its control passed from the hands of merchants as a class to a mixed group who became England's industrial bourgeoisie. Recent research has shown the minimal role of merchants' capital in financing industrial enterprises. In late eighteenth- and early nineteenth-century England, the technical conditions of cotton textile production and iron working allowed small production units to be economically viable. A large number of small units came to characterize the organization of these wage goods firms which, as Table 2.1 shows, constituted the most dynamic core of early industrial growth.

Not only were these firms small, but their rudimentary, labor-intensive technologies of production meant that fixed capital requirements for establishing a factory were small. This conclusion is drawn from direct studies of individual firms; its accuracy as a generalization is supported by Table 2.2, which shows that even in 1851 the productivity of industrial workers was lower than that for agricultural workers. Not only were the financial barriers to setting up a new firm low, but the financing needed was not principally for expensive plant and equipment with long pay-back periods but rather for wages and inventories, outlays which could be recouped much more quickly. These short-term credit needs were met through informal borrowing and lending networks and through credit instruments (for example, letters of credit— developed for mercantile purposes. Once a firm was operating, reinvestment of profits was the major source of financing expansion. The most important qualities for successful entrepreneurship were the ability to deal competently with the vagaries of competitive input and product markets and, perhaps most important, to organize and control a work force in a factory setting. The low financial barriers to entry into factory production and the lack of formal education or even of craft experience for successful industrial entrepreneurship meant that industrial entrepreneurs could be drawn from a wide range of backgrounds. Although the majority of industrial entrepreneurs were from the middle and lower middle strata of English society, there are numerous examples of successful factories being established and operated by people of humble origins. At this time, industrial entrepreneurship was a vehicle for significant social mobility.

TABLE 2.1
The Structure of Early British Industrial Growth

	Index Numbers		*% National Income*	*% Manufacturing, Mining, Building*	
	National Income	Manufacturing, Mining, Building	Manufacturing, Mining, Building	Textile Industry	Iron Industry
1770	100	100	24.0	37.5	n.a.
1821	285	380	34.3	43.9	10.6

SOURCES: B. R. Mitchell, "Statistical Appendix, 1700-1914," in C. Cipolla (ed.), *The Fontana Economic History of Europe*, v. 4, *The Emergence of Industrial Societies*, pt. 2, p. 768; P. Deane and W. A. Cole, *British Economic Growth, 1688-1959* (Cambridge: Cambridge University Press, 1969), pp. 156, 166, 212, 225.

TABLE 2.2
Relative Labor Productivity in Agriculture and Industry, United Kingdom

	% Total Production in Sector Divided By % Total Employment in Sector	
	Agriculture, Forestry, Fishing	Manufacturing, Mining, Construction
1801	0.905	0.788
1851	0.935	0.800

SOURCE: Simon Kuznets, *Modern Economic Growth: Rate, Structure, and Spread* (New Haven, Conn.: Yale University Press, 1966), p. 236.

In the early nineteenth century, England's industrial leadership gave it a unique advantage in the world's markets. England's competitive advantage in industrial production underlay Englishmen's vigorous promotion of the self-serving theory of comparative advantage which argued (in static terms) that the removal of all national trade barriers and the development of an international division of labor (with England specializing in the production of industrial goods) would benefit all participating nations (Semmel, 1970). The logic of the argument, the energetic salesmanship of English ambassadors and commercial attachés, the narrow self-interest of agrarian and commercial elites in areas like the newly independent nations of Latin America (discussed in chapter 3), and the formidable power of the British navy led to widespread acceptance of this radical doctrine. (The United States, despite pressure from Southern planters, maintained and even raised its tariff walls.) This mid-nineteenth-century English policy has been aptly dubbed "free trade imperialism," and as Table 2.3 shows, throughout the four or five decades after the end of the Napoleonic Wars (1815), well over half of English cotton textiles and substantial portions of other key industrial products were exported in exchange for imports of raw materials and foodstuffs.

The importance of foreign markets for English industrial goods is well documented and forms part of our conventional wisdom, but too often it obscures the critical importance of home markets. Table 2.3 also shows that nineteenth-century export successes were a consequence of the development of industries initially oriented principally to domestic markets, and the ability of home markets to support early industrial growth was necessary for later efforts to create markets on a global scale.

To understand the development of domestic markets for factory-produced wage goods in the late eighteenth and early nineteenth centuries, we have to look again at the English countryside. As we have seen, eighteenth-century agricultural growth increased agricultural employment, and as a result of the enclosures, this was typically employment as wage workers. This organizational change discouraged extensive household production, forcing agricultural workers into the market as purchasers, and with increased agricultural employment, they, along with urban wage workers in the same situation, became a substantial market for the cheap consumer goods that flowed from factories. So, in addition to aspects previously mentioned, the importance of the countryside as markets for industrial wage goods is yet another dimension in which the English agricultural-industrial dynamic was crucial in English industrial development. Unlike the depiction of agriculture in the so-called dual model of economic development (see the discussion in chapter 8), English agriculture was not backward; indeed, its organizational transformation and progressiveness vitally supported industrial growth by supplying food, labor, foreign exchange for imported industrial inputs, and markets for industrial products.

Returning to the way in which general social conditions supported the production side, the relative openness and prosperity of eighteenth-century English society were necessary conditions for the competitive capitalist form of English industrial growth, because this growth required freedom for the entrepreneurs and freedom for workers. These freedoms, defined negatively in the tradition of liberal political theory, were not parallel: the freedoms of the former were a lack of effective restrictions on their activities and accumulation; and as previously noted, the freedoms of the latter were the lack of access to property and, within these constrained alternatives, freedom from formal restrictions on geographical mobility and choice of occupation and employer. But even in England these freedoms were but tendencies in the eighteenth century, and large-scale industrial growth required the sure establishment of, on one hand, the preeminence of contractual relationships over other forms of obligation, unrestrained mobility of labor, and access to domestic and foreign markets; and on the other, the creation of mechanisms of social control to contain the newly formed industrial proletariat. Under conditions

TABLE 2.3
British Foreign Trade

EXPORTS

	Cotton Manufactures			*Woolen Manufactures*			*Iron and Steel Manufactures*		
	Value of Exports (£ Millions)	% Total Exports	Exports as a % of Total Production	Value of Exports (£ Millions)	% Total Exports	Exports as a % of Total Production	Value of Exports (£ Millions)	% Total Exports	Exports as a % of Total Production
1784-1786	0.9	(a)	16.5	(a)	(a)	(a)	(a)	(a)	(a)
1787-1789	1.0	(a)	22.9	(a)	(a)	(a)	(a)	(a)	(a)
1825-1829	35.0	50.8	53.7	3.0	12.7	16.5	3.0	10.2	16.5
1845-1849	62.7	39.6	61.1	8.3	14.1	24.1	8.3	12.3	24.1

IMPORTS

(% distributions)

	Total Imports	*Food, Drink, Tobacco*	*Raw Materials and Semimanufactured Goods*	*Manufactured Goods and Miscellaneous*
1840	100.0	39.7	56.6	3.7
1860	100.0	38.1	56.5	5.5

SOURCE: Phyllis Deane and W. A. Cole, *British Economic Growth, 1688-1959*, 2d ed. (Cambridge: Cambridge University Press, 1969), pp. 31, 33, 185, 196, 216.
NOTE: [a]Not available.

of competitive industrial capitalism, the diffusion of the new source of economic power among a large number of industrial entrepreneurs, the diverse background of that group, and their financial independence from pre-industrial elites enabled the industrial bourgeoisie (frequently with help from the working class) to wield decisive political power on key class issues and to elevate their aggressive individualism and materialism into the dominant national ideology. That is, competitive capitalist industrialization, by creating powerful new classes with only weak links to pre-industrial elites and culture, was a potent social force which helped to fashion the political and cultural conditions necessary for its continuing development.

The industrial bourgeoisie's influence on the national state was thus effective in removing restrictions on commodity markets and in changing official attitudes, but it must be kept in mind that the English state had only a minor role in actively promoting industrial growth. Even in the domain of social control, the Factory Acts and poor law legislation in the early nineteenth century were merely limited and largely ineffective efforts to regulate employers and ameliorate the misery of working-class life; the industrial bourgeoisie assumed major responsibility, exercised at the site of production, for containing worker unrest. The small numbers of workers in a single factory, the penetration of individualistic ideology among the workers, the recent rural origins of so many workers, the direct and personally exercised authority by employers in the factory, and employment of private police in towns and cities were the most potent mechanisms of social control. The English state in the late eighteenth and early nineteenth centuries was weak, decentralized, and nonprofessionally administered, and its positive programs of social control were few and reactive. The English state's most important role in industrialization was consistent with laissez-faire principles: it vigorously enforced the "rules of the game" (that is, protected property relationships and enforced contractual obligations) when necessary; and it got out of the way of the competitive market mechanism.

It is worth looking more closely at the operation of these competitive markets, which, with the intense competition among many small firms producing practically identical products (for example, cotton textiles), generated price signals to show where sales would be the most profitable and which rewarded perspicacity, innovation, and capital formation by the industrial bourgeoisie. That is, competitive markets performed the technical function of allocating resources among various uses and coordinating production decisions and consumer markets, but the role of their carrot-and-stick incentives went beyond these static functions. Although each, say, textile firm was too small relative to the whole textile industry to influence the price of textiles (in the parlance of economic theory, they were "price takers"), one of them could earn greater-than-average profits, at least for a while, by introducing a cost-saving innovation in its production process. Whether this innovation was a matter of organization or use of a new type of machine (for example, the spinning jenny, self-starting mule, power loom), their high profits rapidly attracted already established firms as well as new entrants to adopt the innovation. After a rather short time, the pressure of expanded supply drove down the product price until average profits again reigned throughout textile production, forcing high-cost producers who were using old techniques to produce more efficiently or to leave the textile line of business. Because cost reductions led to lower product prices and increased output, the benefits of the technical innovations were spread among product purchasers, including forward-linked firms (for example, clothing manufacturers and their customers), as well as to backward-linked suppliers of inputs. In noncompetitive settings more typical of leaders of subsequent phases of capitalist industrialization, however, cost-saving innovations by a particular firm or set of firms were not necessarily reflected, at least not fully, in lower product prices. The benefits tended to be captured, although unequally, in higher profits, wages, and salaries within these firms. As a consequence, the general stimulus was apt to be dampened and muted, and other sources of dynamism had to supplement market mechanisms.

The ways by which competitive markets encouraged allocative efficiency and economic growth were refined into formal analytical models and became enshrined in the ideology of capitalism only after competitive markets had already been relegated to the poorest fringes of the economy, but this should not obscure the extent to which the competitive model accurately describes a portion of the history of competitive capitalist industrial development. But the scope of these economic analyses is too narrow to be of much use, and the sterility of neoclassical marginal productivity theory of wages, with its retreat from value theory, illustrates inability of this kind of analysis to encompass across-class economic relationships. In an effort to distill systematic patterns of industrial development from national histories, it is necessary to incorporate multiple dimensions of national life.

GERMANY: FINANCE CAPITALIST INDUSTRIAL DEVELOPMENT

Before discussing the course of late nineteenth-century German industrial development, it is instructive to see why such development did not occur earlier, as it had in England. The political fragmentation of Germany might seem to offer some insight into this question; "Germany" as a nation did not exist until the unification of 1871; the early nineteenth-century German Confederation was a loose collection of thirty-nine states in which Prussia and Austria were the major rivals for leadership. But by the early 1830s, all the states (with the major exceptions of Austria and Baltic port cities) were economically unified by the *Zollverein* (customs union), in which Prussia possessed well over half of the population, probably an even greater share of the productive capacity, and the most coherent political organization and powerful army. Prussia, rid of Austria, exercised decisive rule over what was to become Germany, and when unification was achieved, the Prussian king (Wilhelm I) became the first German kaiser and his prime minister of Prussia (Bismarck) became the first chancellor of the new German Reich.

Prussia's dominant position in Germany throughout the period is further illustrated by the fact that in 1913, Prussia's fiscal revenues were over forty times the revenues of the Reich and almost twice those of all other provinces together.

Political fragmentation, like the disruption of the Napoleonic Wars, should be included in a full exposition, but the sketch of English history in this chapter offers considerably more suggestive sources of explanation as to why wage goods never became the source of general and sustained competitive capitalist industrialization in Germany in the early nineteenth century. German agriculture was commercialized in that large quantities of its products were sold in domestic and foreign markets, but the organization of agricultural production (semi-feudal east of the Elbe River and small-holding peasants in the south and west) undoubtedly retarded the development of large domestic consumer goods markets and the migration of people from agricultural to industrial occupations. But beyond economic considerations of product and labor markets, the social and political implications of a large peasantry and of a vigorous system of aristocratic privilege vested in the landowning Junkers of the east, both symbiotic with a powerful Prussian state, severely limited early nineteenth-century German industrial growth along competitive capitalist lines. The profound failure of the 1848 revolution demonstrated the resolution and ability of pre-industrial elites and others to prevent the liberal reforms necessary for competitive capitalist industrialization. Another political lesson which 1848 forcefully taught German liberals was that the industrial working class could not be counted on as reliable allies; important segments of the workers threatened to carry the revolt beyond reformist objectives, and this experience revealed to the industrial bourgeoisie new advantages in the Prussian state with its aristocratic and military pillars (Marx, 1848).

Germany did become an industrial power, but not until the second half of the nineteenth century when a nonliberal, finance capitalist form of industrial growth became feasible.[2] Table 2.4 demonstrates that German industrial development was based not on consumer goods as in England but rather on producers' goods—intermediate products like steel and chemicals, and on machine-building industries and other steel-using products. Railway construction was an important stimulus to German industrial growth, whereas in England, it was a result of industrial development. (See Table 2.5 for figures on railway construction.) The military value of heavy industry (including the railroad) made its expansion attractive to the Prussian state and other powerful groups, and the technical conditions of its production made the size and composition of the industrial bourgeoisie less threatening to those who would have fiercely resisted the social and political consequences of competitive industrial growth centered on wage goods.

These intermediate and capital goods were produced in establishments which utilized the most advanced technologies in the world, initially drawn from England and Europe, and later developed within Germany. As a consequence of the scale and capital intensity of the firms in the most dynamic lines of production, German industrial growth did not spread economic power among a large number of owner-

TABLE 2.4
The Structure of German Industrial Growth

	Real National Income	*Industrial Production*		
		Consumer Goods	Producer Goods	Total
1871	100	100	100	100
1913	357	286	625	476

SOURCE: G. Bry, *Wages in Germany, 1871-1945* (Princeton, N.J.: Princeton University Press for National Bureau for Economic Research, 1960), p. 17.

	Distribution of Industrial Value Added		*Rates of Labor Productivity Growth*
	1846-1861	1913	1875-1913
Foodstuffs & beverages	16.0	15.0	0.9
Textiles	23.5	12.2	2.1
Clothing & leatherwork	26.3	17.1	1.6
Woodworking	11.7	10.3	1.6
Paper products	1.0	3.1	3.5[a]
Metals production	1.9	4.7	2.4
Metal working	10.2	20.0	2.2
Chemicals	0.9	3.0	2.3
Stones and earth	5.6	8.5	1.2
Other	2.9	6.1	(b)
Total	100.0	100.0	1.6

SOURCE: W. G. Hoffmann, *Das Wachstum der Deutschen Wirtschaft Seit der Mitte des 19. Jahrhunderts* (Berlin: Spinger-Verlag, 1965), pp. 68-69.

NOTE: [a]1881 to 1913.
[b]Not available.

TABLE 2.5
Railway Mileage
(in thousands of miles and percentage of world's total)

	First Steam Line Opened	*1840 (%)*	*1880 (%)*	*1920 (%)*
Europe	1825	2.5 (46%)	83.7 (38%)	160.0 (24%)
Great Britain	1825	1.5 (27%)	15.6 (7%)	20.3 (3%)
France	1832	0.3 (5%)	14.7 (7%)	25.9 (4%)
Germany	1835	0.3 (6%)	20.2 (9%)	35.9 (5%)
Russia	1837	0.0 (0%)	11.0 (5%)	44.5 (7%)
United States	1830	2.8 (51%)	93.3 (42%)	252.9 (37%)
Canada	1836	0.0 (0%)	7.2 (3%)	39.3 (6%)
Latin America	1837	0.1 (2%)	7.2 (3%)	62.9 (9%)
Asia	1853	....	11.0 (5%)	62.1 (9%)
Africa	1854	....	2.8 (1%)	27.2 (4%)
Australia, New Zealand	1854	....	4.7 (2%)	26.1 (4%)
World	1825	5.5 (100%)	222.1 (100%)	674.9 (100%)

SOURCE: William Woodruff, *Impact of Western Man: A Study of Europe's Role in the World Economy* (New York: St. Martin's Press, 1966), p. 253.

operators of diverse backgrounds; instead it constituted the basis for new concentrations of economic power controlled by those who had access to the considerable financial resources necessary for establishing an enterprise on an economically viable scale. The amounts of fixed capital needed for German industrialization were markedly greater than those needed by eighteenth- and early nineteenth-century English industrial entrepreneurs (see Table 2.6), and this need strained the resources of the relatively poor, capital-scarce area, necessitating substantial institutional innovation. During the 1820s and 1830s a large part of Germany's industrial capital formation was financed by the government(s) and by English investors, but beginning with the rapid industrial growth of the 1840s and 1850s financial capital was increasingly supplied by joint-stock investment banks. The banks were initially established by merchants and probably were fueled primarily by mercantile profits, but by the 1850s external sources of funds were secondary to retained earnings and credit creation for new expansion. These banks did not merely perform the passive function of financial intermediation; instead, the banks financed, directed, and even created industrial enterprises. One indication of how centralized were the financing and control of German banks and industry was the weakness of the German stock exchange, in spite of widespread use of joint-stock organization in both sectors.

The banks also encouraged coordination of production and pricing decisions among industrial enterprises through mergers and agreements. Instead of open, competitive determination of market prices, centralization of industrial produc-

TABLE 2.6
Great Britain and Germany: Some Comparisons

	Gross Domestic Capital Formation (% GNP) Total	*Gross Domestic Capital Formation (% GNP)* Production Equip. & Non-Residential Construction	*Government Consumption (% GNP)*	*Entrepreneurs & Self-Employed (% labor force)*	*Return on Entrepreneurial Equity (% GNP)*
United Kingdom					
1860-1869	9.4	6.3	4.8	13	10
Germany					
1871-1890	18.9	10.6	5.9	n.a.	n.a.
1891-1913	23.0	14.2	7.1	26 (1913)	31 (1913)

	Incremental Capital-Output Ratios (constant prices)
United Kingdom	
1860/69 to 1880/89	3.5
Germany	
1871/80 to 1891/1900	4.5
1881/90 to 1901/13	4.8

	% Total Production in Sector Divided by % Total Employment in Sector Agriculture, Forestry, Fishing	Manufacturing
United Kingdom		
1801	0.905	0.788[a]
1851	0.935	0.800[a]
Germany		
1882	0.775	0.839
1907	0.707	1.320

SOURCES: S. Kuznets, *Modern Economic Growth: Rate, Structure, and Spread* (New Haven, Conn.: Yale University Press, 1966), pp. 168, 236, 252; P. Deane and W. A. Cole, *British Economic Growth, 1688-1959* (Cambridge: Cambridge University Press, 1969), pp. 142, 143, 146; W. A. Hoffmann, *Das Wachstum der Deutschen Wirtschaft Seit der Mitte des 19. Jahrhunderts* (Berlin: Springer-Verlag, 1965), p. 33; B. R. Mitchell, *European Historical Statistics, 1750-1970* (New York: Columbia University Press, 1975), p. 156.

NOTE: [a]These figures include production and employment in mining and construction as well as manufacturing. If mining and construction employment were excluded from the denominator of the 1851 figure, the ratio would be 1.04. In 1851, British mining employment was 4.1% of total employment, construction 5.2%, and manufacturing 33.0%. Other separate manufacturing totals are not available.

tion and mutual recognition of interdependence led to the formulation and administration of production and marketing decisions by negotiation among interested parties. Industrial cartels—the adaptation of an organizational type with a long history in Germany—embraced most of the firms which constituted the dynamic core of German industrial growth, and although they did not replace market forces (particularly for exporters), cartels did substantially reduce competition among producers.

The labor market in which the large industrial firms operated was also considerably less than free. Workers in the leading industrial firms, no doubt helped by the large scale of the plants in which they worked, formed strong labor unions at an earlier stage of industrial development than did their British counterparts, and negotiations between them and cartels of employers was closer to the conditions of bilateral monopoly than of competition. The lower labor-to-output requirements of steel, coal, chemicals, and machinery production meant that the formation of an industrial labor force was a considerably more modest endeavor than it was for English wage goods production. There was no functional need to remove the legal barriers on geographical mobility by agricultural workers on eastern latifundia nor to destroy the freeholding peasantry in the south and west to supply the factories with vast numbers of people. Similarly, population growth did not make the same vital contribution to German industrial growth as it did in eighteenth-century England.

The strength of the industrial workers' unions, their relatively small numbers, and their productivity compared to agricultural workers and those producing consumer goods (in which artisans and handicraft workers, whose numbers even by 1891 were half again all factory workers, were prominant—see the fourth column of Table 2.6 for some comparative data) set them apart from the general working population in income as well as work life experience. Thus, even though modern sector workers possessed considerable political influence in an early stage of industrial growth, their position in respect to other German workers helps explain the style of German working-class politics, its susceptibility to nationalist appeals in times of crisis, and its ultimate inability to push German social and political change in different directions. The dogmatic character of the Social Democrats' agricultural reform program, which had virtually no appeal to peasants and agricultural workers, is a prime example of this political ineffectiveness in mobilizing other groups of workers (Gershenkron, 1943, pp. 28-32; Mitrany, 1961, pp. 40-51).

The types of products which constituted Germany's leading industrial lines also had far-reaching implications for the nature of demand for industrial products. The military usefulness of these products made them valuable to the German state which was determined to reassert its military superiority on the continent and to resist the threat from the British. The state directly and indirectly was an important source of demand for these products (for example, by purchasing armaments and ships, and building and operating railroads) before exports became significant (see Table 2.6 for government consumption), and promoted militaristic nationalism into the dominant ideology of industrial development.

The patterns of factor mobilization and market development required by this style of industrial growth were the general economic ingredients for the "revolution from above," a process through which industrial development was possible without disrupting Germany's pre-industrial social and cultural forms and replacing them with liberal institutions and values. The fact that these economic ingredients were present did not make the outcome easy or inevitable, but it is a matter of historical record that it did happen. The centralized and bureaucratic Prussian state and the ideology of German nationalism were specifically German components of the success and character of late nineteenth-century industrial development in Germany. It was this powerful state, directed by Bismarck, which mediated the conflicts between the Junkers and the agents of industrial growth, balancing conflicting interests with tariffs, labor law, social insurance schemes, and suppression of the left, and convinced both agrarians and industrialists that national corporate aspirations transcended their short-run interests (Kocka, 1978, pp. 514-515). This process was long and difficult, but the relatively few industrial leaders, the acceptability of their backgrounds and values to the aristocracy, and revolutionary agitation among the best-organized workers facilitated the "marriage of iron and rye" which was consummated in the 1870s when a trade depression slowed industrial growth, and large-scale wheat exports from the Americas threatened Junker foreign and even domestic grain markets. Struggles between industrial and agrarian interests continued with periods of relative decline and resurgence of the major sectors' political influence, but they were limited battles in which each respected the legitimacy of the other's interests (Barkin, 1970; Gerschenkron, 1943, pp. 51-88; Lebovics, 1967).

The industrial bourgeoisie and ideology (nationalism in the case of Germany) were, as in England, important in containing the working class, but the political strength of the workers required considerably more positive state participation in social control. Bismarck's creative mix of brutal repression and sweeping social insurance and welfare legislation was very effective, in large part because of the industrial workers' distance from the majority of German workers (including their relative advantages in current arrangements).

A final contrast with competitive capitalist industrialization is illustrated by German agriculture, which as the last set of figures in Table 2.6 shows, lagged far behind industry in output and growth of productivity. Because it was not required to be a source of labor or product market demand, it could remain backward. Industrialization and urbanization did increase domestic market demand for agricultural products, but the demand was met principally by switching from foreign to domestic markets and by imports rather than by increased domestic production. German agriculture by the end of the nineteenth century did show some growth in productivity, but as in the case of industrial consumer goods, agricultural growth was the result of the industrial development (application of domestically produced farm machinery and chemical fertilizers) rather than a source of that development.

This is an outline of the forces which by 1913 had made Germany a conservative industrial society, combining the conservatism of its own past with the finance capitalism of other historical origins. Two central points must be made especially clear. First, social and cultural forms in industrial Germany were not determined by finance capitalist industrialization but flowed in a relatively smooth, non-dialectical manner from pre-industrial society. That is, finance capitalism did not force Germany into conservative industrialization; it was simply that Junkers and other economic and political elites along with peasants and urban craftspeople would go along with industrialization only as long as it was conservative. The abortive revolution of 1848 and the reaction of the 1850s demonstrated that the influential and powerful strata of German society understood the origins of English liberalism and of the French Revolution well enough to ensure, at least as a veto group, that the liberal competitive path of industrial development simply was not an option that could be exercised.

Having emphasized the essentially permissive nature of economic forces, we come to the second point. No matter how strongly the Prussian state, the Junkers, the peasants, and other forces may have wanted conservative industrialization, their desire would not have been enough to create it if there had not been an alternative to competitive capitalism. Referring back to the standard approaches to the study of comparative industrialization in chapter 1, German pre-industrial society did not just add a conservative patina to a competitive capitalist industrialization; the politically dominant forces in Germany took advantage of fundamental changes in the character of industrial capitalism which were the direct legacy of earlier competitive industrializations.

FINANCE CAPITALISM AND IMPERIALISM

To appreciate the type of global economic system created by finance capitalism, it is useful to compare late nineteenth-century Germany with England in the same period, rather than comparing their respective periods of industrialization. In this second type of comparison, we have seen that such features as the relative importance of producer goods industries, heavy participation by banks, a powerful central state, economic power highly concentrated in a few large enterprises, a segmented working class, and formation of cartels distinguished the early stages of German finance capitalist industrialization from the atomistic conditions which characterized the formative period of competitive industrialization in England one hundred years earlier. Even more revealing with respect to this argument as well as to a theory of imperialism is that these very features became apparent, at least as strong tendencies, in England during the same period (Ashworth, 1960; and 1962, pp. 86-101; Hobsbawm, 1964). In the last decades of the nineteenth century, the expansion of heavy (capital and intermediate goods) industries relative to consumer goods in the English economy tended to increase overall industrial concentration. This growth of heavy industry reflected developments in industrial technology, effects of the mid-century domestic railroad boom, and in respect to machine-making firms, increased backward-linked specialization resulting from the expansion of the market. In the early years of the Industrial Revolution, for all intents and purposes, England did not possess a capital goods sector; it was not unusual for the workers recruited to work in a new plant first to build that plant and the capital equipment before operating it. Factories using machines to build machines resulted from the success of factories using machines to produce consumer goods.

The expansion of capital and intermediate goods production worked against decentralized economic, social, and political institutions even in England where liberalism as an ideology and an organizational reality had attained the greatest height in Europe. Because of this context, centralization did not reach the degree it did in Germany, probably to England's economic disadvantage. By the turn of the twentieth century, liberal institutions were already inefficient for coordinating and stimulating large-scale industry, and the liberal heritage was a definite disadvantage for England in competing with the economically more dynamic Germany. But even in England, the rise of heavy industry had definite consequences: (1) rise of the corporate form of firm organization and of big financial institutions for the establishment and operation of large firms, which, as in German finance capitalism, worked to further industrial combination even among consumer goods firms; (2) promotion of a distribution of income skewed so strongly toward owners of property that it reduced the likelihood that aggregate demand would be sustained at adequate levels, thus reducing the returns on domestic investment; (3) the need by large firms to monopolize raw material sources so as to prevent the erosion of market power by the entry of new firms into their lines; and (4) giving an organizational coherence and eventually the financial resources to the largest and most profitable firms' workers. These workers constituted an "aristocracy of labor" which in the early years was the vanguard of a militant working-class movement. Conceptually distinct from the aggregate demand/surplus realization problem of (2) above, a large capital goods industry chronically operates at less than full capacity and is a source of economic instability: any change of demand for consumer goods has a magnified effect on the demand for capital goods, for the principal customers of produced means of production (for example, machinery) are consumer goods firms whose demand for machinery is much more volatile than is the demand for their products. The destabilizing impact of the capital goods sector on general economic activity was recognized by Marx—the "crisis of proportionality"—and figures prominantly in conventional business cycle theory. Considering the market structure of capital goods, Lenin (1917, p. 28) concluded that ". . . monopoly which is created in certain branches of industry, increases and intensifies the anarchy in capitalist production as a whole." The creation (or re-creation) of a strong state apparatus in England was a response to the need for managing and directing a more complex and unstable economy and for containing the workers.

Although these processes worked in very different contexts, they were visible in both England and Germany in the late nineteenth and early twentieth centuries, and when one adds the fact that there was more than one nation with these characteristics and that the international rivalry and resulting militarism further strengthened the central state, we have encompassed virtually all classical explanations for the late nineteenth-century European scramble for colonies presented in theories of finance capitalist, or "new," imperialism.[3] Although people continue to argue about which elements were most important in generating the imperialistic impulse at this time, it is sufficient for our purposes simply to note their interdependence and common source in the character of the finance capitalist phase of capitalist development. These pressures together made foreign expansion, frequently with the establishment of formal colonies, a very attractive policy for all nations that were firmly embedded in the finance capitalist phase, although there were marked differences of degree among them—the U.S., with its hugh domestic market, extensive natural resources, and nonrevolutionary working class, felt these pressures least. The increased penetration of peripheral economies supplied markets for capital and intermediate goods which were used to produce and transport foreign raw material and foodstuffs. Moreover, exports from these peripheral countries enlarged foreign markets for consumer goods from the core economies as well as foreign demand for additional capital goods, for example, urban streetcars and public utilities in the raw material exporting nations. The resulting exports of capital and consumer goods helped maintain sufficient prosperity in the core economies to meet some of the demands of some of the domestic workers, and the whole foreign enterprise served as a vehicle to develop latent nationalism and racism into a potent instrument of social control even for those workers not directly benefiting from the material rewards of imperialism. Imperialism appeared to be the answer to too many problems to be resisted by governmental authorities; to explain this phenomenon one need not rely on a mechanical economic theory of politics in which the most powerful industrialists and bankers are seen to control political decisions.

The distinguishing feature of finance capitalist expansion, as Lenin brilliantly argued, was the export of capital. Even in the 1880-1914 period, however, there was still considerable foreign economic activity of types which had been dominant in earlier epochs, reflecting then-current development levels of the forces of production in the imperialist nations: the international exchange of commodities for commodities of competitive industrial capitalism; pursuit of commercial profits and fiscal revenues by shipping and wholesaling tropical produce (such as sugar, tea, coffee, tobacco, and so on) throughout Europe, as in sixteenth- and seventeenth-century mercantilism; and the extraction of tribute from foreign colonies—shades of the Ottoman, Incan, and Roman empires. But the export of capital was the defining characteristic of finance capitalist imperialism, and it is imperative that this activity not be obscured by the financial side of the operation. The crucial aspect of exported capital in finance capitalist imperialism was not the bundling up of monetary notes and shipping them overseas. When British (or

German, or French) capitalists invested in a railroad in Argentina or in nitrate production in Chile, the resulting sales of British-produced rails, engines, rolling stock, and mining equipment abroad directly raised profits for leading industrial branches of British finance capitalism. But in addition, the application of these produced means of production in Argentina and Chile lowered the costs of producing Argentine wheat and meat and Chilean nitrates and of transporting them to England; the profits from the British capital invested in Argentina and Chile helped the English pay for the imports of wheat, meat, and nitrates; and the foreign exchange received by Argentinians and Chileans from the exports financed imports of other British-produced goods. The process cheapened industrial inputs and foodstuffs (and thereby money wages for labor power in England), thus raising the rate of return on capital operating in England. The foreign markets for capital goods thus helped the production and realization of profits for heavy industries, and secondarily, the expanded and domestic markets for British consumer goods producers. All of this was *not* the consequence of financial operations in and of themselves; the central factor to emphasize is the export of "real" capital (produced means of production), whether that export was financed by English purchase of foreign government and private bonds, by credit extended by British banks to British capitalists, by the reinvestment of profits extracted through earlier foreign investment, or whatever.

Table 2.7 shows the magnitude and direction of foreign investment just prior to World War I (Table 2.5 on railway construction is also instructive), and as we will see in chapters 4 and 5, this phase of colonization and economic penetration was much more significant for South America than the earlier free-trade imperialism of competitive capitalism.

RUSSIA: THE FAILURE OF FINANCE CAPITALIST INDUSTRIAL DEVELOPMENT

A large part of the economic and social changes in Russia between the Crimean War (1855-1856) and World War I can be seen as responses and reactions to efforts by the Russian state to industrialize along the conservative lines of Prussian finance capitalism for the purpose of military strength. The emancipation of the serfs in 1861 and the judicial and administrative reforms of the same decade which strengthened central control were necessary for pursuing an industrialization policy, and although the precise effectiveness of the state's role is debatable, Russia did experience substantial industrial growth during this period. From around 1870, the state's vastly expanded program of railroad construction was the backbone of domestic industrial growth (see Table 2.5). Preferential purchases from domestic producers, credits, direct subsidies, tariffs, profit guarantees to new firms, as well as complementary policies like establishing national mail and telegraph systems, helped to spark industrial growth of an estimated annual average of 5 to 7 percent between 1860 and 1913. Although growth was uneven during

TABLE 2.7
Distribution of Foreign Investment, 1914
($ U.S. millions)

	Europe	*(% distr.)*	*United States Canada*	*(% distr.)*	*Australia N.Z.*	*(% distr.)*	*Asia*	*(% distr.)*	*Africa*	*(% distr.)*	*Latin America*	*(% distr.)*	*WORLD*	*(% distr.)*
United Kingdom	1,050	(9%)	7,050	(64%)	2,200	(96%)	3,550	(50%)	2,450	(61%)	3,700	(42%)	19,500	(44%)
(% distr.)	(5%)		(35%)		(11%)		(18%)		(13%)		(19%)		(100%)	
France	4,700	(39%)	500	(5%)	100	(4%)	1,250	(18%)	900	(22%)	1,600	(18%)	9,050	(20%)
(% distr.)	(52%)		(6%)		(1%)		(14%)		(10%)		(18%)		(100%)	
Germany	2,550	(21%)	1,150	(10%)	.....	....	700	(10%)	500	(12%)	900	(10%)	5,800	(13%)
(% distr.)	(44%)		(20%)		.....		(12%)		(9%)		(16%)		(100%)	
United States	700	(6%)	900	(8%)	.....	....	250	(4%)	....	....	1,650	(18%)	3,500	(8%)
(% distr.)	(20%)		(26%)		.....		(7%)		....		(47%)		(100%)	
Other[a]	3,000	(25%)	1,500	(15%)	.....	....	1,350	(19%)	200	(6%)	1,050	(12%)	7,700	(17%)
(% distr.)	(39%)		(19%)		.....		(18%)		(3%)		(14%)		(100%)	
WORLD	12,000	(100%)	11,100	(100%)	2,300	(100%)	7,100	(100%)	4,050	(100%)	8,900	(100%)	45,450	(100%)
(% distr.)	(26%)		(24%)		(5%)		(16%)		(9%)		(20%)		(100%)	

SOURCE: William Woodruff, *Impact of Western Man: A Study of Europe's Role in the World Economy 1750-1960* (New York: St. Martin's Press, 1967), p. 154.
NOTE: [a]Principally from Belgium, Netherlands, Switzerland, Japan, Russia, and Portugal.

this period, intensifying after the Turkish War of 1877-1879, industrial production constituted about 20 percent of Russia's total output by 1913 (Goldsmith, 1961, pp. 442, 464-465). Heavy industry led the advance, and the sector was highly centralized, especially in the last decades before World War I (Portal, 1965, pp. 801, 850-859). The centralization stemmed from emphasis on intermediate and capital goods, using modern technology developed in the West, which encouraged large plant size with high capital-labor ratios, and conserving what probably were the scarcest economic resources: entrepreneurial talent and "disciplined" industrial labor (McKay, 1970, pp. 248-253).

Even after the legal abolition of feudal ties, and in spite of severe population pressure in rural areas, labor mobility out of agriculture was seriously impeded. The predominance of such institutions as the *obshchina* (the field commune) and the *mir* (the villages' communal political and administrative organization which was strong even in areas where land was held by individual households) limited the individual peasant's ability to liquidate holdings and imposed joint responsibility for taxes and quitrents. The reasons why the industrial labor force did maintain close ties with the village thus went beyond the cultural and sentimental (Crisp, 1978, pp. 362-387; Gerschenkron, 1965, pp. 185-210; von Laue, 1960-1961). The Russian government itself wanted to preserve and even strengthen the post-emancipation agricultural system because of its contribution to social stability. This was not the sector's only contribution to the industrialization program, for although agricultural organization impeded agricultural development and hindered migration out of rural areas, the agricultural sector was a major source of government revenue throughout this period, and the peasants were brutally squeezed by government taxes, quitrents, levies, and requisitions (Gerschenkron, 1965, pp. 211-13; Kahan, 1967, pp. 461-64). This was a far cry from the English model of a developing agriculture integrated by market mechanisms into the process of industrialization and supporting that process by supplying foodstuffs, labor power, and a domestic market for industrial products.

Although the role of agriculture in Russian industrialization was more similar to that of Prussia than to that of England, the differences between Russia and Prussia were also vital. In Prussia the Junkers appropriated the bulk of the surplus from agricultural labor, a position in the productive process that they maintained throughout the course of industrialization and which was essential in sustaining their power and status in a changing society. In Russia, on the other hand, the state assumed primary responsibility for appropriating agricultural surplus. In addition to the various forms of taxation, the financial arrangements of emancipation resulted in the bulk of the peasants' paying their quitrents ("redemption payments") to the state which then had separate arrangements with the nobility. The state, therefore, stood in a rentier (rent recipient) relation to the peasants. Although many peasants had continuing obligations to work on a lord's land, pay him part of the harvest, and so on, these were increasingly honored in the breach, and the major burden on the peasantry came from the state's various extractions;

accordingly, it was the army and police, arms of the state, that kept the peasants in line, not a landlord class.

Ironically the nobility's control over emancipation, resulting in such favorable financial settlements, led to the virtual demise of that class which, in one historian's words, "had been the chief foundation and support of the government" (Robinson, 1932, p. 131). In spite of government efforts in the last third of the nineteenth century to shore up the position of the nobility through the establishment of the Nobles' Land Bank and the granting of substantial powers in local government, the loss of position in the production process led to the nobility's social and political decline (Robinson, 1932, pp. 129-137). The industrialization program with its fiscal imperatives contributed to this decline, and the nobility as a group, for reasons of financial and occupational abilities as well as cultural inclination, could not find a new base in industry (Gerschenkron, 1965, pp. 210-211; von Laue, 1960-1961).

The new bourgeoisie, however, based on the expanding sectors of industry and mining, was not in a position to fill the gap in the social structure left by the decline of the nobility. Again, like their counterparts in Germany, there were, compared to England in the early days of its industrialization, relatively few entrepreneurs and, in addition, their influence was significantly reduced by governmental distrust (Crisp, 1978, pp. 384-86) and by the large proportion of foreigners controlling Russian enterprises. The strong fiscal position of the czarist government and the stability of the Russian ruble in international money markets—both significantly due to the pressure exerted on the peasantry—enabled Imperial Russia to be an important recipient of the large-scale foreign investment that flowed out of the developed Western European economies in the late nineteenth century, seeking high financial returns and greater utilization of domestic productive capacity for capitol and intermediate goods. By 1941, foreigners, principally French, German, Belgian, and English, held 48 percent (8.8 million rubles) of the Russian treasury's direct debt. In addition they held over 871 million rubles of other securities guaranteed by the Russian government (a substantial proportion being railroad bonds), and 422 million rubles of Russian municipal debt (Feis, 1930, p. 210).

More important for our purpose was the magnitude of foreign direct investment in Russian industry and mining. John P. McKay (1970, pp. 26-27) estimates that between 1880 and 1906, over 53 percent of new common stock subscriptions in Russian industrial enterprises were purchased by foreigners, and Table 2.8 shows the patterns of total capitalization and foreign ownership by branch (also see Lyashenko, 1949).

The penetration of foreign capital, actively encouraged by the Russian government (Kaser, 1978, pp. 471-478), supplied advanced industrial technology, personnel capable of organizing and running a modern industrial enterprise, and access to foreign sources of savings—all vital for a poor country in which large portions of whatever capital had been accumulated were not available for industrial

TABLE 2.8
Capitalization of Russian Manufacturing and Mining

	1880			*1900*			*1915*		
	Total Equity	% Distr.	Foreign Equity as % of Total Equity	Total Equity	% Distr.	Foreign Equity as % of Total Equity	Total Equity	% Distr.	Foreign Equity as % of Total Equity
Food	82.4	29	8	158.3	11	7	447.8	13	8
Textiles	109.0	39	7	373.7	27	20	729.2	21	21
Leather	3.9	1	75	16.5	1	35	54.2	2	26
Wood	5.0	2	4	17.8	1	44	74.4	3	32
Paper	(a)	(a)	(a)	31.8	2	20	93.2	3	20
Mining, metallurgy				472.2	34	72			
Engineering, machinery	69.0	24	41	177.3	13	71	1,700.0	50	63
Cement, ceramics, glass				59.1	4	45	129.9	4	14
Chemicals	10.5	4	15	93.8	7	31	173.2	5	41
Total	279.9	100	18	1,401.5	100	45	3,402.0	100	41

SOURCE: John P. McKay, *Pioneers for Profit: Foreign Enterpreneurship and Russian Industrialization, 1885-1913* (Chicago: University of Chicago Press, 1970), p. 33.
NOTE: [a]Not available.

investment (Portal, 1965, p. 825). Such competitive advantages enjoyed by foreigners undoubtedly stunted the development of a domestic bourgeoisie. Although this foreign-based, surrogate bourgeoisie might cooperate with domestic industrialists in business matters (such as forming cartels), they had little interest in domestic politics beyond what immediately affected their interests, and it is not necessary to rely on the sense of superiority displayed by the Western Europeans toward Russia and all things Russian to appreciate how unlikely they were to establish social ties or political alliances with the domestic bourgeoisie and traditional upper classes. In addition, there is no convincing evidence—in fact there is evidence to the contrary—that foreign financiers and industrialists were able to exert any significant influence over the Russian government through the fact that they were based abroad and important to Russia's industrialization program (McKay, 1970, pp. 274-286).

Even in respect to power on the plant level, the industrial bourgeoisie in Russia, foreign and domestic, was weak and dependent on the state. Its authority over workers was sharply reduced from the mid-1880s when, faced with waves of strikes, the state increasingly tried to assume the paternal role vis-à-vis the workers at which the employers had failed. Feudalism in the factory has worked under certain circumstances (Abegglen, 1958; Geertz, 1963, pp. 82-141), but in nineteenth-century Russia the *mir's* legal right to call back to the village so many factory and mine workers, as well as the predominance of foreigners in the upper echelons of the larger enterprises, made it difficult for workers to identify very closely with their employers. To an ever increasing degree, the government, through regulation and direct involvement in negotiations, became the body with actual authority over wages, hours, fines, housing, and work conditions. The government took explicit responsibility for controlling and disciplining strikers with the police and the army and through police-established labor unions. The government's efforts, however, alienated the employers while transforming the workers' economic demands into political struggle, and the strikes continued (Rimlinger, 1960).

By the turn of the twentieth century, then, the Russian government had been quite successful in its industrialization policy: with the aid of modern industrial technology and foreign capital and entrepreneurship, a sizable industrial sector had been formed without destroying the traditional organization of village life or decentralizing political power. The costs of these successes, however, were formidable. Industrial growth of the financial capitalist type, with heavy government participation and emphasis on capital goods for armament production, can proceed for extended periods of time independent of the material welfare of the general population, and reliance on foreign factors of production with the attendant foreign repatriations possibly increased the downward pressure on living standards. Indeed, aggregate consumption levels of the peasantry rose little during the period and per capita levels, in view of population growth, were probably declining (Goldsmith, 1961, p. 454). The industrial work force did not fare much better, even with considerable industrial growth.

Such conditions put considerable pressure upon the institutions and forms of social control. The peasantry, who had borne much of the burden, was increasingly rebellious while the function and authority of the landed nobility had been undermined. Along with the structure of the old order, the traditional cultural and ideational counterparts were also seriously weakened in this process, and new, stabilizing ideologies and institutions had no chance to replace them, even in the modern sector. For there, the creation of a militant industrial proletariat had taken place without a cohesive and powerful bourgeoisie.

The Russian state, then, directly confronted the increasingly rebellious, producing classes with only the power of the army and police to maintain social order. Industrialization had indeed brought greater integration to Russian society, but it was an integration that helped focus protest by peasants and workers within a society so fundamentally divided from the polity that even nationalist myths were ineffective as a means of social control.[4] Yet even under these conditions the state survived the 1905 revolution. With the increasing efficiency of modern weaponry, even a poorly organized state that has outlived the original basis of its existence, a state without social roots, is harder to topple, and Imperial Russia weathered 1905, however badly shaken and qualified.

Western scholars have frequently interpreted the last decade of czarist rule in ways that make the 1917 Revolution appear external to Russia's social processes, a historical accident brought on by World War I and representing a severe setback to prewar progress.[5] Their argument is that the spurt of industrial growth between 1908 and 1914, in which for the first time consumer goods and private bank participation were notable, demonstrated that the Russian economy had matured to the point that self-sustaining industrial growth without overt government direction and participation was possible and that political reforms and Stolypin's agrarian reforms, virtually dissolving the *obshchina* and *mir,* heralded a new era of social stability and industrial growth along German lines. There is evidence that casts serious doubts on efforts to represent this brief period as socially and politically stable in the urban areas (Haimson, 1964 and 1965; von Laue, 1963, pp. 307-14), and the agrarian reforms increased social differentiation and conflict among the peasantry while the benefits from the reforms were little more than bare tendencies for most of the rural population by 1914 (Robinson, 1932, pp. 208-265).

The argument for the self-sustaining nature of Russian industrial growth between 1908 and 1914 is usually based on the relatively active role that private banks took in financing industry, distinguishing this period of rapid industrial expansion from the 1890s. It is misleading, however, to infer from this that the private sector in Russia was generating its own investable funds. The combined growth in public sector deposits and credits and foreign deposits in private joint-stock banks between 1910 and 1914 was 64 percent of the private banks' growth in current accounts and deposits between 1908 and 1914 (Crisp, 1967, pp. 194, 220), and furthermore, the increased (par and face) value of foreign-owned common stocks in Russian corporations and banks between 1908 and 1914 was over 56 percent of the total increase (McKay, 1970, p. 27). These figures do not support the contention that Russian industrialization was self-financing in this period.

No more successful are these scholars' efforts to represent Russia's role in World War I as external to the industrialization process. Even if industrialization in itself did not directly cause Russian participation in the war, as is probably true, the two phenomena are intimately related in that both industrialization and the war stemmed directly from the Russian state's aspirations to great power status in Europe.[6]

So Russia did enter the war, and the war contributed to the success of the Revolution through the suffering it inflicted on the population, and possibly more important, by diverting the army away from maintaining internal order while diluting it with large numbers of peasant draftees, many of whom deserted with their weapons. The Bolshevik Revolution ended any hopes for capitalist development in Russia, and the elimination of foreign leakages and the reduction of consumption by at least nonproducing classes made larger investable surpluses available from domestic sources. Yet, it is interesting to note that the Soviets' eventual tightening of political and economic controls and the coercive appropriation of rural product were actually extensions of mechanisms employed in nineteenth-century Russia.

Finance capitalist industrial growth in Russia during the late nineteenth and early twentieth centuries was in some ways an economic success and in virtually all ways a political failure. Because the technical requirements of financial capitalist industrialization did not require mobilizing a large labor force or developing internal consumer markets, as in the case of competitive capitalist industrial development, industrial growth could proceed with minimal organizational changes and stagnant or even declining levels of productivity and standards of living in agriculture. The agricultural sector could be squeezed by direct, coercive measures (which in Russia undercut the nobility) to make available the products needed to support domestic nonagricultural populations and the external balance. The pressure on living standards was intensified by population growth which made no functional labor supply or market contribution to industrialization but exacerbated social unrest. The growth of the modern sector lent little support to capitalist institutions, for the proletariat remained in dire poverty, the industrial bourgeoisie was politically weak, and capitalist industrial growth was further discredited by appearing to be a foreign invasion.

As the German case indicates in a general way, some of these problems could have been ameliorated by government policy, but under conditions of finance capitalism, relief measures did not necessarily appear to policy makers as technical requirements for continued industrial growth, but rather as purely social policies which might actually slow it down. In the initial decades of this type of industrial growth, the centralization of the process's management was such that both growth and welfare (as well as social change) were policy phenomena which in engineering terms seemed like independent and even competitive uses of funds rather than mutually necessary conditions of a single organic social and economic process.

The availability of foreign capital to Russia further contributed to the apparent independence of continued industrial growth from domestic social conditions. To proceed in this manner, of course, put intense pressure on mechanisms of social control: intermediate social strata, ideology, and the military. Foreign investment, the character of emancipation, and the state's fiscal imperatives weakened the first two in Russia, and the world war neutralized the last; thus there could occur a successful revolution which, in the name of workers and peasants, proposed an alternative to finance capitalist industrial development.

SOME PRELIMINARY OBSERVATIONS

The historical example of competitive capitalist industrialization has exerted a profound influence on our conceptions of what industrialization is all about. Some of this influence is exerted by the emphasis put on study of English and U.S. history in English-speaking nations, but its most subtle and pervasive route is through generalizations abstracted from that history and embodied in theoretical principles that purport to be universal. Both liberal and Marxist theories of economic growth and change are direct products of English history, and through such theories, competitive capitalist industrialization has indelibly colored our perceptions and the organization of our thinking about industrialization processes in general.

The recognition that real gains in the productivity of human labor could occur in a sector other than agriculture is clearly one of the most important principles extracted from late eighteenth- and early nineteenth-century industrial growth, and it contains the strong corollary that material gains enjoyed by one nation or one group within a nation need not necessarily have been at the expense of other nations and groups. Although older conceptions about the nature of economic growth can still be found in recent scholarship,[7] and resource and environmental concerns have qualified optimism about unlimited economic expansion, the essentially technical principle of net gain has indeed been confirmed by subsequent industrializations. Not so with other theoretical tenets deduced from competitive capitalist industrial development. Important examples include the following, which are found in various mixes in both liberal and Marxist theories: there is an "economy" with its own laws of motion distinct from social and political institutions; industrial growth is a natural and inevitable consequence of capitalist organization and economic "freedom" (the stronger, pre-Soviet statement that such organization and freedom are necessary for industrial growth still appears occasionally); and industrial growth is a powerful social and cultural force that can reshape all dimensions of pre-industrial society, promoting liberal social and political forms and ideologies. Because these theoretical convictions and expectations are based on the historical experience of what Marx called the "truly revolutionising path" of competitive industrial capitalism, it is worth reviewing some key aspects of finance capitalist industrial development.

By the late nineteenth century, the central role of the industrial bourgeoisie, as an active independent agent of social and economic change (a class *for* itself as well as in itself) had been qualitatively affected. Such features as the predominance of large-scale enterprise, state sponsorship and guidance, and foreign ownership in leading industrial firms diminished the need for widespread, aggressive, private entrepreneurship to promote industrial growth. Entrepreneurship was not the only factor so affected. The mobilization of an industrial work force became a much more modest process and no longer required reaching into every sector and region of the nation to free labor power from precapitalist social and geographic restrictions. But in finance capitalism, capital was the factor required at an increased rate, a rate that precluded the casual, rather ad hoc arrangements which prevailed in the early stages of English industrial growth. Institutions and procedures had to be created to insure the adequate availability of capital, and large banks, the state's fiscal powers, and foreign investors performed this function. The patterns of the mobilization of key productive factors required for industrialization, then, changed to reduce the requirements for large-scale inputs of entrepreneurship and labor—socially very disruptive aspects of competitive capitalist industrialization—and to emphasize the inputs of capital mobilized by centralized, stabilizing institutions. Since large consumer goods markets were not necessary to support finance capitalist industrial growth, demand conditions supported and extended these centralizing tendencies.

It is these related and mutually reinforcing changes on the supply side and demand side, inherent in the historical development of industrial production, which inexorably altered the nature of industrialization as a social process even before the end of the nineteenth century. Industrialization no longer had to come from below, transforming all dimensions of pre-industrial social life, but could come from above, preserving and strengthening traditional hierarchies and cultural forms. The functional relationship between industrialization and liberalism, between industrial capitalism and individualism, democracy, and an open, decentralized market economy was thus broken. The bourgeois revolution, as the dialectical consequence of competitive capitalist industrialization, can be seen as a historically restricted phenomenon which by its very success created its own negation. Yet, as vividly illustrated by Russian history, the industrial bourgeoisie and other powerful social classes retained a necessary role in supporting the central state and in controlling the working classes.

Table 2.9 summarizes the key differences between competitive and finance capital industrial development. All these differences are either ignored or subordinated to insignificance by stage theories of economic growth, sociological "modernization" theory, and any attempt to extract lessons from history by explicit analogy or by use of universalistic theories emphasizing similarities of industrial development. For the same reasons, efforts to account for differences by attributing them exclusively to the peculiarities of individual national histories are incomplete.

TABLE 2.9
Competitive and Finance Capitalist Industrial Development: Characteristics, Conditions, and Mechanisms

	Competitive Capitalist Industrial Development	*Finance Capitalist Industrial Development*
Characteristics of leading product lines		
Type of product	Wage goods	Intermediate and capital goods
Production processes and industrial structure	Labor-intensive technology; many small firms	Capital-intensive technology; few large firms
Necessary conditions for growth of leading product lines		
Factor mobilization	Need for large numbers of aggressive entrepreneurs and availability of massive labor and modest capital inputs	Need for some entrepreneurs sensitive to social and political parameters and availability of modest labor and massive capital inputs
Product markets	Wage workers, domestic and foreign	State, other productive enterprises, and foreign investment
Social and cultural order	Unrestricted geographical and sectoral mobility of productive factors	Unrestricted geographical and sectoral mobility for *industrial and urban* productive factors
	Considerable occupational and social mobility	Some limited opportunities for occupational and social mobility
	Status derived largely from position in private production process	Some status from control over large-scale productive assets, although other factors may continue to exert decisive influence
	Ideology of aggressive, competitive individualism; industrial bourgeoisie's drive to accumulate productive assets unencumbered by government regulations and cultural restraints of social responsibility or "irrationality"	Ideology of nationalism, which may mitigate industrial bourgeoisie's drive for private accumulation
Political order	Decisive political influence exerted by industrial bourgeoisie as a class, expressing	Considerable political influence wielded by owners of large-scale industry, and the

(continued)

TABLE 2.9 continued

	Competitive Capitalist Industrial Development	*Finance Capitalist Industrial Development*
Political order	its economic power, supported at crucial junctures by working class	conflicts within the propertied class (e.g. agriculture vs. industry) both require and are a source of significant independent political power vested in central state
Mechanisms		
Coordination of economic activity	Decentralized market system	Cartels and state
Principal agents of social and cultural change	Industrial bourgeoisie	Industrial bourgeoisie and state, the latter able to negotiate the minimum changes necessary to accommodate industrial growth without destroying the pre-industrial social and cultural order
Social control	Industrial bourgeoisie at production sites and liberal ideology; state enforces private, "free" contracts	Industrial bourgeoisie and nationalist ideology; state redistributes income for social and political stability, not economic stimulus, and uses police powers when necessary

Regarding this last point, however, Table 2.9 represents only one side of the two-part approach described in chapter 1. The historical conception of industrial development proposed there is best represented by the metaphor of dual historical movement: national configurations of social, cultural, and political life continually change; and the processes of capitalist industrial production also change. Table 2.9 portrays only the second side, but it can be used as an effective guide to understanding the implications of the first. The conditions necessary for competitive capitalist development were not even approximated in early nineteenth-century Germany, and those necessary for finance capitalist development were not present in Russia during the late nineteenth and early twentieth centuries. Capitalist industrial development occurs only when local conditions are close enough to the requirements of the phase of industrial production current at the time that some domestic groups could successfully seize the opportunities and possibilities of industrial development.

The general approach outlined here goes substantially beyond the models of industrial development offered in the literature of comparative economic history and development in crucial ways. By focusing on dual historical movement in this way, we can better distinguish the particular from the general and construct historical models of industrial development without either flattening and distorting individual national experiences beyond recognition or introducing special ad hoc explanations to account for diversity. As a consequence, we can see both material success and failure as well as the past and the present through a unified, consistent analytical framework which does not press data into rigid categories. But this approach was not fashioned for Europe, and it clearly is time to turn to South America.

NOTES

1. Deane (1967) and Landes (1969, pp. 41-123) are good places to begin for information about leading sectors, firm scale, technology of production, population growth, the roles of agriculture and of the state, and the importance of eighteenth-century England's relative social and political openness. In addition, see Gatrell (1977) for the structure of the cotton textile industry in the early nineteenth century; Bergier (1973, pp. 404-412), Mantoux (1961), Marglin (1974), and Pollard (1968) for the origins and practices of the industrial bourgeoisie; Crouzet (1972) for the volume and sources of industrial capital; Bairoch (1973) and Jones (1975) for agriculture; Lazonick (1974), Mantoux (1961, pp. 136-180) for the enclosures; Thompson (1963) and Pollard (1978) for the working class and social control; and MacDonough (1977) for the halting beginnings of government centralization in the 1830s and 1840s and governmental ineffectiveness as a regulator of the economy through the middle of the century.

2. Kent (1978) is a short, readable political history, with a good bibliography, of Bismarck's role in German unification and of the place of Prussia in both the Confederation and the Reich. Gerschenkron (1943) and (1966, pp. 5-30, 353-364), Henderson (1975), Hoffmann (1965), Kocka (1978), Landes (1969, pp. 193-358), Milward and Saul (1977, pp. 17-70), and Stolper (1967) are good sources for the composition and technology of the most progressive lines of industrial production, agricultural organization and stagnation, slow growth and backwardness of consumer goods industries, the sources of financial capital, and the role of the state. Borchadt (1973) is best on interpreting the meaning of these economic processes. Dahrendorf (1969), Gillis (1965), Hamerow (1958 and 1969), Rimlinger (1971), Tilly (1956), and Wehler (1970) are good treatments of the state in general and its labor policies in particular, including the revolution of 1848 and the subsequent reaction. For more specific facets of German industrial growth in this period, see Landes (1965 and 1966) for industrial structure in comparative perspective; Tilly (1967) and the debate cited in Komlos (1978) for banks; Wehler (1969, pp. 112-193) on ideology; Dahrendorf (1969, pp. 208-213) and Sagarra (1977, pp. 175-227) on social and cultural continuity; Henderson (1954) for early transfer on industrial technology to Germany; Maschke (1969) on cartels, and Wunderlich (1961) on agricultural labor.

3. Hobson (1902), Lenin (1917), and Luxemburg (1913) are the principal representatives of what I have called the classical theories of imperialism. Kemp

(1967), Owen and Sutcliffe (1972), and Barratt Brown (1974) are critical surveys of these theories, and Wehler (1970) is an excellent interpretation of late nineteenth-century German expansion along the lines suggested by them.

4. In this interpretation I have emphasized the second of the two polarizations Leopold Haimson (1964 and 1965) found important in prerevolutionary Russia. Also see von Laue (1963, pp. 307-314) for a similar emphasis. Although definitely not George L. Yamey's intention, the argument in his excellent article (Yamey, 1965) gives strong and perhaps necessary support to this position.

Rogger (1961-1962) traces the inability of Russian nationalism to exert political influence due to the isolation of the Russian state from the rest of society. For this degree of centralized authority which distinguished the Russian autocracy from the West, see Brutzkus (1966, pp. 121-123) and Szeftel (1963).

5. ". . . if the First World War had not occurred—or had occurred a decade later—Russia would have almost certainly have made a successful transition to modernization and rendered itself invulnerable to Communism, . . . that peculiarly inhumane form of political organization, . . . a kind of disease" (Rostow, 1960, pp. 163-164). For a similar though less crude view of czarist Russia's development and the accidental nature of World War I, see Gerschenkron (1966, pp. 20-22, 138, 354-355).

6. Gerschenkron (1966, pp. 131, 142, 193) recognizes this. For a better statement of these interrelated goals, see von Laue (1963, pp. 303-312).

7. Brenner (1977) criticizes Emmanuel Wallerstein's and André Gunder Frank's conception of underdevelopment which retains "fixed pie" notions of economic growth; Brenner's article is an excellent interpretation of fifteenth- and sixteenth-century economic growth, but it is marred by overgeneralization. Weaver (1978) argues against economic interpretations of U.S. racism which employ conceptions of capitalist growth similar to those of Wallerstein and Frank.

3

POLITICAL INDEPENDENCE IN LATIN AMERICA, 1750-1860

By 1825, after two decades of tumult and destruction, the Spanish empire in the New World had disintegrated, and all Spain's mainland possessions had successfully asserted their political independence. The convulsions did not come to an end with the overthrow of Spanish control, however; for years thereafter, elites in the newly independent areas struggled to create viable political institutions to replace the colonial apparatus. Widespread chaos and the great regional differences in the character of the wars of independence and of the political arrangements that eventually succeeded them have made a coherent, comparative historical interpretation of this period difficult.

For North American historians, considerably more than for their Latin American and European colleagues, these problems are exacerabated by the liberal historiographical tradition in which they work. To focus narrowly on prominent individuals, the influence of ideas, and the interaction of various elites, as is the usual practice, simply does not provide sufficient analytical scope to encompass and comprehend the diverse forces which promoted independence and shaped political institutions in the new Spanish American states. Some individuals were clearly influenced by European and North American political thinking, and the elites definitely were the initiators and arbiters of much that did happen, but they—individually or collectively—did not make history just as they pleased. To understand the events in early nineteenth-century Spanish America and to explain their variations by region and time, class analysis is a necessary analytical tool. While the wars of independence were essentially conflicts among competing sectors of the elites, the wars occurred within a context of class struggle wherein the producing classes in some areas threatened the entire social order. Thus, those who led independence movements continually fought on two fronts: against Spanish control from above and against working-class insurrection from below. Although often neglected by North American historians, the second facet of these struggles influenced in important ways the regional variability in the direction of the anti-Spanish revolts and the character of the political regimes established in the newly independent nations.

In order to demonstrate the types of questions that should be asked of historical materials, the first section of this chapter outlines the nature of the Spanish-American independence movements. This will serve as the background for the second section which discusses efforts to create new political institutions in the post-independence years. Although I present substantial historical data, my primary intention is to show the potential that a class analysis framework that incorporates broad aspects of social life has for explaining and interpreting political change.

COLONIAL LATIN AMERICA AND THE WARS OF INDEPENDENCE

The colonial revolts in Spanish America were confused, ambiguous affairs whose regional variations shattered the superficial, and actually illusory, veneer of uniformity that Spanish culture and colonial administrative organization lent to diverse areas. Regional differences in geography and in the nature of the indigenous peoples whom the Spanish conquered demanded flexibility in the method of mobilizing labor, resulting in significant differences in colonial social organization and administrative practices.[1] In the Antilles and tropical coastal areas, the indigenous peoples' casual economic and political organization made them of little economic value to the Spaniards, and the Spanish established plantations worked by nonnative black slaves. Finding densely populated, hierarchical agricultural societies in the highlands of Mexico and Peru, the Spanish were able to take over existing methods of appropriating surplus practically intact through *encomiendas,* a system for exacting tribute which was gradually replaced by semi-capitalist haciendas. In the same areas, the adaptation of an already existing institution of forced labor quotas became a conscripted wage labor system for mines and the few mills producing coarse textiles. Another distinct regional mode for organizing labor in Latin America was represented by seminomadic herdsmen—the *vaqueros, llaneros, huasos,* and *gauchos*—who were loosely organized by a proprietor to work cattle ranches in outlying plains of northern Mexico, inland Venezuela, Chile, and the La Plata provinces. In important ways these regional societies were as different from each other as each was from the pomp and splendor of the viceregal courts in Mexico City and Lima. (See Table 3.1 for population estimates.)

With this diversity, it is necessary to establish a general framework through which struggles for independence in particular areas can be compared to each other. The first step is the explicit recognition that the wars of independence were not waged by working classes against nonworkers; rather they were conflicts between two strata of the nonproducing class. The predominant force in the independence movements was the American-born Spaniards (*criollos*) who controlled most of the productive resources, principally land and labor power.[2] Thus the relationship

TABLE 3.1
Some Population Estimates for Colonial Spanish America Around 1800

Race		*Region*		
		Mexico		7,000,000
		White	1,100,000	
Spanish-born	30,000	Indian	3,500,000	
Criollo	3,000,000	Central America and Antilles		2,500,000
Mixed races	6,000,000	New Granada (Colombia, Venezuela, Ecuador)		2,500,000
Indian	7,500,000			
Black	750,000	Peru (including Bolivia, and Chile)		3,500,000
	16 to 17 million			16 to 17 million

Major Cities	
Mexico City	140,000
Lima	80,000
Quito	70,000
Buenos Aires	60,000

SOURCES: A. C. Wilgus and R. D'Eca, *Latin American History* (New York: Barnes and Noble, 1963), pp. 93-95; C. Gibson, *Spain in America* (New York: Harper & Row, 1966), pp. 117-118.

central for understanding the independence movement is between the *criollos,* on one hand, and the Spanish colonial system personified by the king and his Spanish-born agents in the New World, on the other. But for the association between the two groups to be appreciated in its social and historical setting, one must study it within the context of the larger class dynamics of producers and nonproducers.

Nevertheless, most historians tend to focus exclusively on the *criollos* and their problems in isolation, because it is clear that the development of the forces of production, and thereby of the *criollos'* class position, was seriously retarded by Spanish colonial organization and the regulation of production and commerce. These constrictions derived from the fact that the overriding purpose of establishing and operating the Spanish colonial apparatus in the New World was to finance the Spanish crown's European adventures, and the mines, principally the silver mines of Mexico and Peru (including present-day Bolivia), were considered to be far and away the most important resource. The *criollos'* function in this royal design was the mobilization and control of the labor power required to extract, refine, and transport the ore and to supply foodstuffs to the mines and the urban administrative centers. In addition to these primary functions, colonization of outlying areas was encouraged to protect against encroachment by other Europeans who might threaten the mines and transport routes. The narrowness of Spanish interests in the New World colonies, reflecting the low level to which the forces of production were developed within Spain, distinguished Spain from other colonial powers even in the sixteenth century and increasingly diverged from Northern and Western European colonial policies as time went on.[3] As a consequence of these limited aims, Spanish policy did not encourage, and often actively discouraged, any colonial economic activity that might conceivably have impinged on the yield from the mines. Thus even the production of tropical commodities like spices, sugar, tobacco, and dyes that played such an important role in the colonial practices of the more commercially minded nations of Europe were only barely tolerated by the Spanish authorites for strategic reasons, specifically, populating and securing outlying areas against foreign encroachments which might have threatened specie production and transport.

As a result of this conception of how to benefit from colonies, joined with Spanish fears of *criollo* separatism, the American-born *criollos'* activities were strictly bounded, especially in the sixteenth and seventeenth centuries. Even when granted, titles to the land were extremely insecure, and colonial law, by carefully circumscribing landowners' political and juridical authority over their labor force, obstructed the translation of landownership into social and political power. Exploitation of the indigenous population and of black slaves was subject to detailed legislation, and although enforcement was uneven and erratic, laws often prevented landowners and mine operators from obtaining free and sometimes even cheap labor. Along with limits on how much of the product those controlling the means of production could take away from the workers who produced it (surplus appropriation process), the sale of the commodity (surplus realization) at favorable prices was difficult, for commodity markets were heavily burdened by regulations, taxes, monopolies, and the colonial economic structure. Local markets for crops other than food were very thin, and high transport costs plus the low proportion of the population that was in the money economy narrowed local markets for foodstuffs. More important, returns from exports were kept low by the Spanish requirement that all trade be funneled through Spain, transported by an inadequate fleet system, subject to high export duties, import duties, and a general turnover tax, and monopolized by interlocking trans-Atlantic merchant guilds (*consulados*) made up by fewer than fifty wholesale houses and shippers who baldly manipulated prices to the disadvantage of American producers and final consumers. Finally, tithes which were collected and distributed by the crown bore heavily on the proceeds from agricultural and mining production, and wealthy *criollos* were frequently the target of the Inquisition which, in effect, operated as a capital levy. Altogether, the *criollos* appeared to have had difficulty in supporting an urban upper-class life based on land and semi-servile labor (Brading, 1973).

The *criollos'* position in colonial society was further weakened by the crown's overt discrimination against them in granting titles of nobility and appointments to positions in the upper reaches of the political and ecclesiastical bureaucracies. The *consulados* were also dominated by the Spanish-born, and the colonial social and economic structure offered few opportunities for independent professionals and discouraged industrial entrepreneurship more effectively than did mercantilistic prohibitions. Although occupational discrimination was based on royal need for political loyalty and fears of separatism or on protection of the *consulados'* monopoly position, it was buttressed by a mythology of *criollo* inferiority. These myths employed the same elements frequently used to subordinate social groups: early maturation and decline, laziness, dishonesty, tendency to dissoluteness, and so forth.

These discriminatory policies were important to the *criollos,* varied over time and by region, the early eighteenth-century *criollos* generally were in the anomalous position of being in charge of the principal means of appropriating surplus while suffering the ignominy of financial insecurity, political impotence, discrimination, and ridicule. This list of the ways in which the Spanish crown's control in the colonies, operating through its Spanish-born agents in the New World, worked to the disadvantage of the *criollos* is pretty standard fare in textbooks; sometimes static descriptions of the economic aspects alone are held up as a sufficient explanation for the wars of independence.[4] But it was not in the early eighteenth century that the *criollos* made a concerted effort to shape their political milieu into one more consistent with their requirements; this happened only in the early nineteenth century after many of the colonial restrictions had been loosened. For the causes of these *criollo* revolts, we have to look more closely at the organization and development of colonial society.[5]

Economic expansion in the nations of Northwestern Europe in the eighteenth century increased the demand for the specie, sugar, tobacco, cotton, dyes, spices, vanilla, grain, hides, hardwood, and other items produced or capable of being produced in the New World. These opportunities increased the economic costs for the *criollos* of being politically tied to Spain, for Spain had by then become a backward nation in Europe, due probably in good part to its colonial possessions which had retarded the internal transformations necessary for creating a modern economy and society. The material costs to the *criollos* were reduced by extensive contraband trade, but the prevalence of this illegal activity only underscores the inadequacy of Spanish economic relationships with the colonies. The Bourbon economic reforms initiated by Charles III in the tradition of enlightened despotism in the last half of the eighteenth century (Barbier, 1977), most notably the considerable freeing of trade, served as a temporary palliative and contributed in important ways to the substantial colonial prosperity around the turn of the nineteenth century. Although the Bourbon reforms included other changes that directly benefited the *criollos,* like the sale of important offices to the highest bidder, *criollo* or Spanish, overall they probably worked to increase *criollo* dissatisfaction with the whole colonial system. For instance, the effective rate of taxation was also raised, and even though *criollo* after-tax income rose, the visible burden of direct tax payments replaced the more subtle cost of market prohibitions and monopolizations. More important, however, is that trade liberalization released a dialectical movement that is obscured by considering only the increased prosperity. First of all, many *criollos,* particularly those in secondary and commercial activities but also some landowners, depended on colonial economic restrictions for their positions and suffered from the reforms (see, for example, Hamnett, 1971, pp. 95-105). Furthermore, even for those *criollo* landowners who benefited from liberalized trade, increased returns came not only from higher prices, but also from the greater volume of goods marketed in response to the higher prices. In the colonial context of static labor productivity, increased marketings simply meant increased pressures on consumption levels of producers already integrated into the colonial economy and incorporating new groups of producers not yet so integrated. Both facets of this tendency brought landowners up against colonial labor policies and against the Church as protector of the Indians, a competing landowner, and creditor. Even under the most favorable conditions where marketed output could expand easily, as in the litoral around Buenos Aires, the increased value of produce from the land developed the forces of production to the point where remaining restraints appeared more confining than the earlier, tighter ones (Ferrer, 1967, pp. 43-44, 53-57).

Although it is helpful to put some historical motion into the conception of the *criollos'* burdens, the focus is still inadequate for understanding the timing and regional variations of the wars of independence. For this purpose, we must place these previous observations in proper perspective; there were crucial elements of reciprocity between the *criollos* and the colonial administration. The *criollos* as a class received substantial advantages from Spanish rule, advantages which had effectively bound them to the empire for nearly three centuries. Investigating these advantages requires greater emphasis on the *criollos'* position in colonial society; it is too easy to lose sight of the fact that all the disadvantages of Spanish rule that the *criollos* experienced were disadvantages because, and only because, the *criollos* were sitting on top of an exploitive relationship with the producing class, composed principally of indigenous workers and black slaves. This second, more basic relationship between producing and nonproducing classes is what gives historical depth to the *criollo*-Spanish relationship, and it is the source of the changing balance between *criollos* and Spanish colonial administration. At its core, the crown and its representatives protected *criollo* privilege in the Indies; Spain stood as the guarantor of a social order which freed *criollos* from work by insuring the operation of the various means of appropriating surplus on which that order rested.[6]

Heightened market opportunities for New World commodities from the mid-eighteenth century onward increased pressure for more output from producers. Whether direct cause and effect or not, the riots in Mexico City and Quito, the recurring Andean rebellions, the Venezuelan slave revolts, the Haitian blacks' revolution, the *jacquerie* by the followers of Hidalgo in central Mexico, and the

Indian risings in Guatemala served as vivid reminders to the *criollos* that colonial society in the late eighteenth and early nineteenth centuries was threatened from below. England's seizure of Cuba in the 1760s and Trinidad in the 1790s and Popham's raid on Buenos Aires in 1806 similarily kept alive fears of a foreign invasion which would not be to the *criollos'* advantage. In each of these cases in Spanish America, the *criollos* and the Spanish united to put down the common enemy.

Spain's ability to protect the *criollos* militarily from internal and external assaults diminished sharply through the eighteenth century; although Charles III's establishment of a colonial militia was a sound fiscal move that also created new opportunities for aspiring *criollos,* it was also public notice of Spain's military weakness.[7] Another important component of Spain's role as guarantor of *criollo* privilege was the Church, acting as a stabilizer for the system as a whole, and the crown itself served as a powerful unifying symbol to all layers of colonial society. But to increase crown revenues and direct authority, Bourbon reforms weakened the political and social authority of the first (Bauer, 1971; Hamnett, 1969), and Napolean dealt a severe blow to the symbolic (and military) dimensions of the second when he invaded Spain, his ally, and forced the abdication of Charles IV in favor of his brother, Joseph Bonaparte.

Even in these circumstances, however, the *criollos* as a group were reluctant to break with Spain. The removal of the royal capstone from the colonial administration, structured with complex checks and balances and ambiguous overlappings of duties and responsibilities to ensure centralized Spanish authority resulted in the chaotic disintegration of the empire down to small, local, warring components. Spain successfully reasserted her imperial authority in the New World (except in La Plata) between 1814 and 1816 after Ferdinand VII's restoration, but Ferdinand was restored under the aegis of the republican Constitution of 1812, which contained several clauses openly antagonistic to the interests of the *criollos.* At this point, not only was the Spanish government too weak to protect *criollo* interest, but with the republicans even its intentions could not be trusted. Thus between 1815 and 1824 the *criollos* fought the wars of independence in a relatively well-organized manner, complete with heroes, and the mainland Spanish colonies became independent nations.[8]

What had been a relatively *quid pro quo* relationship between the *criollos* and Spanish turned against the *criollos* in the eighteenth and early nineteenth centuries. Of course it is possible to sustain an unequal relationship over considerable periods of time, as in the case of the *criollos* vis-à-vis Indians and blacks, but the very conditions which caused the terms of prevailing arrangements to turn against the *criollos* testified to Spanish inability to supply the necessary force and deception to maintain these arrangements. That is, the inability of the Spanish crown and its New World agents to secure the *criollos* against revolt from the workers indicated their incapacity to contain *criollo* separatism.

This level of analysis, however, is much too general to distinguish the usefulness and explanatory power of one historiographical framework over another. A considerably more important indication of the value of the class analysis approach is in respect to the regional diversity of pace, form, and consequence of the wars of independence. The areas in which labor was mobilized in relatively nonrepressive forms and where open class conflict was least apparent were the centers of the independence movement. On the plains of Venezuela and Argentina and in central Colombia and Chile, Spanish control was of minimal importance to the *criollos.* For instance, the major function of the Spanish in the outlying areas was to hold frontiers against raids by nomadic Indians, and even those responsibilities were increasingly assumed by colonial militia and private armies.

In Peru, on the other hand, a large indigenous population had been incorporated into the bottom of colonial society, and through a variety of directly coercive mechanisms, such as debt peonage, conscription at subsistence or below-subsistence wages, and collective tributes, they and the black slaves on the coastal plantations produced the surplus value which nourished the social order. The primary concern in Peru was internal control and stability, particularly after the Indian revolts of the 1770s and 1780s which reached a climax in the major rebellion led by Tupac Amaru II, and Spanish administration was an important and visible instrument of maintaining the *criollos'* positions (Campbell, 1979). Although Spanish weakness did stimulate some *criollo* agitation for independence, the risks in such a move were so clear that the Peruvian *criollos* were too divided for an effective separatist effort, and Peru essentially had to be conquered by San Martín's and Cochrane's forces from the south and Bolívar's armies from the north.

Indian uprisings, particularly the Hidalgo revolt of 1810, put the *criollos* of Mexico and Central America under pressures roughly analogous to those on their counterparts in Peru. They sat out the ambiguous changes in Spanish internal politics after Ferdinand's restoration, but the Spanish republicans' resurgence in 1820 presented too serious a challenge to the *criollos.* In 1821, the Mexican *criollos* broke with Spain and attempted to set up an independent Bourbon monarchy. The aristocratic *criollos* in Central America followed shortly, declaring their independence, in their words, "to prevent the consequences that would be fearful in the event that the people should declare it" (Humphreys and Lynch, 1965, p. 25).

Finally, to complete the comparisons, it is instructive to look at the Spanish islands in the Caribbean. Black slaves outnumbered whites, and the Haitian revolution gave these arithmetic ratios a stark concreteness. As a result, no strong independence movement emerged anywhere in the Spanish Antilles until decades later.

The purpose of these brief sketches has been to convey the regional diversity of what in the hemisphere as a whole added up to the Spanish-American wars of independence. Real chaos prevailed during these years, but that chaos had its roots in the social order and was itself a social process whose understanding is necessary for studying subsequent developments. Through a historiographical framework that places the methods of labor mobilization and the state of the class struggle at the center of analysis, this important diversity can be appreciated while meaningful comparisons can be made by relating differences to a general unifying conception of social change.

While a fuller account of colonial Latin America must include the position of the peoples of mixed race (*castas*),[9] the methodological proposition should be clear: it is imperative to locate the *criollos* in respect to the social relations of production and surplus appropriation mechanisms in order to understand *criollo*-Spanish relations, the internal and external conditions (including ideas, personal aspirations, and so on) affecting these relations, and the divisiveness among the *criollos*. But, as set forth in chapter 1, this approach must be applied in a flexible manner in order to avoid a tendency to deduce complete and tautological explanations for everything. It is clear that this approach has its full share of basic assumptions about how a social system functions, forming an underlying "ideal of Natural Order" (Toulmin, 1961, pp. 44-82) that influences the direction of inquiry; nevertheless, when applied as a set of structured questions rather than as a determinate system, it has an open-ended quality which does not supply the answers but requires that they come from the historical materials. In this form, the approach can be helpful at different levels of research, from Spanish America as a whole down to an individual hacienda or plantation.

THE NEW POLITICAL ORDERS

The decades of instability and violence that followed the wars of independence in Spanish America have often been treated as the struggle between dictatorship and democracy embodied in flamboyant *caudillos* and idealistic liberals. But the use of abstract categories and the focus on individuals obscure the patterns of class forces which were competing for institutionalization in the political life of the new nations. First and most important, the turbulence of the period must be seen in light of the *criollo* elite's efforts to forge a class that would be sufficiently unified and powerful to give political structure and geographical definition to the new nation states. In that the overthrown Spanish authority had actively discouraged the development of horizontal economic and political linkages within colonial society, creating the conditions for class rule was a difficult and protracted process even where it was successful.[10] During the colonial period there was only slight economic interdependence among regions, political organizations for concerted action existed only at local levels, and the wars of independence shattered much of what had existed. Mining and herding activities in those areas which were scenes of battles and passing armies were especially vulnerable to physical destruction, and the dependence of mining on an organized work force transplanted some distance from home meant that the mines were harder hit by the dispersal of workers. Production in crop-growing areas was also disrupted, for even temporary loss of centralized political authority led to the breakdown of coercive schemes for labor mobilization such as slavery and debt peonage, and even of property ownership (Griffin, 1949).

Being involved in extended military operations was hard on the elites in other ways as well. In these times of social disorganization and flux new individuals rose to positions of prominence by sheer effectiveness in fighting and in organizing others to fight. Military power was often translated into personal economic power by the acquisition of land—land formerly belonging to royalists, sheltered Indian communities, the Church, or to those simply unable to protect it for reasons of death, absence, or lack of armed strength. A good number of these new leaders neither were white nor could they pass for white, and although the commanders of the patriot armies acted quickly and brutally to ensure that they were not representatives of their class and race origins (for example, Bolívar's execution of General Piar, a Venezuelan mulatto), the upward social mobility of no-whites accelerated the breakdown of the caste dimensions of class that had been declining at least since the eighteenth century (Mörner, 1967). While limited mobility generally is beneficial to class society because it enlists the services of some of the most able individuals from the lower orders and reduces ossification at the top, in early nineteenth-century Latin America it weakened the hold of racial myths which had helped the white elite remain united.

Upper-class coherence was a problem in the new nations even apart from race and the disruption caused by the wars, for conditions of production from which different elites drew their strength were varied and required different and conflicting forms of political organization. The core of the disputes which wracked the new nations concerned the political forms most appropriate for class rule. The character of class rule in question was not total and complete control, for the effective exercise of political power in class societies generally requires alliances among sectors of the upper classes. Such alliances restrict the ability of any one portion of the possessing classes, even those that might have powerful foreign allies, to enjoy clear and consistent hegemony, as the interests of different sectors of that class run afoul each other at some level. In many of the new nations of Spanish America it was painfully clear that the area of agreement was only at the most general level: establishment of a political system that would help protect the class system as a whole while having minimum independent capacity to threaten the existence and development of that system. These qualities, however, are internally contradictory, for a powerful state organized to protect a given class system is precisely the one that is potentially the most threatening, a dilemma which in the history of European and North American capitalism led to the political doctrines and practices of separation of powers in an effort to achieve protection without the threat. The separation of powers into different branches of government did not adequately resolve the contradiction in Spanish America, however, and elites in the new nations had to make definite decisions concerning which aspect of the political system was to be stressed at the expense of the other. Where present, the dangers of having the class system overturned by assaults from below were always the overriding consideration, taking precedence over fears of possible encroachments by a powerful state, and the manner by which different elites controlled the working classes conditioned their respective positions on the type of political structure preferred for the new states.

In those areas in which the class system was in complete disarray or where it was obviously vulnerable to assaults from actively discontented producing classes, political authority was maintained by the clear and constant threat of naked force, including frequent use of private para-military forces. Fearful upper classes tolerated, even promoted, this system but never liked it. First of all, it was expensive in the use of resources; and second, it was risky, not only because such control in the early nineteenth century was uncertain and inefficient but because it made the possessing classes dependent on people and groups of people who might or might not be reliable guardians of upper-class interests.[11] Thus, in this view, as in the liberal view, governance by overt force did symbolize failure, but a failure of upper-class power and organization rather than of morality and freedom.

In most of the new nations the upper classes were not under such extreme pressure, and the preferred means of class rule that emerged embodied two distinct (and European) conceptions of the ideal political order which usually corresponded to the programs of Conservative and Liberal parties in their formative years. The Conservative vision resembled the colonial polity with its system of rather explicit social control. The major institutions were a powerful, centralized state apparatus (in its extreme version buttressed by the symbolism of a monarchy) which through an elaborate bureaucracy and strong military carefully regulated social and economic life. The second major pillar was the established church, whose moral authority was strengthened by a monopoly on education and on birth, marriage, and death rituals, and by the possession of extensive political and economic power. Although this political system exercised social control directly and was envisioned as a means to preserve class society for the benefit of the possessing classes, it had the marked drawback that upper-class political power was indirect. Political power was vested in entrenched institutions that were at least potentially impervious to influence by even the most influential.

The liberal ideal of political organization was more conducive to direct class rule, but its method of social control was considerably more indirect. It worked through an articulated structure of decentralized primary and secondary institutions—property and contract relations, disestablished church, public schools, formal and informal associations, family, and so on—which exerted the economic, social, and ideological pressure necessary to sustain class society. Although violence still had an important role, it was exercised chiefly at lower levels of social organization by policemen, foremen, teachers, parents, and the like against what were perceived to be individual problems. Only when one or more of the basic structures was threatened were centralized instruments of violence such as the army applied by those at the higher levels in national politics. As long as decentralized institutions effectively precluded challenges to the structure of class privilege and power from the range of legitimate political activity, the apparent openness, competitiveness, and flexibility of political processes in themselves could serve as a stabilizing device. The greater the confidence in the effectiveness of the institutions of control, the more the franchise could be broadened and the less electoral manipulation was necessary. Central government was presided over by an executive with a short term and by a bureaucracy in which personnel in the top positions changed with the executive, thus guarding against entrenchment and insulation from influence.

In many of the newly independent nations, of course, the distinctions between the conservative and liberal programs were not as sharp as those described above, but the differences were still substantial and reflected the judgments of different sectors of the elite about how much direct pressure was necessary to keep the producing classes working for them and about whether the pressure could be adequately exerted at the point of production or required application at a systemic level. Mine owners, for instance, favored direct coercion from a central authority, while landowners engaged in market production with a docile labor force and allied with urban merchants generally favored a looser and more malleable political system requiring considerably less tax support. An important group that stood outside this continuum were the large *haciendas,* generally in the interior, which had no labor control problems and slight, if any, connection with the market. The elites of these primitive, largely self-sufficient units were often antagonistic to any type of national government which might impinge on their authority over personal fiefs.

This statement of alternative political ideals is not meant to suggest a linearly deterministic scheme nor to impugn the motives of individuals who espoused one form or another. It simply recognizes that those on top of the new nations' various surplus appropriation mechanisms, in spite of differences over particulars, were sufficiently powerful that collectively they could assure the demise of any set of political arrangements incompatible with the interests of the class as a whole. This did set definite limits on what was possible in practive and influenced the ascendance of certain ideas at particular times. Nevertheless, the stream from which the ideas flowed—Spanish and European (including Anglo-American) intellectual and cultural traditions—had its own history, not independent of material developments but with considerable integrity of its own. A comprehensive view of the new states' political formation must include the cultural and material spheres and their dialectical interaction.[12]

Attention to the social and material spheres, however, makes more intelligible the nature of Spanish-American conservative and liberal policies. The conservatives were not, for instance, economic reactionaries, and conservative regimes, for example, Páez in Venezuela and García Moreno in Ecuador, were often distinguished by active programs of public works and reconstruction and of promoting local manufacturing, albeit under strict institutional controls. The social conservatism of the liberals' political radicalism, however, is even more problematic for North American liberal historiography than materially progressive conservatism. Liberalism cannot be equated with freedom and liberty (or liberation), however; liberalism is a theory of class society. The less free and the more unequal the society to which its essentially permissive tenets are applied, the more obviously are liberal conceptions of freedom and equality beneficial to the possessing classes and brutalizing for the working classes. In early nineteenth-century Spanish America this can be seen most clearly in the economic sphere. Individual ownership and utilization of property was an ideal wedge for breaking up the Indian communities in order to gain access to their labor power and land. The same principle, buttressed by liberal secularism, was used against the Church's wealth and power, and the promotion of individually negotiated contracts as the sole regulator of worker-owner relations, another element of liberal freedom, meant freedom for employers to squeeze workers without state interference.

Casting the discussion in this manner emphasizes what is too often forgotten in Latin American histories: class societies are not a product of nature; considerable human effort and struggle are necessary to create and maintain a system in which some people do the work from which others derive the benefits. Furthermore, as brief as this outline is, it supplies a more illuminating framework for the comparative study of the post-independence struggles in Latin America than, say, the frequently used groupings of landowners as conservatives and urban dwellers as liberals (for example, Johnson, 1958, pp. 15-26). Only a theory of history in which the influence of ideas is conceived of as the principal moving force could explain such a dichotomy, but the more important criticism is simply that there were too many liberal landowners and conservative merchants for this division to be useful (Safford, 1972). A framework grounded in class analysis lends itself to the finer distinctions required for comparing the complexities of this period's politics; I have used it to emphasize the initial difficulties in overcoming the legacy of colonial economic and political organization and the ravages of the wars of independence in order to contain the producing classes within a national political system.

From this view of the period's politics, serious problems result from using stability and instability of the new nations' political life as a central organizing device for comparative study; such a taxonomy obscures the wide variety of social currents embraced by each category. One type of stability is exemplified by Paraguay, where a good part of regional production in the colonial period had been organized and controlled by the Jesuit missions. After Charles III's expulsion of the Jesuits in the 1760s, there was no elite strong enough to take charge of the newly independent nation. The consequence of such upper-class weakness in the face of hostile neighbors in the east and south was the ascendance of Francia, whose absolute dictatorship further stunted class development. Ecuador's possessing classes, on the other hand, were considerably stronger, and the society still possessed sufficient internal structure after independence for them to be able to break away from the Gran Colombia confederation and fashion a stable and strongly conservative state to contain working-class restiveness. Chile was an outlying province with considerable autonomy under colonial administration, and Peruvian markets for such Chilean products as wheat, livestock products, and wine had led to the formation of a vigorous, market-oriented upper class composed principally of landowners and merchants who had few labor control problems. These conditions were not seriously disrupted by the wars of independence, and an aristocratic republicanism emerged early with relatively little strife.

The formative period of post-independence Brazil, although different from Spanish America in that it did not begin with a violent break from Portugal, can also be understood in these terms. Brazil gradually, even cautiously, evolved from a backward colony (for example, there were no printing presses or universities until the nineteenth century), to a co-kingdom (1815), to an independent monarchy (1822), and finally to a republic (1889). During the reign of Pedro II (1840-1889) the landed and urban elites in the south, directly or indirectly related to the expanding coffee export sector, developed to the point that they broke the power of the northern sugar aristocracy and established the semi-liberal political forms of the Republic needed for their further development (Dean, 1971; Furtado, 1963, pp. 119-192; Galloway, 1971; Meade, 1978; Seckinger, 1977).

Political instability also embraced a variety of social currents too important to be obscured by using instability itself as an organizing device. For instance, there were the instabilities of Peru, Bolivia, and Mexico which had been centers of Spanish colonial administration where the wars were extremely destructive. The possessing classes in these nations had neither the confidence in their control of the producing classes nor the unity to create a political alternative to military rule, and the tensions and personal ambitions within the victorious armies led to frequent wars and rapid turnover of the generals at the top.[13] Such a situation contrasts sharply with that in Venezuela, where the conservative Páez regime threw off Bogotá's hegemony within the Gran Colombia confederation and suppressed revolts by coastal workers, in this case introduced to class struggle by royalist troops. The successful establishment of class rule, however, created the conditions in which intra-class conflict grew up within it as a liberal opposition, which then resulted in considerable turmoil. Colombia's experience was roughly analogous to that of Venezuela's in this respect, but in addition it clearly illustrates the nature of conservative-liberal competition. As bitter as such intra-class strife became, the possessing classes could unite quickly when class rule as a whole was threatened, as in the case of the overthrow of a reformist military government in 1854 and removal of the artisans from the political arena.

The Colombian case introduces a new social group into the discussion which so far has been conducted in terms of the various surplus appropriation relations between landowners and workers, planters and slaves, mine owners and miners, and merchants allied with one or another segment of the possessing classes. Artisans, however, were representative of the petty mode: they were workers who owned their own means of produciton and stood outside any of the established appropriation mechanisms. Typically organized in guilds, they produced a wide variety of consumer goods for local markets, including such items as textiles and clothing, furniture, shoes, pans, glassware, and jewelry. In some lines, notably textiles, they competed with primitive factories, but foreign competition was the major threat, and the activity of artisans along with the early factories declined during the Bourbon trade reforms. Artisans were still numerically important, however, during the early years of the national period in the densely populated highland areas of Colombia, Mexico, and northwestern Argentina (near the Bolivian mines) where geography made transportation costs from the coast extremely high for imports. Some political accommodation with the artisanal group was necessary in these areas. In Colombia and Mexico the new governments made explicit, though short-lived, efforts to promote domestic industrial production that initially benefited the artisans. The Colombian experiment, which involved tariff protection, loans, and limited monopoly franchises for selected commodities and producers, came to a rather abrupt end in the 1840s and 1850s when Colombian tobacco exports became lucrative and steamboat service on the Magdalena River opened the interior to cheap imports (Safford, 1965; Harrison, 1952). The resulting shifts in political power led to the freeing of trade, and the artisans entered politics to defend themselves from ruinous competition. Their subsequent suppression by the combined upper classes was only a temporary victory for free trade—limited protection was established again in the 1880s—but it was more important, at least to the victors in 1854, that they would be the ones to decide (Bushnell, 1956; Urrutia, 1969, pp. 30-44).

The dynamics in Mexico were not dissimilar to those in Colombia, but the Hidalgo revolt in 1810 and the continuing post-independence riots by miners and other workers put the survival of the social order into greater question. In this context measures had to be taken to avoid severe urban unemployment in this most highly urbanized of the new Spanish-American nations (di Tella, 1973). During the late 1820s and 1830s the Mexican government set up a sophisticated industrial promotion scheme, complete with a development bank, but the whole program soon foundered (Aubrey, 1949; Potash, 1959). Even when the government-subsidized factories finally began production, their employment effect was late and probably negative, because particularly in textiles their production displaced artisan and older factory production. Internal convulsions and the war with France in the 1830s and with the U.S. in the 1840s strained governmental fiscal powers, leading to raids on the development bank's funds, and confirmed the military's rise to power. Pressure to make good on defaulted foreign loans and the revival of export production from mining (with British capital) and agriculture for European markets put irresistible pressure on protection. So the structure for promoting domestic industrial growth was dismantled in the 1840s and 1850s, and the army remained the principal guardian against working-class insurrection.

In Argentina, like Chile an agrarian province of the Spanish empire with a relatively docile labor force, free versus protected trade could in itself become a major source of intra-class conflict. Artisans were involved, but the struggle was primarily one of the inland elites producing such commodities as wine, textiles, and sugar for domestic markets against coastal landowners and merchants oriented toward export markets. The correspondence of the protagonists to distinct regions meant that issues such as the regional distribution of customs revenues collected in Buenos Aires were also involved, but the geographic clarity of the division helped make the victory of the coastal export interests in the civil war decisive (Burgin, 1946; Ferrer, 1967, pp. 65-73).

Free trade was a major policy issue in Latin America, and as mentioned in chapter 2, it was vigorously promoted by the British. Nevertheless, it was a policy issue which generally surfaced as an effort to influence an existing political system, occurring subsequent to the establishment of class hegemony and cutting across conservative-liberal lines drawn over the political organization of social power. Although free trade is usually identified with liberalism, it concerns market relations of commodities rather than social relationships of production, and thereby can stand apart from more fundamental aspects of social and political organization. Two nineteenth-century examples of neutrality of free trade in this respect were the high tariffs of liberal United States and the free trade feudalism of southeastern Europe.[14] In other words, it was only after the surplus appropriation mechanisms has been secured within a political system that serious conflicts developed over free trade. This is not to say that surplus appropriation and surplus realization are independent processes, for surplus realization supplied the resources to the elite and to the supporting institutions necessary for sustaining and reproducing the appropriation mechanism, thus influencing the outcome of intraclass conflicts. Nevertheless, while foreign markets were the only feasible outlet for the produce of Spanish-American plantations, haciendas, and mines, the free trade issue represented a matter of *relative* access to foreign markets. The alternative was not the export prohibitions of national economic self-sufficiency and independence, except possibly in Paraguay—and there is some doubt even about that (Cooney, 1972)—but a regulated and qualified engagement in foreign markets.

The initial effect of the integration of the new nations into world markets was on the import side. The most active foreign penetration in the years immediately following independence was by British merchants who were selling, not buying. (As noted in chapter 2, this competitive capitalist phenomenon was qualitatively different from Spanish mercantile policy, which retained its family resemblance to the character of British economic penetration of peripheral areas during the seventeenth and early eighteenth centuries.) The disruption of the Spanish-American wars of independence and the undeveloped domestic transport facilities impeded export production and delivery, while the post-Waterloo depression in Europe weakened foreign demand for Spanish-American commodities but intensified English producers' own export promotion efforts (Furtado, 1976, pp. 39-44). Severe balance-of-payments crises and frequent depreciations in the value of local currencies resulted, and the erection of tariff barriers was an obvious reaction to external disequilibria (as well as a source of revenue for the financially pressed new governments).

But some foreign markets were stronger than others; even in the early years the pattern of foreign trade influenced the rise and fall of different sectors of domestic elites in the new nations. As an example, foreign market conditions for tropical agricultural exports (sugar, cocoa, dyestuffs, and so on) were the worst, adding to the problems of plantation-based elites already hard hit by the frequent granting of manumission to slaves for service in the armies during the wars for independence. This weakness made them vulnerable to assaults by other sectors of the national elites producing commodities like hides and minerals with better foreign markets. This unevenness of domestic development with the consequent internal shifts of political power allowed the ascendant elites in the Spanish-American nations where slavery had survived the immediate post-independence period (on the coasts of Venezuela, Colombia, Ecuador, and Peru, and in the interior of Argentina) to abolish it altogether in the 1850s. Within the nations, general emanicipation further reduced planters' political power as well as the threat to social stability posed by slave revolts. This diminution of political power had important ramifications for subsequent political developments. As slavery in these nations had required a strong central authority for its continued viability, planters had strongly supported the "genuine" conservatism in the sense outlined earlier. Their eclipse eased the transition toward more liberal forms in those nations where competing elites were based on less troublesome modes of labor mobilization. The tendency can be seen most readily in Colombia and Argentina, to a lesser extent in Venezuela.

Foreign investment in the first few years of independence made some contribution to building political institutions, but its direct influence was slight relative to internal processes. Apart from some English efforts in Bolivian and Mexican silver mines, foreign investment in these early years was principally British portfolio purchases of the new governments' bonds, seemingly independent of the structure and composition of the particular governments (Rippy, 1959, pp. 17-26). Altogether, British investment in Latin America amounted to approximately 30 million pounds sterling by 1826, and this source of revenue temporarily relieved the governments from having to make hard decisions about who was going to have to pay how much tax. But when these loans were defaulted, as they almost universally were, virtually no new foreign capital entered Latin America for the next twenty-five years. The mechanics of the loans are interesting; they were purchased principally by British financial houses at sizable discounts and sold to the public by means of intensive and misleading advertising at considerable profit for the underwriters. In that the reduced proceeds of the loans received by the Latin American borrowers directly or indirectly went to purchases of imported British goods, their subsequent default by the Spanish-American borrowers meant that the whole operation involved a transfer of income from the ultimate bond holders to British bankers, merchants, and export producers, and to Latin American governments and purchasers of imports (Rippy, 1959, pp. 19-22, 26-42, 172-174). The Latin American nations, however, were under very definite pressure for repayment, complete with occasional naval blockades, and as repayment was to be in pounds sterling (or francs, dollars, and so on), the bonds' redemption necessitated export earnings.

Rosa Luxemburg (1913, pp. 419-445), drawing on Tugan Baranowski and

Sismondi, contended that these defaulted loans to Latin America (and to Egypt and Turkey) were used by the British to force the new nations into the world market as exporters of primary products and importers of manufactured goods, thus condemning them to dependency and underdevelopment. This general type of proposition is common in much recent scholarship on Latin America, and chapter 4 and succeeding chapters will deal at length with various aspects of this theme. The basis for my critique, however, has already been laid in this and the preceding chapter.

There is no question but what the British had definite, though changing, interests in Latin American participation in world markets, and they pressured governments to that end throughout the nineteenth century. As has been demonstrated in this chapter, however, when the terms of the internal struggles wracking the new nations of Latin America are appreciated, to attribute Latin American engagement in international commodity and capital markets solely or even principally to coercion by foreigners is highly dubious. Portions of the Latin American possessing classes were willing and eager to take advantage of world market opportunities to consolidate and extend their positions vis-a-vis domestic working classes and competing segments of the elites (Smith, 1969; Platt, 1968, pp. 308-368; Platt, 1972). The relative political stability of the late nineteenth century indicates that the strategy worked. The content of conservative-liberal rivalry in national politics, although occasionally still extremely violent (for example, Colombia), changed so that competition was between political parties within at least nominally republican political institutions on what earlier would have been seen as liberal terms; the programmatic differences between the parties had narrowed to the point where frequently the parties were distinguished principally by the personalities of their respective leaders.

While integration into the international divisions of labor did retard domestic industrial growth, it is a mistake to portray industrial development in early nineteenth-century Latin America as being some deeply felt national aspiration, welling up from a strong consensus but suppressed by the British. The conflicts within the nations of Latin America in the first few decades after independence were certainly not concerned primarily with promoting industrial growth, even in Colombia and Mexico. They were over who would exercise domestic political power, and in this process, international economic relations and resources were crucial in determining victors and losers. Industrial growth, particularly with the implications of its competitive capitalist form, was simply not in the interests of anyone who counted politically; in this context, to speak of transcendant national goals is to commit an egregious error by using an inappropriate unit of analysis. Moreover, even if none of these considerations had pertained, industrialization still required specific social and economic features, lacking in early nineteenth-century Latin America and far more fundamental than those that English influence or the will of local elites were capable of determining in one direction or another. Chapter 2, including Table 2.9, shows that much more than relative prices was involved in industrial development.

These observations go to the heart of the historiographical argument made in this chapter. Latin American national elites overwhelm the historical record, particularly primary source materials (largely written by members of the upper classes), and historians frequently are more interested in and identify more easily with the refined strata of society. Because these elites were the most receptive to currents of European culture, welcomed foreign economic help in exploiting domestic natural resources and labor power, and yet were wary of foreign political hegemony, one of the major consequences of excluding from study the constant effort it took to create and preserve the system which underlay elite status, is a consistent exaggeration of the importance of external influences in shaping Latin American societies. The tendency to view these societies as having been molded, for better or worse, by foreign influences is apparent in interpretations of the early nineteenth century and all but overwhelming for the latter half of the century when large-scale export economies were created in Latin America (see chapter 4). While there is no doubt that developments in and influences from Europe and North America were felt strongly in Latin America, an understanding of the direction or even the importance of their effects requires adequate appreciation of domestic structures and relationships, especially the varied forms of labor mobilization. Class analysis, as a unifying analytical framework for comparative history, supplies this crucial dimension of explanation.

This framework will be applied in succeeding chapters, but the character of the class forces change significantly. While competitive capitalist industrial development was not feasible in early nineteenth-century Latin America, significant industrial growth of this type did occur in several nations in the first decades of the twentieth century. This was during the global phase of finance capitalism, however, and chapters 4 and 5 show the conditions of that growth and why its off-phase character worked against the self-sustaining economic expansion necessary for national industrial development.

NOTES

1. On these particular points, see Foster (1960); Phelan (1960); and Service (1955). Good surveys of the literature on Spanish-American colonial society are Bowser (1972); Lockhart (1972); Mörner (1973); and Spalding (1972).

2. More precisely, I am talking about white males born in the Americas. For an idea of the position of women in Spanish colonial society, see Lockhart (1968, pp. 150-168); Mörner (1967, pp. 21-34 and *passim*); and Wolf (1959, pp. 218-224).

3. For the economic history of Spain during the colonial period, see Vicens Vives (1969, pp. 291-604). Wilson (1967) is an excellent survey of European mercantilism which brings out the peculiarity of Spanish colonial policy, Parry (1971) presents the details of that colonial practice, and Weaver (1976) locates the character of Spanish expansion within a historical view of capitalist development.

4. Although certainly not a conventional textbook, Frank (1972, pp. 46-54), is a striking example of this type of interpretation.

5. Humphreys and Lynch (1965) is a good critical discussion of the role of ideas in the independence movement, stressing the manner in which the conservative colonial society itself filtered out revolutionary social and political aspects of Enlightenment thought and allowed only the natural science portions to take root. Representative of the strong idealist tradition in the historiography of this period is Johnson (1964, p. 21): "They [the wars of independence] were . . . the manufacture of the fecund minds of a few learned individuals, primarily under the influence of Rousseau. . . ."

6. This aspect of the *criollos'* position is seldom dealt with in the historical literature. Stein and Stein (1970, pp. 110-111) mention it in passing, while Lynch (1973, pp. 340-341) gives the concept more prominence.

7. The role of the Spanish troops was, of course, dual; they also suppressed the *comunero* revolt in Colombia during the early 1780s, a movement with considerable *criollo* support (Phelan, 1978).

8. I am using the periodization of the wars suggested by Parry (1971, pp. 344-360), which Graham (1972) develops more fully.

9. Mörner (1967, pp. 75-90) and Wolf (1959, pp. 233-256) are good discussions of the social status of the *castas* in colonial society and their role in the wars of independence.

10. Even in the nineteenth century class societies did not always produce class-dominated states. Marx and Engels (1846, pp. 59-60), Marx (1852), and Engels (1884, pp. 320-321) explore the historical conditions of class balance by which the state can have considerable independence from even the most powerful classes.

11. These interests I refer to, here and elsewhere, go beyond simple wealth and income maximization; they include the panoply of power, prestige, and personal freedoms that go with being on top. Also included in this is conformance to ethical notions of "right" and "good" that, as Alfred Marshall observed somewhere, serve to make those who are comfortable feel comfortable (and those are not comfortable, resigned). After achieving a comfortable minimum, members of an elite might well trade off some additional income, if necessary, for other advantages of elite existence.

12. Ashcraft (1972) argues this general position forcefully. For Latin America's political tradition in the nineteenth century, see Hale (1972) and Morse (1954 and 1964).

13. Brading (1973, pp. 411-412) distinguishes sharply, and I believe accurately, between the military *caudillos* of Peru, Bolivia, and Mexico from those, as in Argentina and Venezuela, who were agents of class power. Halperin-Donghi (1973) also contains some good discussions of their differences.

14. Emmanuel (1972, pp. xii-xx) has an informative and amusing description of liberal economists' failure to sell free-trade policies to liberal U.S. politicians, and Mitrany (1930, pp. 63-64) shows the importance of free trade for late nineteenth-century Romanian boiars. It misrepresents the political struggle of the period to elevate free trade so that it appears to be the sole, or even central, source of conflict, as does Frank (1972, pp. 51-62).

4

LATIN AMERICA IN THE INTERNATIONAL DIVISION OF LABOR, 1840-1914

Continuing economic development in late nineteenth-century Europe and the U.S. heightened those economies' demand for raw material inputs to use in their expanding industries and for foodstuffs to feed their rapidly urbanizing populations. As described in chapter 2, this enlarged demand in the core economies was complemented by the need to find markets particularly for capital and intermediate goods whose productive capacity tended to outstrip sustained levels of domestic demand for machinery, steel, metal products, chemicals, and so on. Dramatic advances in transport technology lowered transport costs to the point where for Europe, Latin American natural resources became economically feasible sources of raw materials and foodstuffs, and these exports were facilitated by large-scale direct investment from the core nations in support activities like transportation and public utilities and less typically in the production of the export commodities themselves, for example, Mexican metal mining and Chilean nitrates. (See Tables 4.1 and 4.2 for its magnitude, sources, and effects on rail mileage.) By the turn of the twentieth century, most of the nations in Latin America were firmly enmeshed in an international division of labor in which they exported primary products, and with these earnings, minus transport and capital charges, they imported manufactured goods. Latin America's role in this global system was substantial; it has been estimated that of total world exports of particular primary groupings in 1913, the Latin American nations exported 17.9 percent of the cereals, 11.5 percent of the livestock products, 62.1 percent of the coffee, tea, and cocoa, 14.2 percent of the fruits and vegetables, 25.1 percent of the rubber, hides, and leather, and significant proportions of various minerals (Furtado, 1976, p. 51).

The contributions foreign trade and investment have made and are making to the economic advance of the nations in Latin America continue to be the subject of intense debate, and this chapter attempts to clarify some central analytical

TABLE 4.1
Foreign Private Direct Investment in Latin America, 1914
(millions of $ U.S.)

	United Kingdom	*France*	*Germany*	*United States*	*Others*[a]	*TOTAL*	*% Distribution*
Argentina	1,502	289	235	40	1,151	3,217	
Bolivia	17	25	.....	2	.....	44	
Brazil	609	391	.....	50	146	1,196	
Chile	213	.....	56	225	.....	494	
Colombia	31	1	.....	21	1	54	
Costa Rica	3	.....	.....	41	.....	44	
Cuba	170	.....	.....	216	.....	386	
Ecuador	29	2	.....	9	.....	40	
Guatemala	44	.....	12	36	.....	92	
Mexico	635	.....	.....	542	.....	1,177	
Peru	121	1	.....	58	.....	180	
Uruguay	154	.....	2	.....	199	355	
Venezuela	30	2	15	38	60	145	
Other & Undistr.	.....	.....	.....	41	.....	41	
TOTAL	3,585	711	320	1,394	1,559	7,569	
Agriculture	12	.....	.....	239	4	255	3.4
Mining	101	3	.....	415	11	530	7.1
Petroleum	4	.....	.....	136	.....	140	1.9
Railroads	1,667	152	15	305	203	2,342	30.9
Public Utilities	549	17	75	127	149	914	12.0
Manufacturing	83	.....	.....	17	462	562	7.4
Other	2	.....	.....	34	449	485	6.4
Undistr.	1,170	539	230	121	281	2,341	30.9
TOTAL	3,585	711	320	1,394	1,559	7,569	100.0

SOURCE: U.N. Economic Commission for Latin America, *External Financing in Latin America* (New York: United Nations, 1965), p. 17.
NOTE: [a]Principally Belgian, Dutch, Portugese, and Swiss capital.

TABLE 4.2
Railway Mileage in Latin America, 1860-1920
(mileage in 1,000 miles and % of world railway mileage)

	First Steam Line Opened	1860		1880		1900		1920	
		Miles	%	Miles	%	Miles	%	Miles	%
Latin America	1837[a]	0.5	0.8	7.2	3.2	34.5	7.4	62.9	9.3
Mexico	1850	0.0	0.0	0.7	0.3	8.3	1.8	13.0	1.9
Chile	1851	0.3	0.4	1.1	0.5	2.7	0.6	5.1	0.8
Peru	1851	0.1	0.1	1.3	0.6	1.1	0.2	2.2	0.3
Brazil	1854	0.1	0.2	2.1	1.0	9.5	2.0	17.7	2.6
Argentina	1857	0.0	0.0	1.6	0.7	10.4	2.2	21.2	3.1

SOURCE: William Woodruff, *Impact of Western Man, A Study of Europe's Role in the World Economy, 1750-1960* (New York: St. Martin's Press, 1967), p. 253.
NOTE: [a]Cuba

issues which appear to have been missed in the voluminous literature. It focuses on the theoretical premises of the debate because divergent conclusions stem less from conflicting evidence than from the different ways in which similar empirical material is organized and interpreted.

Like most writers, I see the major division of opinion to be between those working in the Anglo-American tradition of neoclassical economic theory and those identified with "dependency theory," based in large part on the analyses of the United Nations Economic Commission for Latin America (ECLA) in the late 1940s and 1950s. Unlike other writers, however, I perceive the differences between these approaches to be less significant than their common assumption that the growth-inducing or retarding effects of foreign trade and investment in Latin America (or elsewhere, for that matter) are due principally to the availability of economic resources. The first section of the chapter, after a brief survey of the two approaches, presents an alternative approach which calls into question the very terms of the debate. The second section presents short case studies of Argentinian and Peruvian experiences with international commodity and capital markets in the nineteenth century to establish a basis for additional comparative material and to elaborate on the general points made in the first section.

COMPARATIVE ADVANTAGE, DEPENDENCY, AND STAPLE THEORIES

In the neoclassical tradition, the central conceptual framework guiding economic research on the relation between foreign trade and economic growth is the theory of comparative advantage (or comparative costs).[1] The theory derives directly from David Ricardo's observation that international commerce enables a nation to specialize in those commodities which it can produce relatively cheaply, exchanging them on the international market for those products it produces relatively expensively at better terms than are available domestically. This activity raises the real income of all trading partners and parallels Adam Smith's discussion of the benefits from division of labor among individuals within a society.[2] These static gains from changing the composition of national production have implications for growth, for the rise in real income increases in some aggregate sense a nation's potential investable surpluses. Buttressing this conclusion are such works as those by J. R. Hicks (1959, pp. 132, 183-185) who recognized that international trade allows a poor country with a small market to exchange products of "low growth potential" for products of "high growth potential" (for example, trading bananas for drill presses) and to realize the efficiencies of large-scale production, and by Gottfried Haberler (1959, pp. 10-15) who stressed the flows of investment, technology, and skills that accompany international trade. Combining the static and dynamic elements, neoclassical trade theory has been made into a logically coherent and powerful argument for the important contribution that participation in the world economy can make to a poor nation's economic advance.

On the surface it appears that the optimism of the extended comparative advantage model has to be considerably qualified in order to fit anything resembling the historical experience of Latin American nations. The most frequently used procedure for dealing with the inconsistency between theory and history is simply to sidestep the issue, asserting that the economic expansion expected to be derived from foreign trade's allocative and dynamic effects did not occur because these nations did not possess the "prerequisites to economic growth." Theorists' reliance on Rostow's tautology preserves economic theory's system of abstractions (and thereby the academic division of labor). But by using this tactic, these scholars explicitly acknowledge both that the theory is not able to consider the effect of international commerce on economic growth beyond the availabilities of economic resources as well as that these economic variables are of secondary importance in explaining growth and development. Moreover, the theory's incompleteness is misleading, for it implies that economic phenomena do not have profound influences on social and political structures, a methodological position which reflects the explanatory limits of the neoclassical economic model rather than the processes of Latin American history.[3]

Unlike neoclassical trade and development theory, dependency models are explicitly formulated to explain Latin American *under*development. While those classed as dependency theorists include an extremely wide ideological range, their common analytical theme is that the particular manner in which the nations of Latin America have been integrated into the world economy has adversely affected the amount of benefits, in terms of economic resources, that those nations have received from trade and foreign investment. Reflecting the spectrum of thought within the dependency school, the diagnoses range from the relative lack of resources that were made available to the Latin American nations to the loss by

Latin American nations of resources through international economic relationships.[4] These differences among dependency theorists, however, are matters of degree within a strongly shared conviction that the principal obstacle to Latin American development has been and continues to be such mechanisms as the repatriation of profits from foreign investment and declining terms of trade for their primary product exports.

At best, these intellectual efforts offer some mild qualifications to the optimistic conclusions of comparative advantage thinking, and at their extreme suffer from serious logical and empirical error. To focus on the flow of repatriated profits in isolation from the whole process of foreign investment, including its productivity and the distribution of the increased product among domestic as well as foreign factors, is analogous to exploring only costs in cost-benefit analysis. Even more disturbing is the frequency with which the repatriation of profits from Latin America to the industrialized nations is labeled surplus appropriation.[5] This labeling indicates serious confusion; repatriated profits are an international transfer of *already appropriated* surplus, and the distinction is crucial. The Marxian conception of surplus appropriation, rooted in the labor theory of value, is a method for studying the class relations, superstructural forms, and the materially progressive or nonprogressive character of a particular society. But when it is used, essentially metaphorically, in a Leninist scheme of worldwide division between proletarian and bourgeois nations without sufficient attention to the class relations within the respective nations, the concept of surplus dissolves into a quantitative aggregate denoting amounts of economic resources, which then is used abstractly to identify *national* rather than class relations. These are categories from conventional economic theory, no matter what one may call them, and they are of only limited usefulness in revealing the contribution made by foreign trade and investment to Latin American underdevelopment.

The argument about secularly declining terms of trade for primary products involves problems of measurement, ambiguous evidence, and doubtful logic, all of which were extensively dealt with during the 1950s and 1960s.[6] Finally, there is the frequently heard assertion that foreign trade and investment forced Latin American nations into a disadvantageous role in the international division of labor. As primary product exporters, so the argument goes, Latin American productive resources were channeled into the least dynamic sectors while their trading partners' specialization in manufacturing promoted technological change, urbanization, and other national and cultural benefits denied to "hewers of wood and drawers of water." The argument harks back to Friedrich List's "natural inferiority of agriculture," a position which certainly has not been universally true.[7] Moreover, even recognizing the presence and bald exercise of European and U.S. power in nineteenth-century Latin America and the repressive forms of labor mobilization within the nations, international commerce and finance in Latin America were principally guided by markets and Latin American possessing classes rather than by foreign politicians or military forces. Unlike areas subject to foreign colonial legislation, the Latin American national governments of the nineteenth century were not prevented by foreign armies and navies from promoting industrial growth through commercial and fiscal policies as in contemporary Germany, the United States, and Australia.[8]

As mentioned in the prefatory remarks, however, my central thesis is that the very terms of the debate between those using neoclassical theories and those employing dependency theory formulations are inappropriate for studying the growth-inducing or retarding effects of foreign trade and investment in Latin America. As should be clear by now, a crucial point of agreement between neoclassical and dependency theorists is what constitutes a satisfactory explanation of the developmental effects of foreign trade and investment, and that explanation centers around the availabilities of economic resources. Thereby the variables entering the arguments are distributive shares of income generated by foreign-owned capital, relative prices of commodities in international markets, international financial flows stemming from aggregate trade and payments balances, and the like. These are the homegrounds of orthodox economic theory, the area of its greatest explanatory power and precision, and the theory of comparative advantage remains a cogent argument, in narrow economic terms, for the important potential contribution that foreign trade and investment can make to poor nations' material advance. This does not mean that it offers an adequate explanation of the Latin American nations' historical experience in world markets, however, because the availability of economic resources is as far as economic theory can go toward investigating the relation between foreign trade and investment and economic development. As has been noted, when faced by intractable historical evidence that in many areas these resources were not translated into sustained economic expansion, economists working in the neoclassical tradition are forced to resort to such quasi-explanations as the lack of "prerequisites of economic growth." The position taken by dependency theorists is a mirror image of this, for using the same focus they regard the lack of economic growth as *prima facie* evidence that the resources from foreign trade and investment were not forthcoming, and they concentrate their efforts accordingly. This is a vivid illustration of the intellectual hegemony exercised by neoclassical trade theory; even when its conclusions are not helpful, conventional theorizing can still define the terms of the debate for those critical of the theory.[9]

This surprising methodological consensus obscures the serious problems that lie in the very terms and focus of the arguments. Given that a nation, that abstract category of neoclassical trade theory (and of liberal thought in general), did receive some net economic resources through its involvement in international markets, it is the next step, the use of these additional resources—the manner in which the opportunities they represented for change and growth were or were not realized in a particular historical setting—that is crucial but not explored. The very structure of orthodox trade theory which enables it to deal successfully with the question of aggregate resources renders its focus inappropriate for this second layer of inquiry, and scholars interested in social change and economic growth must use a different approach that can relate foreign trade to domestic social structure to economic development and underdevelopment, without short-circuiting these processes in the manner of economic theory.[10]

The most promising candidate, in my opinion, is the staple theory of export-led growth—a staple being a resource-based product. Harold Innis is generally credited with the original formulation of this theory in the 1930s, and from Innis its most frequent use has been in interpreting Canadian economic history.[11] This is not without irony, for it is Canadian history which appears most threatening to those who wish to demonstrate that no benefits have been or are likely to be received by staple exporters trading with powerful, industrialized nations. Both Hans Singer (1950, pp. 484-485) and Andre Gunder Frank (1967, pp. 11, 56), as examples, propose complex and implausible explanations for Canada's apparent success in building on exports of primary products for domestic economic expansion.

Although the staple theory has not received the intensive care and nurture bestowed on the neoclassical model, some major refinements of it have been made, most notably through the work of Robert Baldwin and of Albert Hirschman.[12] The staple theory focuses attention directly on the ways in which a nation's export commodities are produced and the manner in which such production relates to national production as a whole. The scale, organization, and factor mix of export production will depend on the particular production function of that commodity and on the availabilities (costs) of different factors from domestic and foreign sources, whether the entrepreneur is strictly a profit maximizer or not. Once these choices are made, however, export production will affect national production in ways that can be identified through the various market linkages introduced in the imput-output discussion in chapter 1.

For instance, family farms were economically efficient units for growing wheat in the nineteenth century while large-scale plantations characterized sugar and cotton production. A few plantation owners employed large numbers of unskilled laborers, yielding a sharply skewed distribution of income distinct from the more egalitarian diffusion of income in a system of family farms, thereby influencing the pattern of consumer demand derived from export-generated incomes. Specialized luxury goods—frequently imported—and services are the dominant pattern of consumer demand in plantation economies, while the family farms are more likely to create a broad market for consumer goods capable of being mass-produced locally. This is the first linkage effect, the income multiplier: the degree to which those earning income in the export sector stimulate economic activity in other sectors of the local economy through their demands as consumers.

The other linkage effects depend more on the specific nature of the export commodity itself and its location within a general input-output system. Backward linkages are new production induced by the export sectors' demand for inputs: fertilizers for agricultural export production; saws for a timber industry; power generation for a wide variety of export activities; and transportation facilities and construction materials for virtually all. Forward linkages are those which involve further processing of the staple; examples include a timber export leading to the establishment of furniture and newsprint firms, oil production for export encouraging the creation of refineries and petrochemical plants, and so forth. Similarly, heightened commercial and financial activity is integrally linked to export production. There is strong interrelation between what is produced and how it is produced, and the sources of the various linkages frequently overlap, but it is still apparent that some types of export commodities are better stimuli for general economic growth than others (Caves, 1971, pp. 433-437).

Properly speaking, the staple theory is more a typology than a theory. As such it is not inconsistent with neoclassical gains-from-trade arguments, and in fact it offers a method for systematically disaggregating these gains and tracing the impulses from the export sector through the national economy. Even more important for our purposes, however, is the focus of staple theory. By emphasizing *production* rather than exchange as the central subject of study, the staple theory can provide a systematic organizing device with which one can relate economic activity to other dimensions of social life and thus avoid the barren narrowness of conventional economic analysis. Again, Robert Baldwin's seminal 1956 article is the principal reference. He posits two newly discovered uninhabited lands equidistant from the nation acquiring the two new colonies. The colonies are identical in all respects except that one is appropriate for producing an export from the now-familiar large plantations, and the other exports a commodity in which a family farm organization is the most efficient. Although Baldwin treats the linkage effects in detail, he also lays the foundation for a broader analysis. Those who establish the large-scale plantations in the first colony are drawn from the ruling country's wealthy elite, since setting up a plantation requires substantial capital outlay, and they recruit labor from among the very poor and unskilled. From this beginning one can see how the social dynamic is likely to play out. The economic and cultural distance between owners and workers has overtones of caste, for there are extremely few avenues of upward mobility for those on the bottom. The technical requirements of plantation production are such that there exists no skill ladder up which a laborer, or even successive generations of laborers, might work, and the advantages of large-scale enterprises in this product preclude a laborer's establishing a new plantation even if land has a price of zero. Retreating to subsistence farming remains the only domestic alternative to plantation work even if land is available and no effective labor control measures exist. The plantation aristocracy embraces a culture which is externally oriented and disdainful of business affairs and manual labor; political life is highly centralized and authoritarian, and per capita economic growth is neglible. In contrast, the modest capital requirements of establishing a family farm in the other colony draw migrants from the ruling country's middle classes, and the automistic and egalitarian character of productive organization encourages the formation of a society that would warm the heart of any liberal theorist: it is open, flexible, decentralized, hardworking, democratic, and materially progressive.[13]

As with any historiographical model, the staple theory expanded in this manner must be used with care. Richard Caves, for one, calls into question the linear determination of social and cultural forms by the economic and technological, suggesting that causation is just as likely in the opposite direction; for example, certain types of societies tend to produce sugar (Caves, 1971, p. 432). This apparently is a reaction to Baldwin's rather mechanical presentation of cause and effect, but the fact remains that even when formulated in such a stark manner, the expanded staple theory offers considerable insight into the comparative histories of the "newly settled regions" in the New World colonized by the English, areas affording some control over the migrants' backgrounds. It provides a vehicle for understanding the evolution of large-scale sugar, cotton, and tobacco plantations based on slave labor in the British West Indies and the U.S. South, and the reasons why grain-growing family farms were established in the Canadian prairie provinces and the U.S. Midwest. Moreover, focusing on staple exports, or more to the point, on the organization of production, contributes to an understanding of why the slave plantation society in the southeastern United States had more in common with the British West Indies (and Spanish, French, and Portuguese sugar areas as well) in social organization, political styles, cultural patterns, and economic dynamism that it did with other regions within the United States. Approaches emphasizing cultural and ideational influences are much less instructive.[14]

What should concern us at this point, however, is not testing a hypothesis but formulating a set of propositions that will fruitfully guide historical study. In this more general endeavor, there is nothing in the structure of the expanded staple theory to prevent its being applied flexibly: the new types of economic activity (in this case, the organization of export production) exert new pressures which work on established institutions and the consequences are a combination of prior conditions and new influences. Conceiving of the model in this way retains the principal causal flow but increases its applicability.

This greater flexibility is vital when we turn, finally, to the histories of the nations in Latin America, for large-scale export sectors were established in societies with long histories. Nevertheless, as shown in chapter 3, the social and political institutions of the newly independent nations of Latin America were in considerable flux, and exports had been an important activity in many of the areas during colonial times. Moreover, it is misleading to conceive of the new export economies founded by English migrants to the New World as having been set up in essentially *tabula rasa* conditions, for the migrants themselves were products of a cultural heritage, responded to the indigenous people they found, and brought in new cultures with African, Asian, and other European peoples. I am not arguing that the backgrounds in which export production flourished in the different areas were the same, but that their differences were a matter of degree capable of being handled within a flexible version of the expanded staple theory.

ARGENTINA AND PERU

The staple theory enables us to compare and make intelligible the diverse effects which integration into international commodity and capital markets had on different Latin American nations. Argentine and Peruvian experiences with foreign trade and investment clearly illustrate the range of those effects, and therefore those nations' histories are useful benchmarks for comparative study.

Argentina's history exemplifies the need to avoid mechanical technological determinism. At the turn of the twentieth century, Argentina was the world's third largest exporter of wheat, and as noted above, the efficiency of small-scale productive units in nineteenth-century wheat growing was of decisive importance in the economic and social development of the U.S. Midwest and Canadian prairie provinces. Although Argentina, probably more than any Latin American nation, can be considered an area of recent settlement in the nineteenth century, Table 4.3 shows that a wheat economy grew up *within* an established export system based on cattle and sheep.[15] The expansion of wheat growing and export, therefore, fitted into and strengthened an existing economic system in which an *estanciero* oligarchy controlled vast tracts of land, reflecting the efficiencies of large-scale ranching, and dominated Argentinian social and political life. Conforming to the technical conditions which encouraged the owner-operated family farms in North American grain-growing areas, Argentine wheat was grown in small units, but in a system of tenant farming and sharecropping. Through these arrangements, the *estancieros* without outlay or risk received income from underutilized or new lands which served to hedge livestock price fluctuations while they retained the appreciated value of the land. The last was particularly important, for crop farming broke up the soil and destroyed the pampas grass, and at the end of the three- to six-year contract period, the tenant farmer was usually obligated to plant alfalfa (from seeds supplied by the *estanciero*) before quitting the plot. The costs of these improvements, necessary for supporting the recently introduced high-quality shorthorn cattle, had proved to be prohibitive for *estancieros* who had tried to do it over extensive areas by hiring labor directly.

Grain growing offered employment opportunities for immigrants that cattle and sheep grazing never could, and even the conditions of tenant farming in Argentina attracted European immigrants, particularly Italians escaping the convulsions of Italian unification. Argentina finally experienced the large-scale European immigration that had long been the dream of Argentine liberals. Nevertheless, the tenancy arrangements sharply reduced much of the dynamism from the grain growing and export that might have been expected from the North American experience. The tenants, with their short-term, ungenerous contracts, had neither the incentives nor the means for making intensive capital improvements in the form of buildings, equipment, irrigation, or land fertility, and their major productivity increases in making the land better for livestock were captured by the *estancieros.* Thus, virtually all the backward and income-multiplier linkages from

TABLE 4.3
Argentina: Changes in the Composition of Exports, 1875-1914
(% of export value of items listed in 1910-1914 prices)

	1875-1879	*1890-1894*	*1910-1914*
Wool	52.9	38.3	13.7
Hides	38.1	25.9	11.6
Meat			
Salted & jerked	8.2	4.8	0.3
Canned	0.0	0.4	0.8
Chilled & frozen mutton & lamb	0.0	2.5	2.3
Frozen beef	0.0	0.0	13.1
Chilled beef	0.0	0.0	1.1
Wheat	0.0	20.4	20.6
Corn	0.0	4.4	19.1
Linseed	0.0	2.6	10.8
Oats, barley, rye	0.0	0.0	3.9
Quebracho	0.0	0.5	2.6
TOTAL	100.0	100.0	100.0
Index numbers of growth of total exports of items listed	100.0	213.2	587.4

SOURCE: Carlos F. Diaz Alejandro, *Essays on the Economic History of the Argentine Republic* (New Haven, Conn.: Yale University Press, 1970), p. 5.

the production of wheat so important in North American grain growing were cut off. Still, export production of meat and wheat was the basis of considerable economic activity, principally in and around Buenos Aires. Forward-linked firms milled wheat, slaughtered cattle and sheep, packed, stored, and loaded the meat and wheat for shipment to Europe, and marketed and financed the exports. Extensive railroad lines were built and operated to transport the wheat which, unlike sheep and cattle, could not walk to the port (see Table 4.2). In addition, although the social and technical conditions of meat and wheat production restricted the development of rural consumer goods markets, income-multiplier linkages, principally through the purchases by the large number of workers employed in the forward-linked industries but augmented with those employed by the government and by elites in domestic service, construction, and crafts, formed a sizable urban wage goods market. In the first decades of the twentieth century, local manufacturing firms made textiles, shoes, soap, furniture, pasta, beer, wine, paper and ceramic products, pots and pans, and other commodities for workers; in 1913 and 1914, the total output of the manufacturing sector (including the export processing firms) produced around 15 percent of Argentina's gross national product (compared to 37 percent from agricultural activities). All this economic activity centered in Buenos Aires supported a thriving cultural life and considerable civic pride, and it certainly did not occur to residents or visitors that this "Paris of the New World" was the capital of an economically underdeveloped nation.

In many important ways, the Guano Age of Peru (a favorite classroom example) was very different, as the extraction and export of guano was an excellent example of an enclave industry. But it was an enclave for particular reasons, and care must be taken not to dismiss its effects. Between 1840 and the outbreak of the War of the Pacific in 1879, Peru exported 10.8 million tons of guano, principally to Europe, which sold for the equivalent of over $600 million.[16] This rich fertilizer was the excretion of a certain type of bird eating a certain type of fish, and for centuries the birds had been depositing it on an uninhabited collection of rocks several miles off a sparsely inhabited coast. No rainfall washed out the nitrogen from the guano. In addition to its physical isolation, the particular nature of guano and its extraction precluded most of the linkages. The mountains of guano were cut and broken up with light tools and wheelbarrowed to the chutes through which gravity propelled the chunks to the holds of waiting ships. The simplicity of extraction and direct loading and the lack of any needed processing effectively cut off any significant forward or backward linkages, even warehousing, internal transportation, or dock facilities. Coastal estates in Peru continued to use some guano, but this does not seem to have been associated with the growth of guano exports.

It is through the income side that guano export had its major effects on Peru. A portion of the export sector's income, of course, was lost to the domestic economy through payments to foreigners, in particular through Peruvian entrepreneurs' need for European capital to set up guano extraction on a large scale—principally workers' housing and modest equipment—and their continued reliance on foreign merchants to transport and sell the guano in distant markets. There were also foreign leakages in labor costs as well, for labor was already in short supply (at the prevailing wage, at least) on the coastal plantations, and most of the guano work force was indentured Chinese, supplemented by convicts and army deserters. While it is unlikely that much of the workers' low wages were sent abroad, a good part of the total labor cost was payment to foreign labor contractors who "recruited" and transported the Chinese.

In spite of foreign leakages, the evidence is clear that the bulk of income from exports of guano was received and spent by Peruvians. The Peruvian government quickly asserted its ownership over the guano deposits as soon as their value became evident in the 1840s, and throughout the period, and as Table 4.4 shows, guano exports were the major source of government revenues. Therefore, before exploring the income-multiplier linkages which resulted from the expenditure policies, it is important to note what these revenues meant for the position of the government within Peruvian society. Although actual governmental receipts were typically in the form of foreign loans secured against future guano sales, guano exports constituted a source of immense governmental income independent of the consent of any domestic constituency. Moreover, the organization of the

TABLE 4.4
Peru: The Evolution of Government Revenues, 1847-1880
(100,000 pesos until 1862; in 100,000 soles thereafter)

	Total Government Revenues	*Revenues from Guano*	*Guano Revenue as Percentage of Total Gov't. Revenues*
1847	4.19	0.26	6.1
1851	5.45	0.30	5.5
1855	9.94	4.30	53.4
1862	20.76	16.32	43.3
1864	23.05	18.54	80.4
1880	17.60	n.a.	n.a.

SOURCE: Jonathan V. Levin, *The Export Economies: Their Pattern of Development in Historical Perspective* (Cambridge, Mass.: Harvard University Press, 1960), p. 95.

economic activity from which those revenues were derived neither strengthened existing social elites nor created new ones. Between 1849 and 1869, the government favored domestic over foreign contractors in placing guano sales franchises, but the stratum of wealthy contractors in Lima created by this policy remained directly dependent on government policy—as so dramatically shown by the government's canceling domestic contractors' franchises and granting sole selling rights to Dreyfus and Brothers Company of Paris in 1869.

Thus the guano revenues created in Lima a large, centralized state apparatus which was remarkably immune from influence by even the most influential classes and which was capable of promulgating policies inimical to the interests of the most powerful of domestic groups. In addition to cutting off the income of domestic contractors, two outstanding illustrations of independent state power in the 1850s were the abolition of slavery, which practically destroyed the sugar and cotton planters on the northern coast, and the abolition of the Indian head tax (*contribución de indígenes*) which severely curtailed the *sierra* landowners' control over the Indian population and undercut the autonomy of their local governments.

The pattern of government expenditures did not create the basis of general economic expansion. It created a thin stratum of very wealthy people (including the upper echelons of military and governmental bureaucracies and the domestic contractors) whose consumption purchases employed people in handicrafts, construction, and services. But these workers, even when joined by lower-level government employees, were too few to create substantial local wage goods markets. Government spending on a large number of internal and external wars, transfer payments to the wealthy, construction of public buildings and monuments, and interest payments on foreign debt did not contribute to national productive capacity. Only the railroad construction begun in the 1870s was a major productive investment, but even it was of but little economic consequence until mining and exporting of metals grew in later years.

The guano export boom, then, had a significant impact on the configurations of domestic political power, but it had slight importance for the economy. The Guano Age declined in the 1870s when only lower quality guano remained and competition from natural nitrates was threatening fertilizer markets; it ended cataclismically with Peru's defeat by Chile in the War of the Pacific (1879-1884) which was touched off by Peruvian attempts to impede the extraction and export of nitrates by Chileans allied with British capital. The passing of the Guano Age left very little behind in the way of a foundation for future economic growth.

EXPORT ECONOMIES IN LATIN AMERICA AND ELSEWHERE

The point of these brief sketches is not that Peru failed while Argentina succeeded or even that the sociopolitical structure resting on Argentina's export economy subsequently led to failure while the grain-growing areas on North America succeeded. It is, rather, that economic growth and its lack are not phenomena that stand apart from other dimensions of social life; the impact of international trade and investment on economic diversification and general expansion must be studied through its effect on the broader societies of which the economies were part. It would be hard to deny that "Argentina" and "Peru" in some aggregate sense had access to additional economic resources through their integration in the international division of labor and receipt of foreign investment, even though foreigners also profited from the activities. But to understand how or why different staple exports generated little, some, or considerable sustained growth in different societies, the magnitude of economic resources available and/or retained within national boundaries is only one (and perhaps a minor) influence. As a result, conceptual frameworks which focus narrowly on quantitative aspects of economic resources will always have to rely on external, ad hoc explanations for the variety of national experiences with foreign trade and investment. For orthodox economic theory, the problem lies more in its system of abstractions (that is, in what it chooses not to explain) than in the way the selected variables are related, and those dependency theorists who deny the logic of neoclassical trade theory while allowing themselves to be confined by its scope inhabit the worst of all methodological worlds.[17]

The importance of relating export activity to the social and political dynamics of the nations in which it takes place is indicated by comparing Chile's experience as an exporter of natural nitrates with the Peruvian Guano Age. The superficial similarities of the two nations' export characteristics—"minerals" whose locations were physically isolated from national centers—leads to their frequent inclusion in the same category of mineral exporters or enclave export producers (e.g., Furtado, 1976, p. 49). In the 1860s, Chilean society was dominated by a consolidated elite of landowners, merchants, and silver and copper mining interests, and the political influence of these groups was virtually uncontested. After the War of the Pacific, however, nitrate revenues began to change the complexion of political power. The prominence of foreigners in exploiting the nitrates reduced the impact of the new source of wealth on the domestic social structure, and the major internal effect of this vast new source of wealth was in swelling the fiscal revenues of the central government. These new resources, derived from activities independent of the domestic elites, reduced the elites' control over the state. When President José Manuel Balmaceda attempted to assert the state as an independent reformist agent in Chilean society, an alliance of domestic possessing classes, aided by the English, overthrew the government in 1891. The victors subordinated presidential power to congress to ensure upper-class control over the state, but unlike the situation, say, in Argentina where political control by export elites was an expression of their social and economic power, control over the Chilean state became a key *source* of social and economic power for the national elites.[18] Thus export enclaves in Chile as well as Peru tended to lift the state above society, but these tendencies worked on different social and political contexts, and while altering that context, it impedes understanding of the economic impact of foreign trade and investment on both nations to consider only purely economic phenomena.

But to compare Peruvian and Chilean experiences to other areas with similar staple exports, like that of Mexican metal mining and of Bolivian tin and Venezuelan oil (beginning around 1900 and 1920, respectively), can be interesting and fruitful when done systematically with the flexible version of the expanded staple theory. I have already mentioned this type of comparison in regard to the export of wheat from Argentina and North America, and it could be done for, say, coffee exports by looking at the distinct economic and social consequences of the large plantations in Brazil, Guatemala, and eastern Colombia versus the more atomistically organized cultivation in the Antioqueño region of Colombia and in Costa Rica. Several Latin American nations in addition to Argentina have had experience with a series of export staples, and they suggest another dimension for comparison—over time within a nation. Brazil had four roughly successive major staple exports—sugar, gold, rubber, and coffee—whose production was organized in distinct ways and each of which contributed to the social and economic organization of modern Brazil. Tobacco and coffee had different economic and social consequences in Colombia, and Cuban tobacco and sugar exports created different social systems within one small island.[19]

Unlike orthodox trade theory, which seeks high-level generalizations through a narrow *ceteris paribus* analytical system focusing on exchange, the staple theory can place commodity and exchange relations within their respective societies, through analyzing production. In so doing, the staple theory acts essentially as a set of clearly structured questions, questions whose organization and usefulness are not threatened when very different answers result from addressing them to the histories of different times and places. Large-scale export sectors did not succeed in propelling the national economies of Latin America into self-sustaining growth, but their individual effects were significantly different and should be appreciated as such. Even more different, of course, were the histories of those nations in which staple exports did generate economic diversification and general expansion; but divergent experiences are not a source of embarrassment with the expanded staple theory which can encompass both industrial development and underdevelopment within a unified analytical framework and use this variety to increase and enrich our historical understanding of general tendencies and particular processes.[20] In chapter 5, we will look more closely at the character of industrial growth supported by Latin American staple exports.

NOTES

1. Helleiner (1972) is a compact survey of the economics literature on international trade and economic development. Findlay (1973) is a much more rigorous exposition of neoclassical thought on trade and development.

2. Heckscher-Ohlin analysis attempts to explain the source of the relative cost differentials between nations, and thereby the patterns of trade, by respective national endowments of productive factor proportions. The analysis adds little to the "gains from trade" argument outlined above, rests on a particularly shaky set of propositions, and depends on definitions so broad and elastic that empirical work is difficult. Furthermore, most of the trade and development work seriously employing Heckscher-Ohlin theorizing actually deals with the effect of growth on trade, rather than the converse; for example, Harry G. Johnson (1962).

Hla Myint (1959), stressing pretrade underemployment of productive factors, is probably a more accurate and useful representation of the forces leading to the particular trade patterns of regions like Latin America. Richard Caves (1965) reformulates Myint's classical approach into orthodox substitution theory.

3. Dividing social enquiry into specialized disciplines often has some strange consequences in the study of larger questions. Through such ploys as the "prerequisites of economic growth," economists tend to relegate the explanation of the sources of economic growth to the sociologists, and the sociologists reciprocate by studying only its effects. Touraine and Pecaut (1967-1968) describe these problems as a background for their study of working-class consciousness in Latin America.

4. Hans W. Singer (1950) and Andre Gunder Frank (1967) are prime examples of two poles of dependency theory. Singer's article is essentially a statement of the ECLA position, and judging from the frequency with which it has been reprinted in collections (including Caves and Johnson [1968]—the "official" American Economics Association collection in international economics), it has been adopted by neoclassical economists as the standard criticism of standard theory. Emmanuel (1972) and Amin (1974) are more sophisticated versions of the same general approach. Carlos Quintana (1970) is a very useful compilation of the ECLA position and its evolution. Chilcote and Edelstein (1974, pp. 1-87), Bath

and James (1976), Cardoso (1977), and Fagen (1977) are good surveys of and guides to dependency theory literature, illustrating the difficulty of summarizing it with precision. Cardoso and Faletto (1979), combining dependency theory and class analysis, and Thorp and Bertram (1978), with a strong empirical slant, are two of the best recent works applying dependency theory. For examples of this argument, see Sweezy (1967), Jalee (1969), and Frank (1967). The use of Marxian language by these authors does not indicate the application of Marxian analysis to the issues.

6. For a good critique and bibliography of the declining terms of trade thesis, see Powelson (1977). Cairncross (1961), Flanders (1964), and Nisbet (1970 and 1971) are representative of the more general neoclassical counterattack. Criticisms of dependency theory from other angles are Ray (1973), Cueva (1976), and several articles appearing in various issues of *Latin American Perspectives.*

7. See the discussion in chapter 2 for the conditions under which agricultural dynamism have led to industrial growth. In addition, the citations in notes 11 and 14 of this chapter describe the role of agriculture in U.S. and Canadian growth and Youngson (1959, chapter 10), discusses Denmark's experience.

8. Myint (1954-1955) and Geertz (1963) are good studies of the effects of international trade under conditions of formal colonial arrangements. Gallagher and Robinson (1953) cogently analyzes the ability of Latin America to remain formally independent during Europe's nineteenth-century scramble for colonies.

9. The well-known "two gaps" approach of Chenery and Strout (1966) is a good example of conventional theorists' emphasis on problems of resource availability leading to prescriptions of more foreign assistance. The central problem of the inability of poor nations to grow is perceived to be a shortage of domestic savings and of foreign exchange; compare Singer (1950) and Frank (1964).

Kuhn (1962) is an excellent study of the ability of theories ("paradigms") to define legitimate scientific enquiry.

10. Kindleberger (1951) and Hymer and Resnick (1971) discuss and illustrate the inappropriate focus of neoclassical trade theory for the historical study of Europe and of European colonies in Africa, respectively. Baran (1952) is a suggestive study of the connections between international trade and domestic class structure, but his subsequent book (1962) emphasizes international flows of resources.

11. Caves and Holton (1959) outlines Innis's work on codfish and furs and updates it to include timber and wheat in the nineteenth century and minerals and newsprint in the twentieth. Along these same lines see Bertram (1959) and Buckley (1958). The staple theory has also been used to study regional growth in the United States; for examples, see Douglass North (1961) and Perloff and Wingo (1961).

12. Baldwin (1956) and Hirschman (1958). The best expositions of the modern staple theory and its relation to other approaches are Roemer (1970, pp. 5-38), Watkins (1963), Caves (1971), and Hirschman (1977).

13. Although Baldwin's article is frequently cited, it is seldom reprinted. As a prime example of the sociology of economic knowledge, economists have tended to pare the scope of this work down to the traditional variables of orthodox theory, until only the production function and its attendant linkages are left.

Examples of this narrower conception are the discussions in Caves and Holton (1959, pp. 18-21), where social institutions are declared to be outside "professional purview," Roemer (1970, p. 11), and Caves (1971, pp. 423, 432). As a consequence of limiting the scope of the staple theory to that of conventional economic analysis, Caves tends towards the "prerequisites of economic growth" argument of neoclassical trade theorists. Even Baldwin's later work implicitly accepts this narrowed frame; see Baldwin (1963 and 1966).

14. North (1961), using the narrowly economic staple theory, compares the regional economies of the U.S. South, Midwest, and Northeast. Far richer are the comparisons, consistent with the expanded version of the staple theory, in Dowd (1956) and Genovese (1967). If Hartz (1964) had incorporated some material dimensions of people's lives into his idealist approach, he would have had less trouble in explaining the weakness of liberalism in the Southern states.

Rubin (1959) and Keith (1977) contain some excellent comparative treatments of plantations in the Americas.

15. Goodrich (1964-1965). For this period of Argentine history, see Corradi (1974); Diaz Alejandro (1970), Ferns (1960), Ferrer (1967), Hanson (1938), Randall (1977), Romero (1963), Scobie (1964 and 1971), and Smith (1969).

16. Levin (1960, p. 112). The information on Peru can be found in Levin's excellent study, pp. 27-123, Greenhill and Miller (1973), Mathew (1970 and 1973), Piel (1970), Pike (1967), Romero (1967), and Berg and Weaver (1978).

17. Marx (1867, p. 76) expressed a similar opinion about orthodox economic theory: "The categories of bourgeois economy . . . are forms of thought expressing with social validity the conditions and relations of a definite historically determined mode of production, for example, the production of commodities." He goes on to declare, however, that the categories are unsuited for historical study.

18. For this period of Chilean history, see Bauer (1971), Blakemore (1965), Kirsch (1977), Mamlakis (1971 and 1976), Pregger Román (1979), and Pike (1963 and 1963a).

19. For Brazil, see Furtado (1965, pp. 43-92), Dean (1969, pp. 3-48), and Ridings (1978); for Colombia, Berquist (1978), McGreevy (1971), and Urrutia (1969, pp. 25-28, 47-51); for Cuba, Ortiz (1947).

20. For these purposes, the ability to compare differences in a systematic manner is considerably more useful for writing a history of the Americas than one which depends on similarities and parallels. Herbert Bolton is the name usually associated with the latter approach; Hanke (1964) explores the Bolton thesis, but the discussion is marred by being set in a flat "is-it-true-or-false?" frame.

5

THE BEGINNINGS OF INDUSTRIAL GROWTH IN SOUTH AMERICA, 1900-1930

From the preceding chapters it should be clear that earlier industrializations and general theories based upon them must be used with extreme care when studying twentieth-century industrial growth in South America. Industrialization is not a historically uniform process from which a series of salient characteristics can be lifted out of the past and applied generally. One of the most misleading, yet enduring, "lessons from history" in liberal scholarship on Latin America is that of the bourgeois revolution: it is asserted that the twentieth-century industrial bourgeoisie, like their eighteenth- and early nineteenth-century counterparts, can be expected to become a powerful force that will remake an industrializing nation's social and political structure along liberal lines to allow sustained industrial growth. Ironically, this is an ahistorical caricature of Marx's understanding of English history, as Marx himself saw that different paths to industrial development were already being taken during the nineteenth century (Marx, 1848; 1852; 1894, pp. 323-337). Although later industrial growth still does continue to create groups antagonistic to existing social and political arrangements, as chapter 2 shows, there is no historical basis for expecting the industrial bourgeoisie to be among them.

In South America, industrialists were in fact politically quiet, reflecting the particular form of industrial growth they sponsored, a form deeply influenced by prior industrializations. As outlined in chapter 4, industrialization in Western Europe and North America was strongly felt in South America through the core industrial nations' demand for primary products to use as inputs in their expanding economies and to feed their growing urban populations. Technological advances in transportation, also creations of this industrial growth, lowered transport costs to the point where South American resources became feasible sources of supply, and the advantages of new markets for European producers of consumer goods, railroad equipment, power generating machinery, and so on, supported and encouraged the creation of export economies in South America.

The industrialization of Europe, then, by integrating South American nations into a global system of economic interdependence as exporters of resource-based products, conditioned the development of the domestic economic and social structures within which South American industrial growth occurred. In addition, the capacity and eagerness of Western European and North American economies to supply capital goods and industrial intermediate products (such as fuel, lubricants, industrial chemicals, and certain materials) to South American firms producing for local markets, shaped the internal growth of the new industrial sectors.[1] Together, these dimensions of historically cumulative forces worked at different levels to transform general economic *inter*dependence into a dependent form of industrialization.[2] What follows is the outline of a model of dependent industrial growth as it appeared in Argentina, Brazil, Chile, Uruguay, and to a much lesser degree Colombia in the early years of the twentieth century, and the second part of the chapter connects this form of industrial growth to the social and political processes of the period. Figures A.1 and A.2 and Table 5.1 present some indicators of industrial activity at this time.

TABLE 5.1
Indicators of South American Manufacturing Production, 1929 and 1930
(U.S. $1,000,000, 1960 prices, and 1,000 people)

	Manufacturing Output, 1929	*Per Capita Manufacturing Output, 1930*	*Manufacturing Employment, 1930*	
			Factories	Artisanal[a]
Argentina	1,835.8	152.5	390	560
Bolivia			8	117
Brazil	832.6	24.8	510	826
Chile	192.4	44.2	96	161
Colombia	98.6	13.0	70	340
Ecuador			10	132
Paraguay			3	40
Peru			34	308
Uruguay			55	65
Venezuela			20	71
TOTAL SOUTH AMERICA			1,196	2,620
Mexico	573.0	34.4	230	387
TOTAL LATIN AMERICA			1,501	3,329

SOURCE: United Nations Economic Commission for Latin America, *The Industrialization Process in Latin America, Statistical Annex,* mimeo (New York: United Nations, 1966), pp. 27, 23, 16, 18.
NOTE: [a]Firms with fewer than five workers.

DEPENDENT INDUSTRIAL GROWTH

The expansion of export production in several nations of South America led to substantial industrial growth of two principal types.[3] The first was industrial production directly related through forward and backward linkages to production of the export commodity itself, as in the case of plants in São Paulo that made bags for coffee beans or that of the slaughter houses and the establishments for the preparing and packing of meats in and around Buenos Aires (which also served domestic markets). The forward-linked activities tended to take place in port cities rather than in the countryside, because transportation networks were designed for getting the staple from the place of production to the port and characteristically had few cross-linkages, coming together only at the point from which the staple could be shipped abroad. Thus the port city, where unloading and reloading had to occur in any case, was the location at which large and continuous flows of the staple occurred. The same reasons, in reverse as it were, worked to make the producers of inputs of staple production locate at the port cities where they could serve the whole rural market. These distributional advantages, on top of the usual cost advantages which led industrial plants to favor urban locations—existence of social overhead facilities like power, water, workers' housing, and fire protection; a ready supply of labor; organized capital markets and other specialized services—encouraged little industrial activity to penetrate the countryside.[4]

The second prominent type of industrial activity was producing consumer goods for the local market. Domestically produced consumer goods were generally of lower quality than imports and were primarily wage goods—commodities purchased by workers. The most common were the type where transportation costs afforded some significant locational advantage to domestic production over importation.

Reflecting the cheapness and feasibility of transporting raw materials relative to the cost of the finished product, such goods as beer, bread, and inexpensive china and glassware tend to be made near their final markets even if most of the raw materials have to be obtained and shipped from some distance. In addition, the availability of local raw materials gave locational advantages to domestic producers of such commodities as cotton and woolen textiles, shoes, flour, bricks, and noodles in many of the South American nations.

In addition to the protection afforded by transport costs, tariffs helped many local wage goods manufacturers defend themselves from foreign competition. Some of the tariffs resulted from lobbying by local, import-competing producers, but this effort was seldom decisive. A more accurate explanation of the tariff structures in South America in the first three decades of the twentieth century is that tariffs were the major source of government revenue for most of the nations. Even in Chile, where foreign presence in export production led to export taxes as the most important, tariffs on imports were still significant. In part, this reflects the relative ease (efficiency) of collecting this form of tax, compared, say, to sales, property, or income taxes. But beyond this, the pattern of the tariffs strongly indicates the ability of the upper classes to determine on whom the burden of taxation was to fall. Tariffs fell largely on imported wage goods, considerably less on luxury imports, and typically not at all on agricultural machinery, seeds, fertilizer, and other inputs necessary for export production and processing, transportation, and public utilities controlled by politically potent domestic elites and their foreign allies.[5] Clearly a particular tariff that is so high that it virtually precludes the importation of that commodity does not yield much revenue, but the revenue tariffs still raised the domestic prices of these imported wage goods. And it was precisely these cheaper imports for which transport costs were already a higher proportion of final price than for the more expensive imports, and whose production did not require large plants or high levels of technological sophistication. The confluence of these factors is what led to the domestic establishment of plants making such items as coarse textiles, cheap shoes and furniture, certain processed foods (for example, pasta), harsh soaps, inexpensive wines and beers, and some building materials.

The firms producing consumer goods for the domestic market also located in the cities because, in addition to advantages in production costs, most of the market was there. Even firms serving rural workers producing the export staple were situated in port cities because of the transportation network patterns. (Other rural workers constituted little in the way of a market.) One type of market for manufactured wage goods, then, was formed in this way by workers directly involved in the production, processing, hauling, and loading of the export staple, and this market was served by firms located in the port cities.

A second type of urban market for manufactured wage goods was in the political centers where government expenditures, derived directly or indirectly from export activity, supported a wide variety of low-paid occupations—construction workers, clerks, soldiers, and the like. In addition, better-paid government employees, although more prone to purchase imports than local manufactures, spent their incomes in ways that supported service workers and others who in turn purchased domestically produced consumer goods. A third type of urban market for wage goods developed in the cities favored as residences by the families of export elites. Although this class tended to live in cities, away from the source of their income, the elites' expenditure patterns did not give much direct support to urban manufacturers of low-quality consumer goods. The retainers, service workers, and others in a wide variety of occupations catering to their tastes, however, did purchase these commodities and amounted to a substnatial market for local manufacturers.

The nature of urban organization is such that there are always other sources of demand for local commodities, that is, the purchases of those who supply public services—trash haulers, utility workers, policemen, school teachers, transport workers—as well as a whole range of employees engaged in commerce. The inner complexity of city life was developed to the degree that the city served one or more functions relative to the export base: port, government center, or residence of export elite.[6] Buenos Aires and Montevideo were all three for Argentina and Uruguay and were the outstanding examples of export-induced urban growth in South America. The other major industrial cities of this period also combined many of these functions but had to share some of them more than did Buenos Aires and Montevideo. São Paulo, adjacent to the major coffee port (Santos), was the state capital in a highly decentralized political system but had to compete with Rio de Janeiro, a beautiful city for upper-class living, the nation's cultural center, and at that time the federal capital. Similarly Santiago, Chile's national capital in a unitary political system and the seat of learning and upper-class cultural activities, lost some industrial activity to the port cities of Iquique and Coquimbo in the north, nearby Valparaíso, and Concepción in the south. Economic activity in Colombia was even more diffused spatially, for the cities of Medellín, Baranquilla, Cali, and Buenaventura felt the direct impact of the prosperity from coffee exports more than did Bogatá, which nevertheless retained its political and cultural preeminence—in part due to its elevation and more healthful and pleasant climate.

Consumer goods industries which grew up with the export economies began as "finishing touches" fabrication using imported components. In the early match factories of Brazil and Uruguay, for example, imported sticks were dipped into an imported chemical mix and packed into imported boxes. These firms were initially set up in order to exploit some locational advantage, quirks in tax laws of the exporting and importing nations, or simply existing or forthcoming tariff protection.

Import merchants were often key figures in setting up new factories; they had knowledge of the local market, an established distribution network, and access to financing, so that even when they were not actively involved in an entrepreneurial role in the new manufacturing enterprises, they frequently financed these firms and distributed their products—often under false foreign labels to overcome buyer resistance to locally made commodities.

By the beginning of World War I, then, a sizable industrial sector producing consumer goods for local markets was growing up within the export economies of Argentina, Chile, Brazil, Uruguay, and to a lesser degree Colombia, drawing entrepreneurial talent principally from importers, middle-class immigrants, and occasionally from the families of the export elites. These firms were generally small, most employing fewer than five people, but together with the large, relatively highly capitalized, foreign-owned plants processing exports or producing power for the urban centers, factory production became a significant urban activity in those nations. Table 5.2 shows the patterns of industrial production for Argentina, Brazil, and Chile around the height of the export processing-wage goods dependent industrialization.

Export-led industrial development can proceed until industrial growth becomes self-sustaining and relatively independent of the export staple, but to do so,

TABLE 5.2
The Structure of Manufacturing Sectors in the 1920s: Argentina, Brazil, Chile

	Argentina, 1925-1929		*Brazil, 1919*	*Chile, 1929*
	% Output	(Imports as % Dom. Prod. + Imports)	% Output	% Output
Food and beverages	36.6	(5)	26.2	48.3
Tobacco	0.8		5.5	4.6
Textiles, clothing, and shoes	9.8	(45)	38.3	23.4
Leather products	6.5		n.a.	4.3
Wood and furniture	3.2	(37)	6.9	5.4
Paper products	1.9	(31)	1.3	} 2.3
Printing and publishing	9.8		0.4	
Chemicals and pharmaceuticals	5.7	(38)	} 3.6	2.7
Petroleum refining	1.6			
Rubber products	.....	(93)	0.1	.....
Stone, glass, cement, non-metallic minerals	6.9	(27)	5.7	1.3
Metal products	4.5	(65)	4.4	} 7.7
Vehicles and machinery	2.9	(79)	2.2	
Electrical machinery and appliances	.....	(98)	.....	
Other and misc.	9.6		3.5	.....
TOTAL	100.0	(51)	100.0	100.0
Avg. annual manufacturing growth rates, 1920s	7.1		3.0	4.3
Avg. annual GDP growth rates, 1920s	5.9		2.8	8.0
Manufacturing as % of GDP in 1929	22		11	8

SOURCES: Carlos F. Diaz Alejandro, *Essays on the Economic History of the Argentine Republic* (New Haven, Conn.: Yale University Press, 1970), pp. 222, 225; Laura Randall, *An Economic History of Argentina in the Twentieth Century* (New York: Columbia University Press, 1977), p. 117; Henry W. Kirsch, *Industrial Development in a Traditional Society: The Conflict of Entrepreneurship and Modernization in Chile* (Gainsville, Fla.: University of Florida Press, 1977), p. 50; Werner Baer, *The Brazilian Economy: Its Growth and Development* (Columbus, Ohio: Grid Publishing Co., 1979); Martos Ballasteros and Tom E. Davis, "The Growth of Output and Employment in Basic Sectors of the Chilean Economy, 1908-1957," *Economic Development and Cultural Change* 11 (1963), p. 160, Figure 2.

the web of interindustry and income linkages must increase in magnitude and complexity to the point where the sector itself begins to generate an internal, self-feeding dynamism that becomes a source of growth impulses to the rest of the economy (see, for example, North, 1955). For instance, one source of demand for domestically produced consumer goods that has not yet been mentioned came from the workers employed in the consumer goods sector. As the sector grew and employment expanded, proportionally more of the sector's demand was internally generated through the wage incomes from industrial production. As important as the quantitative aspects are, however, scale alone was not sufficient to create the conditions for self-sustaining industrial growth in even the largest industrial sectors of South America.

As we have seen, this industrial growth occurred in a world where developed nations were able and willing to supply the South American economies with industrial products. The usual conclusion is that foreign competition constrained South American industrial expansion by underselling domestic producers of consumer goods. This threat existed, but in addition to the protection inherent in the relatively high transportation cost of importing cheap wage goods, the use of tariffs for revenue purposes enabled local industrialists to obtain tariff protection for a variety of products. Tariff protection of internal markets from foreign consumption varied by country, of course; in Brazil, for example, the reliance on multinational markets for exports, imports, and capital enabled Brazil's government to be more insulated from pressures by particular foreigners than were, say, the Argentinian elites with their considerably closer, almost bilateral relations with Britain. As a consequence the Brazilian government was freer to impose tariffs on imports of cotton textiles than was Argentina.

Nevertheless, penetration of South American markets by exports of manufactured consumer goods from the finance capitalist industrialized nations had less influence on the shape and internal dynamism of South American industrial sectors than did imports of foreign-made capital and intermediate goods. As long as local industrial production was confined to producing consumer goods or processing exports, much (probably most) of the potential energizing effects on the national economy of industrial production was lost. According to the simple Keynesian income-expenditure/multiplier model, the production and sale of machinery (but not consumer goods) induces a net increase in the demand for consumer goods greater than the machinery's value, but this demand-creating effect leaks abroad if the machinery is imported.[7]

The ability of machinery production to create demand for consumer goods is not unique to that activity; the construction of roads, bridges, and statues of mounted liberators creates demand in the same way. In order to understand the crucial role specific to a domestic machine-producing sector in creating a progressive and flexible economy, it is necessary to go beyond the sphere of exchange and consider the technical and structural nature of machinery and its production.[8] On the technical side, a domestic capital-goods sector contributes to spurning growth in an economy by stimulating thought and energy toward raising the productivity of human labor. Machinery adds to the value of a commodity not only by substituting embodied labor power of the machine's fabricators for on-the-spot labor exertion; it also embodies scientific knowledge applied to production (a skilled form of labor power) that creates new and more efficient methods of production. The lack of a domestic capital goods sector thus means the lack of the type of enterprises which have been the source of so much innovation in industrial technology. Innovation is lost not only to manufacturing; it is lost to agriculture, mining, and other sectors, and the loss is most serious where local conditions (for example, climate and the skill level of the work force) present problems different from those areas from which the capital equipment was imported. Aggravating this loss, South American entrepreneurs not only imported their capital equipment but also tended to import the engineers and technicians to operate it. Such recruitment of skilled labor from Europe lessened the need to create national technical schools and local cadres of technically trained personnel, thereby further reducing pressures to explore and develop technology locally.

In its structural role, a domestic capital goods sector creates backward and forward linkages of its own that are important for general, self-sustaining economic progress. The forward linkages induced by domestic machinery production encourage new lines as well as new competition into existing lines of consumer *and* capital goods production. The backward linkages of machinery production add to the pressure exerted by consumer goods manufacturers to develop and utilize domestic resources. A capital goods sector needs steel made of iron, coal, and chemicals; fuels and lubricants require refineries and equipment to explore and develop petroleum resources; and so forth. The production of these intermediate products in turn creates markets for machinery, thus formally acting as both a forward and a backward linkage of a capital goods sector—a situation which further underscores the central importance of capital goods production.

At this point we must inquire why, with the apparent presence of adequate entrepreneurial talent, a capital goods sector so crucial to a progressive and flexible economy did not grow along with the expansion of a machine-using consumer goods sector in South America? One reason is that the development of producer goods firms requires considerably larger markets than those available within the South American nations in the early years of the twentieth century.[9] This obstacle, however, is frequently overemphasized, for it is essentially a start-up problem whose importance a couple of decades of healthy market growth in nations like Argentina and Brazil would have substantially reduced. But there are other reasons. Transport costs of capital goods, unlike cheap consumer goods, did not afford much protection from foreign competitors; transport costs relative to selling price were considerably lower for machines (Merhav, 1969, pp. 35-36; Moneta, 1959, p. 58). This characteristic of capital goods also reduced the feasibility for domestic producers in any one of the South American nations of establishing a capital goods sector and exporting to other South American nations in order to overcome the narrowness of local markets. Location simply did not provide a significant enough advantage over European and North American producers of machinery.

Nevertheless, domestic markets for producer goods could have been protected through tariffs and the sector encouraged by a variety of governmental measures. The central problem was simply that no one important was interested. Such policies would have raised domestic producer goods prices, increasing the cost of inputs (such as machinery, fuels, fertilizers, transportation services) used for export production and processing, thereby reducing the export elites' commitment to such a program. Even more interesting is that by the time domestic consumer goods industries had grown to the point where, given the nations' resource bases, the establishment of some domestic producer goods firms behind tariff walls might have been feasible, local consumer goods industrialists recognized that such a development would not be in their collective interest. It would have raised the costs of their inputs and thereby reduced the level of effective protection represented by a given level of tariffs against imported consumer goods.[10] The South American industrial bourgeoisie, as individuals and as a class, had but little stake in general industrialization; their position and interests had developed within a system of partial, dependent industrialization and were tied to it. The second column of Table 5.2 shows the percentages of total domestic supplies of industrial products imported in Argentina, and the pattern reflects these internal political forces.

Therefore, even in those South American nations which experienced significant industrial growth in the early decades of the twentieth century, market forces and the social relations which grew out of the organization of industrial production were not powerful enough to propel those primary product export economies from a position of international interdependence into anything other than a dependent industrial development that lacked an internal, self-expanding dynamic. Growth in the industrial sectors was closely tied to the activities of domestic exporters, foreign markets for those exports, and foreign suppliers of imports of producer goods. When staple export earnings were good, the income which trickled down induced a high demand for domestically produced consumer goods at a time when the foreign exchange for those producers' purchases of imported capital goods and inputs was relatively available. On the other hand, when external markets for the staple export was poor, demand for consumer goods fell off at the same time that the domestic cost of the imported inputs, and therefore the costs of domestic consumer goods production, rose. The output and profitability of the local industrial sectors was directly related to the output and profitability of the export sectors.

As outlined in chapter 2, the early twentieth-century conditions which created a dependent, consumer goods industrialization in South America were qualitatively different from the circumstances of English competitive capitalist industrialization a hundred years earlier. Although England's industrialization was similar to that of, say, Argentina and Brazil in that it was led by wage goods industries, the relative unimportance of the domestic producer goods sectors in the early stages of English industrialization did not imply a dependent industrialization. Capital goods were still made domestically, but their production took place in small, artisan-type shops or perhaps more typically, at least in cotton textiles, they were made right in the consumer goods factories.[11] No other nation had a developed capital goods sector from which the English imported their machinery, so that with technological advance, the mid-nineteenth-century railroad boom, and the growth of consumer goods production which induced a greater division of labor, a domestic producer goods sector grew into a viable and important branch of industry.[12] The local production of fuel (particularly coal) and of iron and steel in England was similarly stimulated and developed, and the export of cotton textiles and other industrial products at an early stage paid for the imports of cotton and other raw materials.

Probably influenced by the English experience as a historical demonstration that consumer goods can successfully create a dynamic, integrated industrialization and that industrial development is antagonistic to pre-industrial social forms based on agriculture, much conventional reasoning about the relationship between staple exporting and domestic consumer goods production concludes that there was a negative relation between the two. From an exclusive focus on consumer goods production, thus ignoring interindustry linkings (that is, the consumer goods firms' requirements for [imported] intermediate goods and capital equipment) and underestimating the strength of the income-demand links between export production and consumer goods, it is frequently deduced that contracting staple export markets stimulated domestic consumer goods production, because the consequent shortage of foreign exchange gave local producers greater protection against the imports of foreign-made consumer goods. Such conclusions are misleading; indeed, the expansion of South American industrial growth during World War I, frequently cited as an example of how a decline in foreign trade stimulated domestic industrial production, actually suggests the converse.[13] In the early years of the war (1914-1915), the shortage of shipping did curtail trade between South America and Europe, and during this period industrial output in South America contracted. (See Figures A.1 and A.2.) But the remainder of the war years were boom times for most of the South American traditional exports, and domestic industrial production expanded, supported by rapidly rising imports from the U.S. which in large measure substituted for the intermediate and capital goods temporarily unavailable from Europe (Baerrenson, *et al.*, 1965, pp. 19-20). This is precisely the behavior expected from dependent industrialization as opposed to the simpler import-substituting industrialization models. It is true that the World War I period was not quite business as usual, but the disruption in foreign trade was short and mild enough that patterns of industrial dependence were not altered in any important aspect.

Not until the Great Depression of the 1930s did the dependence of internal economic activity have to be directly confronted, but it should be noted that even in the 1920s the overseas markets of some export economies were weakening. There were some problems on the supply side: for example, the geographical extension of export staple production in Argentina, the chief source of export growth in physical terms as there were but slight productivity increases, had run up against natural limits (Ferrer, 1967, p. 124). Problems of demand were even more severe (Glade, 1969, pp. 362-370). Most South American nations' staple exports were meeting increasing competition from other producers (sometimes from within Latin America), and cheap synthetic substitutes eroded important markets. Brazilian rubber exports before World War I and Chilean nitrate exports whose decline pulled down domestic industrial production after the war are examples of these two types of new competition. Resource-saving innovations, rising tariffs, and other trade restraints in the staple-importing nations also reduced the vigor of staple export markets. Various national measures were taken in an effort to maintain the structure of the export economies, the most ambitious being Brazil's coffee price support scheme ("valorization") financed by foreign loans, but entirely new directions in public policy were not taken until the debacle of the depression in the 1930s.

SOCIAL AND POLITICAL PROCESSES

Industrial growth did not challenge the political and economic configurations of the export economies of South America but instead relied on them. As a consequence, the industrial bourgeoisie was unable and unwilling to challenge the social arrangements on which their own position depended; their preeminent ambition was to be accepted as members of the elite on the elite's own terms. This aspiration was not unrealistic, for the elites of these nations did not constitute a closed social estate, and such acceptance was not infrequent for members of the second and third generations of very wealthy industrial and mercantile families (depending also on such factors as religion, culture, national origin, and so on). The political importance of the industrialists as a group was also reduced by the high proportion of the class who were recent immigrants. Only in narrow technical aspects of economic policy did they have any influence, and that political influence which they did have in the pre-World War I period was usually exercised through individual manufacturers' personal connections to the export economy, particularly through importers and members of the export elite. Even in the 1920s, when industrialists began forming trade associations to engage in lobbying and propaganda as more coherent interest groups, they did not collectively represent a significant new force in these nations' social, political, and cultural lives. Nevertheless, the success of the export economies and the resulting economic growth did lead to the rise of new social groups considerably more significant and dynamic than the industrial bourgeoisie, groups whose activities ultimately undermined the political stability created by that economic success.

The first and most important of these was an urban, wage-earning working class, a group drawn or pushed into the cities by a variety of forces. Some were indigenous peoples from the countryside, others immigrants whose contracts in staple export production had expired or who had directly immigrated to the South American cities. Whatever their origins, however, they were free in the double-edged sense that Marx described eighteenth-century English workers: "free from the old relationships of clientship, bondage and servitude, and secondly, free of all belongings and possessions, and of every objective material form of being, *free of all property;* dependent on the sale of its labor capacity . . . as its only source of income" (Marx, 1857-1858, p. 507 [italics in original]). The politically most important parts of the urban working class were those engaged in transportation and factory production, for these activities, like mining, brought large numbers of people together in highly organized, authoritarian working conditions, thereby heightening their perception of common position and encouraging the creation of organizations to promote their interests as a class.

Associations of urban workers had begun in colonial times, so in themselves were not new in South America. But the early forms were mutual assistance societies through which artisans and handicraft workers protected themselves from individual disasters by collective insurance schemes and organized their social and religious lives in ways reminiscent of the guilds of medieval Europe, although they seldom had the power to regulate a trade or craft as did their European counterparts. These guildlike associations survived into the twentieth century along with artisan production, and while several became the bases of political organizations, for the most part, it was the politics of anarchism which reflected the individualistic nature of their work. Their political activity caused episodic violence but had little lasting impact.

The rise of large-scale production units employing wage labor gave birth to new forms of labor organization and working-class politics. The expanding factory work force, added to railroad and other transport workers, stevedores, construction workers, and miners, created unions that acted aggressively to better their lot directly through strikes and political agitation in the early years of the twentieth century. Some of the specific directions the new class struggle took, in particular socialism and communism, showed the influence of immigrant workers with experience in the European labor movement, as in the case of earlier anarchism. But it is a serious mistake to dismiss working-class unrest as merely the product of outside agitators and ideas, as is common practice; the fact remains that the new perceptions and militance were the product of the workers' actual position in the process of production.[14] Exhortations to combine and to assault prevailing structures of privilege and power, no matter how frequent and how strident, would have been futile if these structures had not appeared to have immediate and unfortunate consequences for workers' own lives and the lives of those around them. Large groups of people brought together in a structured work environment cannot be expected passively to endure harsh and demeaning discipline, general powerlessness, and meager and uncertain material rewards and prospects when their everyday experiences invite them to make the connection between their situation and that of others enjoying comfort, status, and security. The labor unrest in the early decades of the twentieth century was a product of the wage labor system, whether in Colombian river transport and United Fruit plantations or Chilean nitrate and coal pits. Outside agitators harnessed and articulated this discontent but did not create it.

The second important group developing in the cities at this time was salaried white-collar employees. Their quantitative rise was less directly the creation of expanding industrial production than was the factory workers', but their occupations were primarily based on the expansion and increased complexity of urban life to which industrial activity was an important contributor. The white-collar workers were (and are) socially and occupationally heterogeneous, including schoolteachers, bookkeepers, administrators, managers, journalists, clerks in shops and offices, and the whole panoply of salaried employees in the public and private sectors. Although independent professionals and even some small entrepreneurs occasionally joined the employees in their political efforts, these white-collar employees were similar to wage workers in that they were not possessors of property and their income was thus derived from the sale of the only commodity they possessed—their labor power. But they were definitely not members of the working class nor should they be considered to have had an identity of interest with them. For the most part, they were literate and frequently formally educated, and the conditions of their work generally gave them opportunities for advancement, an upward mobility which sharply distinguished them from wage workers. Indeed, much of their time and energy were spent in setting themselves apart from the working classes socially and culturally, even when their earnings were but slightly, if at all, above those of the better-paid wage workers. One of the chief devices they used in this effort was to copy consumption patterns of the elites as closely as possible. Consumption assumed an importance for the white-collar workers beyond subsistence and creature comfort in that it involved status and class identification.[15] This consideration was what made so many of the salaried class and their political parties either indifferent or actively hostile to domestic industrialization, believing it would raise the prices they paid for consumer goods.

The lack of internal group coherence as well as unclear relation to the means of production—or to production at all—make it difficult to regard white-collar salaried workers as a class, but in order to avoid introducing new and confusing terms, they will be referred to here as the middle class. At the same time, it is important to remember that they are not the middle class of the English Industrial Revolution. That middle class was the industrial bourgeoisie, in the middle between the propertyless workers and the landed elite, possessing the means of industrial production and in the process of becoming the most economically powerful social group in the nation. The South American middle classes for the most part possessed no such property, and although similar to the English industrial bourgeoisie in their interest in politics, their interest stemmed from weakness rather than strength. As one historian concludes a discussion of South American middle classes' political activity in this period: "The power of the state, therefore, was sought first as a substitute for the economic power which the new groups did not yet have and, secondly, as an instrument by means of which the economic rewards that were otherwise unobtainable could be procured" (Glade, 1969, p. 355). The quotation succinctly points out the two fundamental, interrelated problems of middle-class politics in the first decades of the twentieth century: how to exert political influence and how to translate political influence into measures which would promote middle-class interests.

To begin with the second dimension, the middle classes were vitally concerned with achieving more favorable positions within existing social systems, but their occupational and status composition was so disparate that it was difficult to define concrete policy proposals around which large numbers could be mobilized. Led by Uruguayan and Chilean middle classes, by the 1940s and 1950s the middle classes in the more industrialized South American nations had achieved some significant direct class benefit legislation which increased the distance between salaried and wage workers by statutory provisions. Major examples were minimum salaries (often preceding minimum wage legislation by years), social security systems, and access to consumer credit on favorable terms. But in the early years of the twentieth century when the middle-class parties were first taking shape, the shared goals of the salaried workers were so general that their parties' platforms tended to be very general and open-ended, essentially oriented toward enabling *individuals* of the middle class to get ahead. That is, members of the middle classes organized and fought collectively to institutionalize the means for personal upward mobility. Considerable effort went into expanding opportunities for white-collar workers by increasing government employment *and* establishing the standards and procedures for filling these jobs.

The stress on opportunities for individual upward mobility, however, in spite of its representation as a general principle, was reserved for members of the middle class and their children. A recognition of the limits of these intentions brings into perspective the importance of higher education to the middle class and their political parties. For these non-property-holding strata, a degree from an institution of higher education was the major means by which the middle class could distinguish itself from the working classes. As important as consumption patterns were, formal education was the ultimate certification of middle-class membership, serving as a passport to a white-collar job. A well-developed, publically subsidized system of higher education was particularly desirable, because it lowered the financial barriers to attendance—in effect, through regressive tax systems, by getting the working class to pay for the education of middle-class children. As technical and engineering education remained undeveloped, the only real hope for young people from working-class families to enter the ranks of the middle classes was at its very lowest rungs through normal schools and low-level clerical positions. The universities which certified people for the liberal professions and good managerial and administrative posts were strongly oriented toward the humanities and thus heavily laden with upper- and middle-class culture and values. University admission requirements, including graduation from an academic secondary school, interviews (dress, accent, manners), and examinations on arcane subjects with attention to the form (spelling, grammar, paragraphing, and so on) in which the papers were written, screened out all but the most fortunate and able children of the working class. This system was defended on the grounds of academic standards, irrespective of the standards applied for graduating after admission. Private universities also continued to operate, serving to keep the Church's hand in and to establish an internal hierarchy of middle-class degree holders.

It is important to distinguish the type of political program put forth by the middle-class parties from that of the growing working-class movement. The latter's goals in this period were essentially of direct collective benefit: legitimization of unions and collective bargaining, regulation of wages, hours, and working conditions, establishment of accident and disability insurance, and other aspects of group betterment. Because these proposals were a definite challenge to employers' power, their espousal quickly became cast in overt class-conflict terms when early worker organizations and strikes were brutally suppressed, and the conflict became more generally politicized as the state assumed responsibility for breaking strikes and disciplining recalcitrant workers. Political activity was important for even limited workers' gains, because general policies were necessary to neutralize the police, to protect workers from employers' sanctions, and to make their demands more palatable to employers as a whole by making them generally applicable, that is, not putting one employer or particular group of employers at a competitive disadvantage relative to those who might still freely hire children, avoid supplying safety equipment, or paying insurance.

Middle-class aspirations, on the other hand, did not directly conflict with property interests. Their goals required political activities because state participation, in the form of legislated procedural changes and expenditures, was central to their success, and access to occupations such as legislator and party worker was an important part of the goals themselves. The whole range of middle-class reforms, then, was distinct from those of the working-class movement in that it reflected the heterogeneity of this group and stressed opportunities for mobility by individuals, albeit individuals from the middle class.

This brings us to the second dimension of the problem faced by middle-class politics in this period: even with considerable unity the middle class could exert little political influence, for it did not occupy strategic positions of independent power from which to apply concerted pressure. The greatest advantage and opportunity to influence political decisions came from open campaigns and free elections. Although numerically a small portion of the nations' populations, the middle classes' literacy, urban location, organization and communication skills, and limited goals made them a significant portion of the populace participating within existing frameworks of national politics. Their political style was opportunistic, making and breaking alliances in an effort to increase their influence, but they were continually frustrated in these machinations, because even when they could muster the votes among urban constituents, the votes counted for little. In Argentina, Brazil, and Colombia the elections were regularly stolen, and although electoral fraud was not unknown in Chile, the parliamentary system there gave Congress—and thereby rural bosses—overwhelming governmental power.

Thus the first order of business for the middle-class political parties during this period was electoral reform, which they undertook by attempting to identify their particular interests with that of the nation and by appealing to the universal rights of man (literally male in this instance). The technique of representing special interests as general interests was not the peculiar property of the South American middle classes, but it is emphasized here because although the rhetoric did not appear to make much impression on the propertied or working classes of the period, it deeply influenced liberal, particularly North American, scholars in the 1950s and 1960s. They believed that the middle classes and their parties were progressive, ideologically committed, democratic forces in Latin American politics, representing a safe middle ground between right-wing authoritarianism and left-wing subversion.[16]

The political programs and successes of middle-class parties in the early decades of the twentieth century cannot be properly understood, however, except as they related to the current state of the class struggle between the polar classes of property and wage workers (Miliband, 1969, pp. 32-33). Even in Buenos Aires and Montevideo their relative numbers were too few to compensate for the weakness of their social and economic position. After considerable experimentation, a good number of middle-class political parties discovered in the working-class movements the potential allies necessary to give them the needed political leverage. Prior to this discovery, the middle-class party stance toward the working classes ("the social problem") was at best ambivalent and usually indistinguishable from that of the elite's parties. Those parties looking for working-class support, however, soon developed platforms which included social as well as political reforms and elevated those members who had been advocating such programs into the parties' higher echelons. Even in nations where middle- and working-class alliances were accomplished, they were uneasy and tentative in nature. Both partners were conscious of the risks to their own goals inherent in such arrangements.

The role of the middle classes in the Mexican Revolution was an important lesson to South American middle-class political parties of how not to involve the working classes when working for electoral reform. In Mexico, frustrated by their inability to participate in or influence the autocratic government of Porfirio Díaz, the urban middle classes, who were led by Francisco Madero (a member of one of Mexico's wealthiest families) and supported by industrialists and merchants hurt by preferential treatment given to foreign capital and enterprise, mounted a successful putsch in 1910 against the Díaz regime with the slogan of "effective suffrage, no reelection" and the goal of restoring the liberal Constitution of 1857. Their easy victory was illusory, however, and in the subsequent fight against counter-revolutionary forces the Constitutionalists were forced to appeal to wage workers and especially peasants with vague promises of social reform. The response was literally overwhelming, and the narrow political revoltuion rapidly became a social revolution. As a consequence, the next twenty-five years of Mexican history were dominated by the effort of new and remnants of old propertied and middle classes to contain and control workers and peasants. The presidential term of Lázaro Cárdenas (1934-1940) was the high watermark for creativity in this regard, for it was in this period that the Revolution was formally institutionalized by establishing a corporatist state with welfare trappings to promote a domestically owned capitalist economy that contained some archaic communal elements (*ejidos*) in the rural areas of greatest peasant unrest. Since 1940, government has been essentially a matter of management, although not an easy one.[17]

The Mexican case stands in sharp contrast to that of Uruguay, where the configurations of class forces allowed considerably more room to maneuver. In the small nation (fewer than a million people in 1900), Montevideo held one third of the population while in the countryside, the undisputed base of the nation's economy, the landowners were torn by frequent and violent dissensions among sheep, cattle, and farming interests. With the support of a sizable middle class and a large, active working class that had developed in Montevideo, a capable and energetic reformer, José Batlle y Ordoñez, was elected president in 1903 and dominated Uruguayan politics until his death in 1929. Continuing civil wars in the countryside severely restricted the power of the landowners in national politics, and Batlle utilized these almost classical conditions of class balance to centralize political power and strengthen the apparatus of the state. He was prodded by the pressure of recurring strikes and working-class unrest in Montevideo, with the result that the political and social reforms during the last fifteen or so years of his life were legion.[18]

In the reforms, he was careful to maintain and institutionalize as much as possible the social equilibrium. Extensive labor and welfare legislation for the urban middle and working classes (explicitly exempting the rural sector), vast expansion of white-collar jobs in the government bureaucracy, direct and indirect subsidies (including high tariffs) and discrimination against foreign capital for domestic industry, and subsidized transportation, export processing, credit and financial services, and energy for both agriculture and manufacturing interests were some of the major elements of the Colorado party's program under Batlle. This was all paid for by a diffused system of taxation, mostly indirect, of which tariffs were the largest portion. Although there were voluble protests from the propertied classes about "socialism," the balance struck between costs and benefits to each important group and among competing groups appears to have been quite successful during the 1920s. But social systems continue to change, frustrating attempts to freeze equilibrium conditions—that historically *rara-avis*—and Uruguay's social and political structure that rested on such a balance underwent severe challenges in later decades.

The conclusion for middle-class parties from these two early experiments of using working-class allies seemed to be that the urban working classes could be of considerable help in gaining political office through established procedures. On the other hand, if those orderly procedures, backed by the army and the police, were to fail and fighting broke out, the working classes, particularly those in the countryside, could be extremely dangerous. The Russian Revolution strengthened this conviction.

These lessons appear to have been taken seriously by middle-class parties throughout South America. In Chile, where the urban workers and miners in the north and south were extremely militant—there were some 293 "formal" strikes between 1911 and 1920 culminating in a near revolution in 1920—the middle-class Radical party became strongly reformist in rhetoric. Gaining working-class support, they used it successfully to threaten the narrow electorate into voting Arturo Alessandri into the presidency in 1920.[19] But when the parliamentary form of national government and the middle classes' own temporizing prevented the implementation of any significant social and economic reforms, it took further strikes and disruption to force responsiveness. The result, supervised by the military, was a body of ameliorating labor and welfare legislation, which while of some benefit to the urban working class, actually favored middle-class employees, and a thorough restructuring of national government embodied in the Constitution of 1925.

The Argentine middle classes, on the other hand, operated in a milieu with considerably less working-class pressure, and the political program of its party, the Radical Civic Union, was almost solely concerned with electoral reform.[20] Quantitatively the Argentine middle classes were a larger proportion of the politically significant population than their counterparts in Chile and were able to exert more direct pressure on the ruling classes. In the name of electoral reform, the middle-class political groups, together with some dissident factions of the armed forces and workers, mounted a couple of revolts around the turn of the twentieth century that were easily, almost politely, suppressed. But in 1912, in an attempt to preempt the Radicals' appeal, the oligarchy reformed the electoral process, instituting universal male sufferage (women waited until 1947), a secret, mandatory ballot, and minority congressional representation from individual districts. In spite of the intention of these concessions, the Radical leader, Hipólito Yrigoyen, was elected president in 1916, and Radicals kept the office until 1930.

Much of the electoral weakness of the Argentine working class in this period stemmed from the fact that immigrant noncitizens made up between 50 and 70 percent of the adult male population in and around Buenos Aires. Although this total clearly included men of all classes, the numbers of noncitizens were greater in the lower strata, with the consequence that the vast majority of the working classes were excluded from the formal political process. Nonetheless, workers did band together and strike to improve their lot, but the Radicals, as long as they could depend on the army to maintain the political order, could ignore their demands and even, in 1919, bloodily suppress their activities. In the fourteen years that the Radicals held executive office, no important social legislation was enacted (although the oligarchy's control of Congress contributed to this), and university reform was the only significant change effected during this period.

Altogether, the political ascendance of middle-class radical parties in Chile and Argentina left a record somewhat less than distinguished, but current critical judgments of their performance are often too harsh. Despite North American liberal conceptions, it is unrealistic, given the social and economic position of the middle classes in Chile and Argentina and the class-dominated nature of those polities, to expect Radicals either to desire or to be able to break concentrated economic and social power by legislation. The fact remains that these new elements did serve, no matter how reluctantly, to open up the political process and to begin legitimizing organizations and political activities of the working classes.

SUMMARY AND PERSPECTIVE

South American industrial growth during the first three decades of the twentieth century was led by wage goods produced in small factories. But there ends the similarity with English competitive capitalist industrial development of a hundred years earlier, in large part because South American growth was in the global context of the more advanced phase of finance capitalist industrial production. The ramifications of being off-phase were many, and they undercut the possibilities of creating self-reinforcing competitive capitalist industrial expansion in any of the South American nations.

The sectoral composition of finance capitalist industrial growth in Western Europe and the U.S., together with the particular type of imperialist impulses to which it gave rise, meant that foreign firms effectively supplied the South American economies with capital and intermediate goods, and with the credit to buy them. By itself, this sharply reduced the potential for more fully integrated, backward-linked industrial growth and for technological progress in South America.

Finance capitalism in the core industrial nations also affected the South American social and political configurations in ways inimical to competitive industrialization. Even in those nations where staple export production was under local ownership and control, as in Argentina and Brazil, the process of staples production supported powerful classes who dominated national politics and cultural affairs and were indifferent or hostile to domestic industrialization.

Even in Chile and Uruguay, where economic elites were displaced in the political sphere, the industrial bourgeoisie was not the new political force. As in Argentina and Brazil, the industrial bourgeoisie of Uruguay and Chile suffered serious political disabilities: because industrial growth did not demonstrate the internal dynamism necessary for sustained growth, neither their numbers nor economic power rapidly increased; large proportions of industrialists were recent migrants from Europe; and their position was dependent on state policy for both tariff protection and labor control and on export earnings for their product markets and availabilities of inputs.

The commercial and urban societies created by staple exports expanded the new middle class of white-collar workers who were politically ascendant in all these nations, and when the middle class looked for political allies, they turned to industrial workers as more promising sources of support than the industrial bourgeoisie. The record of the middle-class parties' real support for working-class causes was poor, but this ambivalence certainly was not due to middle-class support for domestic industrial development. The presence of working-class organizations which had to be reckoned with thereby weakened industrial entrepreneurs politically by making the latter more dependent on state policies for labor control and by offering prospects for political coalitions potentially disadvantageous to industrialists' interests. Moreover, it is not clear that individual industrialist's interests would have been served by national industrial development.

As the German experience suggests, such obstacles to competitive capitalist industrialization as politically potent agrarian classes, noncapitalist organization of the countryside, uncertain domestic consumer goods markets, and the rise of politically self-conscious labor organizations could have been much less formidable for finance capitalist industrial development. The obvious question, then, is why was not the finance capitalist path to industrial development pursued in South America at this time? And the equally obvious response is, pursued by whom? For reasons outlined in this chapter, market forces did not promote local production of capital and intermediate goods. Foreign pressures on South American governments certainly would have discouraged any concerted political effort to establish significant capital and intermediate goods sectors, but the major point is that there was no domestic constituency for such a program. As I have mentioned, it did not appear to be in the economic interests of the agrarian, commercial, or even industrial possessing classes, and the political costs of reduced influence over an expanded, bureaucratic state apparatus (to say nothing of the increased taxes to support it) were not attractive either. While the middle classes might have been a source of support for the resulting employment opportunities, important segments of this amorphous group actively fought against any sort of domestic industrialization. Finally, the urban working classes' immediate plight was so desperate that such a long-run program would have been of doubtful interest to them. A strong nationalist ideology and a self-conscious and politically effective military might have helped overcome these obstacles, but neither seems to have had much effect in this direction.

Only in the third phase of industrial development—monopoly capitalism—did South American industrial growth begin to make substantial advances. Chapter 6 shows how the responses to the depression of the 1930s established the bases for monopoly capitalist industrial growth in several South American nations, and chapter 7 delineates the general characteristics of this pattern of industrial growth and their particular forms in South America in the post-World War II decades.

NOTES

1. Although I have already used these terms, it is probably a good time to repeat the distinction between capital goods and intermediate goods. "Capital goods" refers to machinery, tools, and equipment (produced means of production) purchased by firms for use in producing commodities; "fixed capital" includes the plant as well as installed capital goods. "Intermediate goods" are those manufactured materials (as opposed to raw materials) purchased by a firm to be used up in fabricating another product, for example, tires purchased by an automobile-making company. Both capital and intermediate goods are "producer goods."

2. See the discussion of dependency in chapter 4 and the citations in notes 4, 5, and 6 of that chapter for the term's frequently vague and sweeping definitions. I use dependent industrialization in a narrow, technical sense, akin to that of Merhav (1969) and to the "nonintegrated industrialization" of Ferrer (1967, pp. 148-158), and then go on to discuss its social and political correlates in South America without using the term for the whole range of phenomena.

3. In addition to the country studies cited in notes 18-20, see the following for data and interpretations of industrial growth during this period: Cardoso and Faletto (1979), Furtado (1976), U.S. ECLA (1966), and Wythe (1949) for Latin America as a whole; Diaz Alejandro (1970), Randall (1977), and Ferrer (1967) for Argentina; Baer (1979), Dean (1969), Furtado (1965), Nachman (1977), Mattoon (1977), Stein (1957), and Teixeira Vieira (1951) for Brazil; Ballasteros and Davis (1963), Kirsch (1977), Mamalakis (1976), and Pinto Santa Cruz (1962) for Chile; McGreevy (1971), Rippy (1931), and Urrutia (1969) for Colombia; and Thorp and Bertram (1978) for Peru.

4. Alonso (1964) is a concise statement of the principles of location theory; his article is included in an extremely useful collection. Blakemore and Smith (1974) is very good on the development of spatial patterns within the South American nations.

5. Diaz Alejandro (1970, p. 294) argues that the Argentine tariff structure indicates that the tariffs on wage goods were not principally revenue tariffs but must have been deliberate efforts to promote domestic industrial production. He reasons that revenue tariffs would have focused on luxuries and agricultural machinery rather than wage goods, because the tariff-induced price rise in these two types of products would not have discouraged their importation either by reducing total demand for the articles or by import-substitution domestic production, thus yielding higher revenues than tariffs on wage goods. This deductive argument is an excellent example of the dangers of applying abstract principles of rationality and maximization without consideration of the class distribution of political power and tax burdens.

6. Hoselitz (1955) is an interesting typology of cities and their functions not

inconsistent with mine. Morse (1971) is a good discussion of Latin American urban growth in this time.

7. As with the production and sale of any commodity, the selling price of machinery reflects an equal amount of income distributed among those involved in the machinery's production (including those producing inputs), and a sizable proportion of this new income will be used to purchase consumer goods. But the income distributed from the production and sale of consumer goods corresponds to the money value of those additional consumer goods those transactions make available on the market within a given period of time (say, a year). The income created by the production and sale of capital goods, on the other hand, is considerably greater than the corresponding increase in the money value of new consumer goods on the market in that time span due to those transactions. The difference between the consumer goods and capital goods activities in this regard stems from the fact that all income from the production and sale of a new machine accrues at the time it is made and sold while its contribution to consumer goods output is distributed over a number of years and will be less than the machine's purchase price in any particular year. The overall effect of an increase in the domestic production and sale of capital goods in a given year, then, is to induce a net increase in the demand for consumer goods. But this effect is lost to the national economy when those goods are imported. Marx characterized this particular exchange phenomenon as purchases without sales, as opposed to the savings function of sales without purchases.

8. Although in the economic development literature there is general agreement on the central importance of capital accumulation for economic development, the vast majority of growth models focus exclusively on the financial and exchange aspects of accumulation. With concern about savings and investment levels, the price of borrowed funds (interest rates), the operation of financial intermediaries, incentives, and the influence of inflation on all of the above, the more interesting and complicated side of machinery production is generally ignored or else completely hidden by the use of aggregate (average and incremental) capital-output ratios. Lowe (1952 and 1955) are excellent, although complex, attempts to capture the technical and structural character of accumulation in formal models, and Ames and Rosenberg (1965), and Rosenberg (1963a, 1963b, and 1972, pp. 87-110) are good historical and empirical discussions of the contribution by machinery production to economic growth.

9. On the scale requirements for capital and intermediate products as opposed to consumer goods, see Hicks (1959, pp. 184-185, 204) and Rosenberg (1963a and 1963b). The need for large-scale markets for a viable producer goods sector has two principal facets. Large-scale plant size is necessary for efficient production in a significant number of intermediate products (for example, steel and fuels) as well as for some capital goods. While no such technical imperatives govern the size of firms in many lines of machine making, the products are highly specialized, frequently made to individual buyers' specifications, and still require a large total market to generate sufficient demand for such specialized items.

10. Let us take a recent issue over the U.S. tariff structure to illustrate the "effective" or "value-added" tariff concept. If the U.S. imposes a 10 percent *ad valorum* (per value) duty on imports of instant coffee while allowing roasted

coffee beans to enter duty-free, U.S. processors of instant coffee are actually receiving protection far in excess of the nominal 10 percent. If, let us say, the process by which roasted coffee beans are turned into instant coffee adds 20 percent to the coffee's market value, then the 10 percent tariff protecting U.S. instant-coffee producers from Brazilian competition is equivalent, in effective protection, to a 50 percent tariff (10 percent/20 percent). So arises the seeming anomaly that if duties on imported coffee beans were raised, the actual levels of protection for U.S. producers of instant coffee would be *diminished,* making the Brazilian product more price competitive in the U.S. market. The same reasoning applies to the position of South American consumer goods producers with tariff protection but using duty-free imputs.

Johnson (1967, pp. 96-104) clearly explains and applies the logic of "effective protection." Hirschman (1968) is an excellent discussion of many of these problems, including the domestic industrial bourgeoisie's interest in blocking backward linkages.

11. Marx (1867, p. 382) wrote, "There were mules and steam-engines before there were any labourers whose exclusive occupation it was to make mules and steam-engines; just as men wore clothes before there were any such people as tailors." See Ames and Rosenberg (1965) and Rosenberg (1963b) and their citations for the development pattern of capital goods industries in England and the U.S.

12. It is this staging of the process of industrial development which informs the interesting article on the industrial division of labor by Stigler (1951).

13. As one example among many, Baer (1965, pp. 16-17, 26-29) insists that the disruption of foreign trade associated with both World War I and World War II stimulated Brazilian industrial growth. Dean (1969) and Leff (1968, p. 13) cogently criticize his data on industrial output and argue the opposite conclusions.

14. A large element in this overemphasis on outside agitators stems from labor historians' focus on institutional histories of formal labor organizations, leading naturally to a stress on the roles of individuals and groups of leaders (many of whom were immigrants). Representatives of this genre are Poblete Tronosco and Burnett (1960) and Alexander (1962 and 1965), who, while they present useful information about unions, consistently downplay the changes in work and workers' lives that led these people to band together for different purposes at different times. The authors' organizational focus also enables them to denegrate any political assault on the wage system and to advocate collective bargaining as the "proper" and "mature" goal of working class organizations; in this perspective, they are deeply influenced by Kerr, *et al.* (1960). Although the tone is no better, Alba (1968, pp. 203-370) gives more information on working-class politics. Spalding (1977) is the best on urban labor, although he ignores some of the issues I believe are crucial, and Bauer (1979) is excellent on rural labor. Individual country studies, when available, are often better than those that deal with all of Latin America. Among the best are Baily (1967), Dulles (1974), Angell (1972), Morris (1966), Urrutia (1969), and Payne (1965). Erickson, *et al.* (1974) surveys the literature on the labor movements in Argentina, Brazil, and Chile.

15. Mills (1953) is still the landmark work on the general characteristics of this amorphous group. Crevenna (1951) was the basis for much subsequent study of

the Latin American middle classes, and Johnson (1958) is still the best-known work on the subject in English.

16. Petras (1970) is a critical review of liberal scholarship on Latin American middle classes; see also the sound assessments of the political and social role of this group in Nun (1968) and Veliz (1965). The more recent liberal literature is generally less enthusiastic and more realistic about the middle classes.

17. Johnson (1958, pp. 128-152) presents a similar interpretation of the Revolution; Wolf (1969, p. 3-50) is one of the best concise narratives of the Revolution in all its complexity and Dunn (1972, pp. 48-69) and Goldfrank (1975 and 1976), also with comparative intent, pose important questions of interpretation; and Womack (1969) is a brilliant portrait of Zapata as a revolutionary leader. Cosio Villegas (1965) is good on the background to the Revolution. Cumberland (1968) is one of the best general histories of Mexico, Bailey (1978) is a recent historiographical survey, and Reynolds (1970) is a useful compilation of data on twentieth-century Mexico. Ashby (1967), Chevalier (1967), Gonzales Casanova (1970), Hansen (1971), *Latin American Perspectives* (1975), Ross (1966), and Smith (1972) cover important aspects of post-revolutionary Mexico.

18. For Uruguay, see Hanson (1938), Lindahl (1962), Johnson (1958), and Benvenuto (1967).

19. For this period of Chilean social and political history, see Cavarozzi and Petras (1974), Haring (1931), Johnson (1958), Petras (1969), Pike (1963), and Nunn (1970).

20. For background and interpretations of Radical politics in Argentina, see Bailey (1967), Cornblit (1967), Germani (1965 and 1968), Johnson (1958), Romero (1963), and Scobie (1971).

6

DEPRESSION, WAR, AND INDUSTRIAL EXPANSION, 1930-1945

Markets for South American staple exports had been showing some weakness during the 1920s, as we have seen, but the impact of the Great Depression which engulfed the capitalist world in the 1930s was shattering for most South American export economies.[1] The collapse of international markets was made worse for South American exports by defensive protectionist policies employed by the industrialized nations. The total effect was a serious decline in export earnings of foreign exchange which, in turn, dramatically reduced the ability of these nations to import goods and services. The prices of South American exports dropped, but even at lower prices foreign markets in general absorbed a smaller physical quantity of exports; and the prices of South American exports plummeted farther and faster than did the prices of the goods that were being imported.[2] As Table 6.1 shows, these declines were not uniform in their magnitude. In general, the market position of mineral exporters (not including oil) was the worst, while the exporters of non-tropical foodstuffs were relatively best-off. Mexico and Argentina are examples of these two cases respectively. Tropical agricultural commodity exports occupied a middle position between the extremes.[3]

The decline in the ability to import due to contraction of export markets was further exacerbated by the reversal of the direction of foreign investment flows. During the depression, particularly in the early years, the region as a whole experienced net foreign divestment. New foreign investment money coming in was substantially less than what foreigners were liquidating and taking back home. This reversal reduced still further the amounts of foreign currency available for purchases of imports.

The depression, in addition to its effect on the capacity of South American nations to import, led to a drastic decline in domestic incomes derived from exporting. If those engaged in export production had used all their incomes on imports of consumer goods (and nobody else had bought imports), the contrac-

TABLE 6.1
Changes in the Terms of Trade for Latin America:
Argentina, Brazil, Chile, and Mexico, 1925-1929, 1930-1934, 1935-1939
(1925-1929 = 100)

	Qx	*Px*	*Pm*	*Px/Pm*	$Qx\frac{Px}{Pm}$	*Qm*
Latin America						
1930-1934	91	56	73	76	69	n.a.
1935-1939	98	70	78	89	77	n.a.
Argentina						
1930-1934	92	68	85	80	73	68
1935-1939	89	89	88	100	90	77
Brazil						
1930-1934	110	74	124	60	65	52
1935-1939	152	87	196	45	68	73
Chile						
1930-1934	67	53	81	62	42	52
1935-1939	98	35	59	59	58	73
Mexico						
1930-1934	75	82	133	57	45	55
1935-1939	89	137	208	64	61	74

SOURCE: Derived from U.N. Economic Commission for Latin America, *Economic Survey of Latin America, 1949* (New York: United Nations, 1951), pp. 19, 98, 112, 211, 272, 408-409.

NOTE: Qx: Index of quantity of exports
Px: Index of price of exports
Pm: Index of price of imports
Px/Pm: Net Barter Terms of Trade
$Qx\frac{Px}{Pm}$: Income Terms of Trade (Export-based Capacity to Import)
Qm: Index of quantity of imports

tion in the export sectors' income and purchasing power would have had minimal effect on the other sectors of the domestic economy. But as demonstrated in the last chapter, this was not the case, particularly for Argentina, Brazil, Chile, Uruguay, and Colombia. The sectors of those national economies producing for domestic use relied heavily on the export sector to generate domestic demand (income-multiplier linkage) as well as to supply foreign exchange for imported inputs. Furthermore, the loss in income from exporting struck at the keystone of the national elites' power and status; proceeds from exports, whether excercised by governments or by employers at production sites, were the main source of economic resources which sustained the whole social order, that is, kept workers working for owners. When the depression curtailed this source, immediate steps had to be taken to avoid the dissolution of existing social relations of production.

The success achieved by such defensive measures depended on the severity of the externally induced crisis as well as the strength of existing mechanisms of social control, and thereby varied nation by nation. The defensive policies of the South American governments during this period are usually interpreted as attempts to protect the balance of international payments, thus casting the argument in starkly technical, narrow terms. Although the balance of payments deficits were perceived as a serious problem demanding immediate action, international flows of currencies were just one facet of the larger, more pressing problem of preserving the existing social order. This was the real issue raised by the depression.

The changes that occurred in the economic sphere, particularly in regard to the development of the industrial sector, will be the subject of the first part of this chapter, followed in the second section by a discussion of the sociopolitical patterns that both conditioned and stemmed from these changes.

ECONOMIC CRISIS AND REORIENTATION

The depression led to immediate political changes in most South American nations, frequently by means of a forceful overthrow of the existing government. In spite of the varied political complexions of the new governments, the emergency measures the governments of the more industrialized nations took against domestic economic contraction and social unrest were similar in many important respects. Whether the new governments explicitly represented the export interests, as in Argentina, or whether they were middle-class parties drawing strength from the working class, as in Colombia, or whether they were from outside the export-urban political axis, as in Brazil, they made concessions to the urban working classes. In the form of new legislation or through implementation of existing legislation, these concessions included such measures as the legalization of unions, regulation of working hours and conditions, job security, social insurance schemes, and some welfare measures. Strong provisions for the political control of labor organizations were also established. The extent of all such changes depended on the pressure the workers could bring to bear much more than on the ideology of those in government.

Benefits to the lower classes were small pickings, however, when compared to those received by the export elites. Most South American governments subsidized prices for export staples, and all devalued their national currencies during this period. The combined effect was to raise the domestic currency incomes of exporters above what they would have otherwise been.

In addition to devaluation, these governments made other efforts to ameliorate external financial imbalances. During the early years of the depression the governments of all nations except Peru imposed exchange controls which in effect created governmental monopolies in the domestic purchase and sale of foreign currencies, allowing them to control the amounts to be used for different purposes, frequently by charging different prices for foreign currencies according to their intended use (multiple exchange rates). Governments were somewhat ambivalent in their use of general import restrictions, however, because of their eagerness to put the export economy back on the tracks. For instance, President Getulio Vargas substantially raised Brazilian tariffs in 1931, but this appears simply to have been an effort to strengthen his hand in bilateral bargaining; in return for some mild promises from the coffee-importing nations, he undermined the domestic tariff structure. Similarly, under threats of being closed out of the British market by Commonwealth preferences, Argentina signed the infamous Roca-Runciman pact of 1933 (renewed in 1936) which lowered Argentine restrictions on imports from Britain and gave special treatment to British investors. These measures indicate the indifference of those in control of the governments of Argentina and Brazil toward domestic industrial activity and industrialists; they were willing and eager to sacrifice the interests of this sector to gain even slight and uncertain advantages in export markets.

There were limits to the extent of this neglect, however, limits defined by the level of unemployment which the urban working class would tolerate. Urban unemployment was most serious in Chile, the South American nation hardest hit by the depression, and there and to a greater degree in Argentina and Brazil, governmental policies supported the aggregate level of domestic demand. Efforts to preserve upper-class incomes as well as meet other spending imperatives, at a time when their foreign-trade revenues were dwindling, forced reluctant governments into protracted budgetary deficits. And as these deficits could no longer be financed by foreign loans, they had to be financed in a manner that resulted in pumping into the national economy new purchasing power that had to be used for domestic products. Such net demand-creating measures, in conjunction with governmental efforts to channel demand for consumer goods away from the shrunken value of possible imports, began to catch hold in the third and fourth year of the depression, stimulating domestic industrial production.

It is essential to recognize the mediating role played by political decisions in preventing the depression in South America from becoming as deep as it was in the U.S. Ad hoc governmental policies in Argentina, Brazil, Chile, and Colombia to protect upper-class incomes and to control working-class restiveness stimulated domestic demand by means of a Keynesian-type fiscal policy before the publication of J. M. Keynes' *The General Theory of Employment, Interest, and Money* (1936) and before Roosevelt's New Deal in the United States. But the similarity with Keynesian prescriptions should not lead one, in retrospect, to characterize these policies as conscious efforts to promote industrial growth.[4] Nevertheless, irrespective of intentions, these policies did reduce the income-multiplier dimension of dependence that had tied industrial to export growth, and the example of Uruguay shows that the depression, by ruining staple export markets and curtailing foreign investment, would not have stimulated domestic industrial growth through some universal and inevitable import-substitution mechanism had these policies not protected the level of domestic effective demand. Chapter 5 shows that the collapse of the foreign trade sector would simply have been transmitted through contracted incomes and demand levels and dragged down domestic production for domestic markets.

Figures A.1 and A.2 and Table 6.2 show the aggregate changes in industrial activity during the 1930s, but the experience of Argentina, Brazil, Chile, and Colombia are more interesting than indicated by these general measures and will be the focus of this chapter. The stimulus to industrial growth in these nations, resulting from the redirection of domestic demand away from imports to domestic sources in the 1930s, is a matter of general agreement. What has not been given proper emphasis, however, is that this redirection of demand did not encourage the same type of industrial growth as had typified the earlier decades; it involved important changes in the *composition* of demand for domestic industrial output. In contrast, the economies of Peru, Ecuador, and Venezuela, where the effect of the depression was less severe, and of Bolivia and Paraguay, where the social relations of production were not so sensitive to changes in staple export markets, grew and contracted along the lines of dependent industrial growth typical of the earlier decades of the twentieth century.

Governments in Argentina, Brazil, Chile, and Colombia, however, acted vigorously in order to preserve existing patterns of income distribution, and with the scarcity of foreign exchange, even high-income consumers, not just wage earners, had to depend on domestic production. The firms that catered to these new markets, larger than those for wage goods (in purchasing power, not people), were prominent in domestic industrial expansion during the 1930s. The class of industrial products defined in chapter 1 as modern consumer goods no longer could be imported in sufficient volume, and upper-income receivers had to turn to local sources to obtain them. These articles included consumer durables like automobiles, radios, and household appliances, complementary goods like tires and fuels, as well as such items as prepared and processed foods and nylon textiles, which are grouped together with important wage goods categories in Tables 6.3 and 6.4. In spite of the inadequacy of these categories, the two tables still suggest the beginning of important shifts in the composition of production in Argentina, Brazil, Chile, and even Colombia, where manufacturing was dominated by handicrafts and artisan production in 1929 (see Table 5.1). The structures of manufacturing production in Uruguay, Bolivia, and Paraguay retained the older patterns.

The technical conditions of producing these goods involved larger-scale plants, more complex technologies, and higher capitalization than characterized the production of such wage goods such as cotton textiles. Obviously, fine clothes were still made in small shops, but the expansion of modern consumer goods production for upper-class consumers promoted large-scale industrial units which in size and organization resembled public utilities, mines, and some export processing plants more than the industrial firms making consumer goods in the 1920s. The technical and organizational differences between firms producing for

TABLE 6.2
Indicators of South American Manufacturing Activity, 1940
(1960 prices)

	Manufacturing Output				*Manufacturing Employment*			
					Factories		Artisanal[a]	
	U.S. $1,000,000	(1929=100)	Per Capita	(1929=100)	**1,000 People**	**(1920=100)**	**1,000 People**	**(1929=100)**
Argentina	2,446.0	(133.2)	172.9	(113.2)	605	(155)	615	(110)
Bolivia					15	(188)	125	(107)
Brazil	1,361.4	(163.5)	32.9	(132.[illegible])	815	(160)	838	(101)
Chile	275.0	(142.9)	54.3	(122.9)	138	(144)	149	(93)
Colombia	214.3	(216.7)	23.6	(181.5)	110	(157)	340	(100)
Ecuador	58.5		23.7		17	(170)	158	(120)
Paraguay					6	(200)	47	(118)
Peru					65	(191)	331	(107)
Uruguay	167.1		84.7		79	(144)	66	(102)
Venezuela	140.9		38.0		53	(260)	68	(96)
TOTAL SOUTH AMERICA					1,903	(159)	2,737	(104)
Mexico	916.0	(159.9)	46.2	(134.3)	370	(161)	368	(95)
TOTAL LATIN AMERICA					2,413	(161)	3,458	(104)

SOURCE: United Nations Economic Commission for Latin America, *The Industrialization Process in Latin America*, Statistical Annex, mimeo (New York: United Nations, 1966), pp. 23, 17, 18, 20.

NOTE: [a]defined variously by nation: in some, all manufacturing establishments employing fewer than ten workers; in others, fewer than seven workers; and in others, fewer than five workers.

TABLE 6.3
The Structure of Manufacturing Sectors: Argentina, Brazil, Chile, 1939

	Argentina		*Brazil*		*Chile*	
	% Output	Relative Growth[a]	% Output	Relative Growth[a]	% Output	Relative Growth[a]
Food and beverages	29.3	80	28.6	55	36.7	76
Tobacco	0.7	89	2.3	53	5.8	126
Textiles, clothing, and shoes	15.9	162	27.1	97	17.7	76
Leather products	2.5	38	1.7	71	3.9	91
Wood and furniture	4.7	147	5.3	n.a.	5.4	100
Paper products	1.6	84	1.5	} 345		
Printing and publishing	6.1	62	3.6		8.4	279
Chemicals and pharmaceuticals	10.5	144	9.8	76	8.4	311
Rubber products	0.0	.....	0.7	very large	n.a.	n.a.
Stone, glass, cement, Non-metallic minerals	3.8	55	5.9	273	5.7	438
Metal products	7.3	162	7.6	176	}	
Vehicles and machinery	4.9	169	4.4	n.a.		
Electrical machinery and appliances	0.8	very large	1.2	n.a.	8.0	104
Other and misc.	10.3	107	1	n.a.	n.a.	n.a.
TOTAL	100.0		100.0		100.0	
Avg. annual manufacturing growth rates, 1930s	3.4		8.5		2.6	
Avg. annual GDP growth rates, 1930s	1.5		8.4		−0.5	
Manufacturing as % of GDP, 1939	28		14		11	

SOURCES: See Table 6.1, and Markos Mamalakis, *The Growth and Structure of the Chilean Economy* (New Haven, Conn.: Yale University Press, 1976), p. 150.

NOTE: [a] $\frac{\text{\% Change in product output (1929-1939)}}{\text{\% Change in total manufacturing output (1929-1939)}} \times 100$. An index number of 100 indicates that the output of a product category grew at the same rate as total manufacturing output.

TABLE 6.4
The Structure of Manufacturing Sectors:
Uruguay, Colombia, Venezuela, Bolivia, Late 1930s and Early 1940s

	Year	*Food, Beverages, Tobacco*	*Textiles, Clothing, Leather*	*Wood Products*	*Chemicals*	*Metals*	*Other*	*TOTAL*
Uruguay	1936	56.9	19.2	2.8	3.9	8.7	8.4	100.0
Colombia	1945	51.5	23.1	3.0	4.4	3.4	14.4	100.0
Venezuela	1936	58.2	16.7	3.9	9.5	1.8	9.9	100.0
Bolivia	1942	58.3	29.3	6.1	5.0	0.5	5.2	100.0

SOURCE: United Nations Economic Commission for Latin America, *Economic Survey of Latin America* (Lake Success, N.Y.: United Nations, 1949), p. 17.

the high-income consumers and those producing for workers represents yet another vital difference between nineteenth- and twentieth-century industrialization; in nineteenth-century England, wage goods were produced in factories and were the leading growth industries, while luxury consumer goods by and large were made by artisans and handicraft workers using labor-intensive methods. By the 1930s the relative differences in the conditions of production for the two types of markets had been reversed (Felix, 1974, pp. 217-219).

The change in the composition of demand and the pattern of output had significant implications for industrial growth. Although the income-multiplier dimension of dependent industrialization was diminished by government policy, the backward-linkage problem was intensified by the shift to different types of goods whose production required greater inputs of machinery, steel, fuels, lubricants, and other imports. Exchange controls and multiple exchange rates were used to change the composition of imports away from finished consumer goods and toward intermediate and capital goods, but the greatly reduced volume of possible imports still put a strict upper limit on the amounts of these imported producer goods available. This was particularly serious in Chile because its sluggish agricultural sector forced reliance on large quantities of imported food. Severe constraints on the supply side were thus felt throughout the more industrialized South American economies, and demand-pull inflationary pressures existed in the urban areas of South America during the depression years.

The entire range of domestic industry, including wage goods, was affected by the squeeze of rising demand and of constraints on expanding output. Expansion in wage goods production occurred through the addition of night shifts to increase utilization of existing plant and equipment, supplemented by some new, usually small firms employing rudimentary technologies and requiring few imported inputs. As was the case during World War I, many small shops also sprang up in response to the need to extend the operating life of capital equipment by repairing it and making replacement parts. Some of the larger, established firms increased their output of wage goods, occasionally by transforming production processes (for example, cigarettes), and a few initiated or expanded production of higher-quality products more suited to the higher-income customers who were now dependent on local production for consumer goods.

Governmental exchange authorities, for reasons of efficiency or not, allocated the bulk of imported intermediate products and machinery to the larger firms of both the modern and wage goods type, and overall centralization increased in the manufacturing sector producing for both kinds of markets. The centralization process was confirmed and rationalized, from the point of view of large industrialists, by the growing market power of industry associations during these years, which in Brazil, for example, resulted in the expansion of cartels in several lines of wage goods production. Those firms producing specifically for the new, higher-income consumers made the greatest contribution to the centralization process. Foreign-owned firms were important in these product lines and in intermediate goods like fuels and chemicals, particularly after the middle of the decade. As Table 6.5 shows, between 1929 and 1943, total U.S. direct investment in Latin America declined 41 percent, and it increased in only two areas: petroleum less than 0.2 of 1 percent, and manufacturing more than 40 percent, mostly in Argentina, Brazil, and Chile (see also Wilkins, 1974, pp. 167-241). The larger, more industrialized economies of South America, with excess demand for industrial products (and thereby opportunities for high profits), offered attractive markets to producers in the industrialized nations where deficiencies of demand and profits prevailed. Foreign shortages, tariffs, and exchange controls impeded foreign firms' ability to take advantage of these markets by exporting finished consumer goods to them, and U.S. and some European firms established new firms and expanded previously operating plants in South America to avoid these barriers. Aided by their freedom from foreign exchange shortages which restricted access by local firms to foreign capital equipment and intermediate products, the foreign firms in South America prospered and grew. Just prior to and during World War II, foreign capital comprised about 18 percent of total capital in Brazilian manufacturing (30 percent of São Paulo's manufacturing capital) and 25 percent of the capital in Chilean manufacturing (U.N. DESA, 1955, pp. 53, 64, and passim). Although no totals are available for the other nations, the same source lists the substantial proportions of foreign investment in particular lines of manufacturing in other South American nations, especially Argentina.[5]

The large industrial firms, whether owned by local people or by foreigners, used production processes similar to those of the industrialized nations of North America and Europe with concomitant high capital-labor ratios and high labor productivity. The tendency in nations of capital scarcity and labor plenty to use sophisticated, labor-saving, capital-intensive techniques has been termed irrational by many neoclassocal economists; clearly the more reasonable method of production, the argument goes, would have been those that conserved scarce capital and used relatively large amounts of the readily available factor—labor power. Economists have suggested several explanations for this apparent perversity: the greater prestige enjoyed by entrepreneurs employing modern techniques; the scarcity of labor with the necessary skills; subsidies for high capitalization resulting from governmental policies; and the inflated cost of industrial labor above the "real" (opportunity cost) price (White, 1978).

No doubt some of these considerations did influence owners' choices of techniques, but there are other, more compelling reasons for this pattern of decisions concerning production processes. The use of modern industrial technology appears strange only to economists steeped in neoclassical production and growth theory (for example, the Cobb-Douglas production function), which deduces that the productivity of a factor of production declines as it is used more intensively relative to other factors. Recent theoretical work has raised serious doubts about the logic of this proposition (Harcourt, 1972; Nell, 1972), and empirical studies have shown that the technology behind high capital-labor factor proportions increases the productivity of capital as well as that of labor (Felix, 1974).

TABLE 6.5
United States Direct Investment in Latin America, by Nation and Sector, 1929-1943
(millions of $ U.S.)

		TOTAL	*Agriculture*	*Mining and Smelting*	*Petroleum*	*Public Utilities and Transport*	*Manufacturing*	*Trade*	*Other*
Argentina	1929	332	.....	.....	30	148	82	53	19
	1943	380	.....	12	39	182	101	27	19
Brazil	1929	194	.....	.....	23	97	46	16	12
	1943	233	.....	.....	30	88	66	29	20
Chile	1929	423	.....	332	.....	67	7	13	4
	1943	328	8	215	3	66	28	7	2
Colombia	1929	124	16	11	56	25	3	4	9
	1943	117	2	5	75	18	6	6	5
Peru	1929	124		80		11	3	3	27
	1943	71	13	29	11	8	6	3	2
Venezuela	1929	233			226				6
	1943	373			341	8	1		23
LATIN AMERICA TOTALS	1929	3,462	817	732	617	887	231		178
	1936	2,803	400	708	453	937	192		113
	1943	2,721	385	405	618	875	325		113
LATIN AMERICA %	1929	100.0	23.6	21.1	17.8	25.6	6.7		5.2
	1936	100.0	14.3	25.2	16.2	33.4	6.8		4.1
	1943	100.0	14.1	14.9	22.7	32.1	11.9		4.3

SOURCES: U.N. Economic Commission for Latin America, *Foreign Capital in Latin America,* (New York: United Nations, 1954), p. 154 and *External Financing in Latin America* (New York: United Nations, 1965), pp. 32-33.

In other words, while it may appear paradoxical to economists, industrial engineers recognize that a capital-intensive technique, because of its capacity to raise the productivity of all factors of production including capital, may very well be a capital-conserving method of production as measured by capital/output ratios.

In addition to the technical and relative-price aspects of selecting productive techniques, there is a series of other considerations which made the technology developed in Western Europe and North America attractive to those producing industrial goods in South America. First of all, South American factories during the 1930s were rather turbulent places in which work discipline (that is, workers' willingness to submit to owners and their representatives) among increasingly class-conscious workers was tenuous at best. In this milieu, the favored techniques were obviously those requiring few workers, no matter how many poverty-stricken workers lived in the neighborhood (Rosenberg, 1969). Secondly, the technology contained in imported machines was appropriate for South American industrial capitalists in ways that transcended considerations of particular factor proportions. The imported technology was a capitalist technology in that it embodied a design of work organization which ensured the owner and his representatives maximum control over the work process and the product. Work was divided and specialized to the degree that close supervision was possible and individual workers were severely limited in their ability to gain an overview of how the parts related to the whole. A seemingly necessary function for those who coordinated production, bought materials, and sold the product was thus maintained (Marglin, 1974; Gorz, 1972; Braverman, 1974; Edwards, 1979). Finally, the use of modern industrial technology enabled a few firms to produce on a large scale and exercise considerable market power in their product lines. Whether the technology actually reduced per unit costs at higher levels of output or whether it merely permitted higher levels of output without too great an increase in per unit costs, the large-scale producer in small markets could influence prices to his advantage at the expense of suppliers and customers—a strong incentive to employ "inappropriate" technology (Merhav, 1969). Thus, during this period the industrial sectors began to develop their present characteristic pattern of firm sizes: a few very large firms in a sea of very small firms.

Foreign-owned firms were in the forefront of the development of backward-linkage production in which the limitations on imports had created bottlenecks in the expansion of industrial activity. They frequently dominated such lucrative markets as those for rubber products, transportation machinery, fuel and lubricants, chemicals, and electrical equipment. Domestic firms entered these areas as well, and between them progress was made toward filling in the vertical structure of national industry, most notably in Brazil.

The experience of the South American industrial sectors during World War II, however, revealed how slight was the reduction in dependence on imported inputs. Export markets had been slowly recovering from the darkest days of 1932 and 1933; although the 1937 international contraction was a setback, it was short-lived. World War II greatly stimulated demand for South American staple exports and through the income-multiplier linkage was a strong stimulus for domestic industrial markets. Foreign trade pressures during the war were in some respects the opposite of those of the depression years: the warring nations bought large volumes of South American staples but were restricted in their capacity to supply commodities in exchange. The result was that the South American staple-exporting nations built up magnificent balances of foreign exchange and experienced increased inflationary pressures. But industrial growth, despite the beginnings of some manufacturing exports, was constrained by the shortage of imported inputs. (See Figures A.1 and A.2.) This squeeze, following on the heels of the depression experience, further reduced domestic opposition to developing domestic productive capacity in some basic producer goods, and governments moved to establish or enlarge steel, fuel, and energy production. The necessity for imported machinery meant that many of these projects would have to be put off until the end of the war, but industrial development had come of age as an important political goal in South America.

SOCIAL AND POLITICAL TRANSFORMATIONS

Whether or not at the direct behest of landed and export-based classes, the central government in each of the industrially advanced South American nations was forced to intervene in and regulate a considerably larger portion of national affairs than had previously been necessary to maintain and reproduce the social order. In addition to becoming more deeply involved in labor disputes and labor control, central governments were called upon to protect the income of the wealthy classes whose economic base had suffered a severe blow from the collapse of export markets. Policies supporting property income were forthcoming, but by their very success in obtaining such policies the national elites, even in Argentina, Brazil, and Colombia, were being transformed into clients of increasingly strong central states in which power was vested in elaborate, expanding bureaucracies. The elites came to depend on particular state policies in very direct, immediate ways that were quite distinct from the relatively indirect services the classically liberal states had previously supplied in protecting the social system, that is, assuring property rights, freedom of contract, minimum individual and collective violence, and so on.[6] The result was that although the staple export possessing classes' political power was not destroyed, their position was reduced to that of an interest group among other interest groups, albeit a very influential one.

The weakening of the landed classes in Colombia resulted in the election and inauguration of reformist liberal governments with labor support in 1930 and 1934. The change in status of export elites, however, was most dramatic and unequivocal in Brazil, where coffee growers believed that Vargas was not supporting coffee prices at a high enough level. Joined by industrialists unhappy about his tariff policies (but without discernible support from the working classes), they mounted an armed rebellion against Vargas's government from the state of São Paulo in 1932. Vargas successfully crushed the rebellion (in a campaign which included the aerial bombing of the city of São Paulo), and Brazilian politics were never the same again.

A similar type of change was occurring in Argentina, but it did not reveal itself in such a stark manner until the 1940s. In the coup of 1930 the export-based oligarchy had taken state control back from Yrigoyen and the Radical party, and they managed by fraud and force to hang onto it for thirteen years. But even though their control enabled Argentina to be the most aggressive South American nation in trying to keep export markets (particularly Great Britain) open, this was attempted *through* the state. Foreign negotiations, internal price supports for meat and cereals, and regulation of the working classes all led to enlarging and strengthening the state apparatus which later would be used against the landed classes.

In Uruguay and Chile, where the landed classes' control over the state had already been effectively severed, centralized state power still grew, but the patterns were different. The depression destroyed the precarious internal balance of forces that the Uruguayan government had fostered, and the dictatorship of Gabriel Terra emerged, actively suppressing working-class protest. In Chile, the landed classes were relatively insulated from the disastrous decline in Chilean mineral exports. Unlike the situation in the other more industrialized nations of South America, export markets were not directly important to the most powerful agricultural interests, who supplied local markets with grain and meat. They did not do this very well, however, and Chile had to import large volumes of foodstuffs. When the nation's import capacity declined, domestic food prices rose sharply and benefited the landowners. This was the basis of the landowners' short-lived political comeback; after four months of chaos in 1932 (during which a Socialist Republic of Chile was declared), Arturo Alessandri was reelected, no longer as the spokesman of reform and working-class aspirations as he had been in the 1920s, but as the candidate of the landed classes. By 1938, however, the middle and urban working classes reasserted their political influence by the election of a Popular Front government.

Whatever configuration of forces prevailed in national politics, however, the defensive policies that these governments pursued were strikingly similar, all strengthening the state and the urban classes. The expansion of governmental activity swelled government employment of white-collar workers, and no matter what the intentions of expanded state interventions, members of the middle class benefited by increased employment opportunities. Also, whether a government emphasized subsidies to the rich or to the poor, the result was an increase in domestic markets for domestically produced manufactures, stimulating urban industries and increasing the size of the urban proletariat. The expansion of both governmental and manufacturing employment opportunities drew workers from the countryside into the cities and thus expanded markets for domestically produced wage goods and increased the need for public services.

The swelling of the ranks of white-collar workers in the public and private sectors occurred under conditions which significantly affected the attitudes of the middle-class political parties toward industrialization. Perceived earlier as "artificial" and as a conspiracy on the part of industrialists hiding behind tariffs to raise prices of domestic consumer goods, domestic industrial growth began to be supported by the middle-class parties. The change was the result of a confluence of several related factors. First, the expansion of white-collar employment opportunities was clearly related to continuing economic growth, and with the virtual demise of the export sector, domestic manufacturing seemed to be a more promising source of general economic expansion. More particularly, manufacturing was proving itself to be a good source of white-collar employment. Unlike agriculture or mining, it was an urban activity that directly employed a large number of managers, lawyers, accountants, clerks, and the like. Indirectly it led to the employment of people in the public sector for purposes of industrial regulation and encouragement as well as for the services associated with urban activity, such as primary education, mail delivery, sanitation, and law enforcement. In other words, manufacturing as opposed to staple-export activities promoted bureaucratic employment growth in both the public and private sectors.

Another reason for the change in attitude by the middle class toward industrialization was that the export sector had proven itself unreliable as a source of industrial consumer goods. The preceding chapter mentioned the multidimensional importance of consumption to the middle classes. The initial shock of the depression in the early 1930s, the sharp setback in 1937, and World War II demonstrated that if industrial consumer goods were to be available on a regular basis, local sources would have to be developed. The first section of this chapter discussed the economic significance of the shift of higher-income consumers toward domestic sources; the political corollary was that increasing numbers of people had new interest in the expansion of domestic industrial production. Finally, the middle-class political parties' formal and informal political cooperation with sectors of the urban industrial working classes made them more attentive to the health of the industrial sector as a whole in order to draw working-class political support.

Such changes in middle-class attitudes toward industrialization are crucial for understanding the *developmentista* thrust of the post-World War II era, but no less important were changes occurring in working-class politics. During the 1930s and early 1940s, important new tendencies were beginning to surface in the structure of the working class and the politics of the working-class movement, tendencies which were to divide and weaken the workers as a force for general social reform, much less as a threat to the wage system as a whole. In the early days of each nation's working-class movement, there was considerable mutual support given by the working class generally, urban and rural, to the particular organizing efforts by groups of the workers. But the gains that were made soon turned into obstacles to a unified working-class political movement.

One of the earliest and most important divisions among workers was between urban and rural workers. The initial source of this divergence was that agricultural workers were harder to organize than urban workers. Agricultural work on *haciendas* was generally more individual than factory work, separating workers geographically in their work and in their living even when they were not, as so many were, migrant workers following seasonal crops; nature rather than the employer often appeared to be the greatest adversary; and relations between worker and employer were not governed by general, impersonal laws enforced by outsiders. This last condition simply meant that the pure wage system had not penetrated much of the countryside; there the relationship of the worker to the employer involved much more than just an "economic" connection, that is, an exchange relationship conditioned by unequal bargaining strength. The worker-employer relationship was even more complex when the agricultural workers were members of an indigenous village where capitalist relationships simply were not very important.

All of this did not mean that agricultural workers were passive in the 1930s. On the contrary, the frequency of violent rebellions by indigenous workers in the Peruvian highlands and the occupation of lands by peasants in eastern Colombia attest to the aggressiveness of these people. But it was not a movement whose organization, tactics, or goals could easily be fitted into the urban working-class political movement.[7] Obviously, the bloody strikes on the banana plantations on the northern coast of Colombia, where employer-employee relationships and the organization of work more closely approximated that of the factories, mines, and docks, held out greater promise for urban-rural worker alliances. But this was an exception to the general situation in which the numbers and coherence of labor organizations in the countryside lagged far behind those of the cities, even in Argentina, Uruguay, and Chile where cultural and racial differences between workers was minimal.

Another important factor impeding rural-urban worker alliances was that the political influence of the rural propertied classes on the central government was greater than that of the urban propertied classes. When working-class political pressure was exerted, it was usually urban working-class pressure against governments heavily influenced by rural propertied classes. The natural outcome of this pattern was that when concessions were made to the workers, they explicitly excluded rural workers from any of the provisions, thus codifying and widening the gap between rural and urban working-class movements. The continued growth of the urban industrial work force and its productivity relative to their rural counterparts during the 1930s further accentuated the distance between country and city workers.

As industrial expansion in urban areas proceeded, the anarchical organization of capitalist production as a whole (although despotic within the factory) compelled working-class groups to adopt tactics and organizational patterns that also divided the urban wage workers among themselves and affected their impact on national politics. First of all, it was very difficult to form coherent, stable, and effective organizations based on working-class neighborhoods. The residents of working-class neighborhoods tended to be transient and heterogeneous in background and outlook, and to find it hard to focus in common on a concrete, specific cause of their plight. Although not impossible–witness the successful rent strikes in Santiago in the 1920s–it was difficult to sustain solidarity for extended periods of time. People can perceive their common interests much more readily at the work site; whether that site is a plant, a mine, or the docks, the similarities of their positions are likely to be stronger than the differences.

However, in order for workers to use their most potent weapon against employers–the withdrawal of labor services, or strike–employers must be limited in their ability to replace the present workers with others. In skilled occupations (for example, electricians) or in areas of general labor shortage (the mines of northern Chile), employers were handicapped in this regard, but for most South American workers, like those employed in urban textile mills, employers could easily find large numbers of strikebreakers. For those workers' organizations to attain any leverage on employers, they had to engage in political action to force the state not only to recognize and protect legitimacy of unions but to restrict the employers' ability to fire and replace striking workers and their leaders during the initial organizing effort.

This struggle was long and bitter in the nations of South America, just as it has been everywhere, but it was an effort in which all unions and most workers had a stake and in which considerable solidarity was achieved through national working-class centrals. The pressure exerted on the state and on the propertied class was formidable, and although the pace varied by nation and the form of the concessions differed–in some union by union, in others by general legislation, and in others just in practice–working-class organizations in the South American nations with significant numbers of wage laborers slowly gained ground. Certain other groups, who saw in the working-class movement the power that their own organizations lacked and the opportunities that the movement presented for achieving their own ends, lent their support. These groups included dissident elements of the propertied elites and rootless political parties. The most important were the middle classes, who were trying to gain access to national politics and recognition for the organizational efforts of their own lower strata, for example, primary schoolteachers and postal clerks. The anomaly, however, remained. Even as the working classes scored limited successes, these successes turned into obstacles for the working-class movement as a general political force.

This takes us back to look more closely at the principal imperative for organizing the workers of a plant: to deter the employer from subverting and crushing a strike (or any collective action by the plant's workers) by simply replacing that plant's work force. In other words, in order to defend themselves from the employer, the plant's workers first had to succeed in defending themselves from other workers, particularly unemployed workers.[8] Ironically, worker solidarity was further undermined when the workers of an organized plant exercised their protected status by going out on strike, because in doing so, they often disrupted the supply of a good or service important to other workers (for example, bread or public transportation). Even winning that strike meant higher costs for producing that good or service, whether the issue was wages, hours, working conditions, or whatever, and these costs were likely to be reflected in higher prices that other workers paid for the commodity. Labor legislation in the South American nations frequently took into account these divisions among working-class organizations, and indeed the laws were frequently designed to exacerbate divisiveness among workers, as in the rural-urban case, by proscribing any but plant-level unions.

To these inherent, structural features of capitalist organization, which divided organized workers from unorganized workers and individual unions from each other, was added yet another factor. As the industrial sector expanded due to the decline of competition from imports and due to the demand-creating effects of government policies, the size pattern of firms in the manufacturing sector changed. The change in composition of industrial output away from wage goods, the allocation of scarce imported producers' goods to particular firms, and the increased activity of foreign firms led to a centralization and division of the industrial sector into a relatively small number of large modern firms and a large number of small firms. The large firms were more likely to have a unionized work force than were the smaller ones, because their production processes were more sophisticated and demanded a more skilled or disciplined worker—thus making it more difficult for an employer to find replacements—and because, unlike the smaller firms which came and went at a fairly high rate, the larger firms were more stable. These conditions plus the greater number of workers in each of the larger plants and the higher wages they received not only made unionization more feasible in the large firms, but it also resulted in those unions being stronger and better able to obtain benefits for their members than those in the small firms. The employers in large firms certainly were not sympathetic to their workers' organizations and demands, but relative to the small firms, wages constituted a smaller proportion of the total costs of the large firms, the large firms had greater ability to pass increased labor costs on to customers and suppliers than did the owners of small firms, and the large firms were characteristically more profitable. Reflecting the hierarchy of firms in manufacturing, then, there grew a corresponding vertical hierarchy of unions, and those on top, along with the large unions representing workers in similar, relatively fortunate circumstances in other sectors (such as railroads and mining), formed an "aristocracy" of workers.[9]

All the differentiation and division within the working-class movement did not destroy the movement as a political force, however. As the numbers of organized urban workers grew throughout the 1930s and early 1940s, the movement's political influence also grew, but where these tendencies were strong, as in Argentina with the most highly developed industrial sector, its political character and direction changed. The very organizational structure of the movement encouraged so-called trade union consciousness, in which union members and leaders identified their interests as "Company X Workers" or at most as "Product Y Workers" rather than as "workers" or even as "urban workers." The large unions, and indeed all unions, were still capable of concerted, unified action to defend themselves against reactionary policies of the state attempting to reduce working-class status, but this type of political activity pertained to their individual bargaining positions within the wage-labor system. Their willingness and even their ability to mobilize the masses for an assault on the system as a whole was steadily being eroded while the large unions' political influence within the system grew.

Such an analysis of the evolution of the working-class movement is considerably more useful for understanding the changing political role of organized labor in those nations than are patronizing statements about the workers being "bought off." The general structural trends, of course, developed in an uneven fashion and in different national situations, and therefore the changing political character of working-class organizations appeared in different forms, but that variety can be seen to have originated for the most part from underlying structural changes in working-class movements.[10] This perspective helps explain, for example, why the Chilean Popular Front government of Pedro Aguirre Cerda (1938-1941), with the support of organized labor and the Communist and Socialist parties, would pass legislation impeding rural labor organizing and even outlaw strikes by rural unions during the harvesting season, while expanding benefits for urban unions and initiating a program of industrial development. We can also better understand organized labor's acquiescence, even tacit support, for the turning away from reformist to status quo governments in Colombia in the late 1930s and in Chile in the early 1940s. Finally it helps to explain the authoritarian period of Vargas's leadership in Brazil and the rise of Juan Perón in Argentina.

After Vargas's rise to power in the 1930 coup and during most of his first elected term, he appeared indifferent, even hostile, toward domestic industry.[11] The attitude of Vargas and his advisers, like that of the urban middle classes, seemed to be that although domestic industrialization was not "natural" and its protection benefited local industrialists at considerable cost to local consumers, the mistake had been made and the urban working class was not going to disband quietly. While he did grant some concessions to the urban working class, the emphasis was on social control. Vargas's major economic policy efforts were aimed at expanding and diversifying Brazilian exports with the deliberate political effect of centralizing power in the national government at the expense of the state governments in Brazil's federal organization.

Even though Brazil's working-class movement was considerably weaker than that of Argentina and Chile, Vargas began to appreciate the political potential represented by the urban workers as industrial employment grew. This recognition, with the indifferent success of export promotion which was further set back by the 1937 contraction of foreign markets, led him to launch a conscious industrial development program during his dictatorship of 1937-1945. By enacting legislation advantageous to urban labor, he had the support of the most important segments of the working class, who also tolerated his suppression of their left wing. Vargas established a national corporatist structure of functional groups, including labor, industrialists, professional workers, agriculturalists, and so on, through which for the first time the working class had some institutionalized influence on national government. With this political base, he managed eventually to obtain the guarded support of domestic industrialists for establishing backward-linked industries.

Perón's rise in Argentina was also based on the support of urban labor.[12] The repeated, although not very successful, attempts of export-elite governments to give away whatever was necessary to preserve the British market for Argentine exports of cereals and meat had alienated the urban unions and industrialists from the oligarchy's rule, and the 1943 military coup replaced the government. The military rulers were a mixed lot politically, but Colonel Juan Perón, in charge of labor affairs, actively and effectively courted the large unions. With their overwhelming support he was elected president in 1946, and with their support he crushed the left wing of the labor movement. Like Vargas, Perón (with the crucial assistance of Eva Perón) institutionalized labor's role in the political process, but he went far beyond Vargas in developing new bases of labor support by organizing and improving the lot of unorganized labor, including that of the inland cities and rural areas. The big unions themselves had made little or no effort to organize even the new urban workers who had come from the countryside to Buenos Aires in large numbers since the mid-1930s, much less those in the inland city or rural areas. These previously powerless people (*descamisados*—the shirtless ones) became the most important single group behind Perón's regime.

The Peronist experiment was the most thorough demonstration of how the structural features of the more industrialized South American economies impose severe limits on reform. In the next chapter, a general delineation of these South American economic and social structures and the character of monopoly capitalism will serve as the basis for an understanding of the Peronist era in Argentina as well as of more recent processes discernible in other societies on the continent.

NOTES

1. For the scale of the depression worldwide, see League of Nations (1945), Lewis (1949), and Kindleberger (1973). Furtado (1976), Glade (1969, pp. 376-402), and U.N. ECLA (1951 and 1965) survey the impact of the depression on Latin America as a region. For the political and economic dimensions of some individual South American nations' experiences during the depression, see Ciria (1974), Diaz Alejandro (1970), Ferrer (1967), Randall (1977), and Romero (1963) on Argentina; Baer (1979), Dean (1969), dos Santos (1974), Erickson (1977), Furtado (1965), Leff (1968), and Loeb (1957) on Brazil; IBRD (1950), Fluharty (1957), and Urrutia (1969) on Colombia; Ballasteros and Davis (1963),

Cavarozzi and Petras (1974), Ellsworth (1945), Mamalakis (1976), Muñoz (1968), and Pinto Santa Cruz (1962) on Chile; and Benvenuto (1967), Hanson (1938), and Lindahl (1962) on Uruguay; and Thorp and Bertram (1978) on Peru.

2. Changes in a nation's export-based capacity to import are calculated by comparing for two periods the indices derived from multiplying an export quantity index by an export price index and dividing this product by an index of import prices (see Table 6.1). Meier (1968, pp. 41-46) describes several different methods of constructing index numbers to summarize a nation's foreign trade position.

3. Brazil's increased physical volume of coffee exports even during the worst of the depression deserves an explanation. It takes coffee trees several years to begin bearing, and as a consequence, the fixed costs of coffee production (clearing land and planting and tending trees to maturity) had already been sunk before the depression. Thus, for the individual grower, the increase in variable costs (or marginal costs) associated with producing more coffee (minimal tree care, harvesting, processing, and transport) was a relatively small proportion of the total cost of growing coffee in existing groves, and even in the face of drastically falling prices and of destruction of coffee beans through governmental price support efforts, coffee exports increased. The demand for Brazilian coffee seems to have been relatively price elastic and income inelastic.

4. Diaz Alejandro (1970, pp. 103-105) interprets government stabilization policies during the depression as emanating strictly from technical, countercyclical, and developmentalist intentions rather than from a class trying to preserve its position. The policies enacted during the depression are consistent with both interpretations, but it needs to be pointed out that quotations by government functionaries do not disprove the class basis of such policies, as Diaz Alejandro believes. Even apart from outright lying and deception, policies may be proposed and implemented by a set of *técnicos* for reasons very different from those of the propertied classes, with at least political veto power, who allowed them to be put into effect. The fact remains that the demand stimulation was not achieved by handling out money on the corners of working-class *barrios*.

5. A partial list of foreign firms operating in Argentina during the 1930s, not including meat packers, is Cinzano, Bols, Nestlè, Crosse and Blackwell, Harrods, Aden, Goodyear, Lever Brothers, Chesterfield, Ford Motor Company, General Motors, Phillips, General Electric, RCA Victor, Bayer, and Johnson & Johnson (Scobie, 1971, p. 188; Diaz Alejandro, 1970, p. 265).

6. Sweezy (1942, pp. 240-244) clearly brings out the importance of these functions of even the most liberal, laissez-faire capitalist state.

7. This harks back to the "peasant problems" of the German Social Democrats mentioned in chapter 2; Mitrany (1961) discusses the general problem of worker and peasant politics in Central and Eastern Europe, and Mariátegui (1928, pp. 31-76), writing in the 1920s, is a striking example of a South American socialist's ambivalence toward the rural working class as a political force with its own interests. Duggert (1975) surveys Marx's writings on the subject.

8. Payne (1965) shows that where workers do not succeed in this effort to protect themselves from potential replacement, as in Peru, union tactics are very different from those in nations like Argentina, Brazil, Chile, and Colombia where union shops were accorded a modicum of legitimacy.

9. Most commentators on the change in working-class politics emphasize this last, vertical differentiation. Lenin (1917) and Lukacs (1971) are theoretical statements of this process, and the same emphasis is predominant in writings on Latin American working class politics, for example, Angell (1972), Alexander (1962), Baily (1967), Bonilla (1964), Landsberger (1967), Spalding (1977), Touraine and Pecaut (1970), and Urrutia (1969). For similar developments in other labor forces, see Hobsbawm (1964) for nineteenth-century England, Gordon (1972) and Silverman and Yanowitch (1974) for the United States, and Saul (1973) and Weeks (1972) for Africa.

10. Erikson, *et al.* (1974) is not as mechanical as Kerr, *et al.* (1960), but both stress the influence of the political context in which worker movements grew and virtually ignore internal structural changes within the working class. Clearly one must study both.

11. In addition to the citations in notes 1 and 9, see Graham (1969), Skidmore (1967), and Wirth (1970) on the reign of Getulio Vargas.

12. Barager (1968), Corradi (1974), Kenworthy (1967), *Latin American Perspectives* (1974), Potash (1969), and Silverman (1969) offer information and interpretations on the rise and fall of Juan Perón beyond the works cited in notes 1 and 9.

7

THE GROWTH AND STRUCTURE OF SOUTH AMERICAN INDUSTRY, 1945 TO THE PRESENT

Government commitment to promoting industrial growth in the most industrialized South American nations was uncertain and uneven in the years immediately following World War II, but by the end of the 1950s and the beginnings of the 1960s, industrial growth was an important policy goal in virtually all nations of South America. This effort was justified and rationalized in broad, national-interest terms by the United Nations Economic Commission for Latin America (ECLA, or CEPAL–its Spanish acronym). Beginning in the late 1940s under the forceful leadership of the Argentine economist Raul Prebisch, ECLA published a series of empirical and analytical works arguing the necessity of domestic industrialization in order to escape from what was represented as increasingly unfavorable world market conditions for raw material exporters. Like the more recent dependency theories which it inspired, ECLA's diagnosis of Latin American economic problems centered on the economic relations between these nations and Western European and North American industrial centers. Continually declining terms of trade for Latin American staple exports (relative to their manufactured imports) and the volatility of staple price fluctuations, the argument went, have prevented and will continue to prevent the creation of dynamic national economies in Latin America.[1] Although some attention was paid to technical internal factors, ECLA's early analytical and empirical efforts focused on external, international commodity and exchange relations, an orientation that did not threaten South American elites.

Stemming from this analysis, the core of the ECLA policy prescriptions became known as import-substituting industrialization. In practice, these policies were simply a package of subsidies to industrial enterprises effected by government through high tariffs on imported consumer goods, low or negative tariffs on imports of machinery and intermediate inputs, cheap credit (frequently at negative real interest rates) to industrial firms, and public investment in needed complementary services and inputs such as transportation, power, fuels, and steel which private enterprise had not adequately developed. As should be obvious from the previous chapter, this scheme was little more than the systemization and formalization of ad hoc governmental policies that had evolved out of the crises of depression and World War II, and as such, the degree to which ECLA directly influenced national policies should not be overstated. And it is precisely the tendencies and contradictions already apparent in the 1930s and early 1940s which came to define the pattern of industrial growth in the postwar decades. In any case, Tables 7.1 and 7.2 show the substantial Latin American industrial expansion during the post-World War II years.

GENERAL PATTERNS

A special study by ECLA (1977, 427-448) is a good source for comparative data which place Latin American manufacturing growth in global and regional perspective. In Latin America as a whole, the average rate of growth in manufacturing between 1950 and the mid-1970s was 6.9 percent, a respectable figure which was higher than those for the European Economic Community (6.4 percent), the United States (4.8 percent), Canada (5.0 percent), and Australia and New Zealand (5.4 percent) but a bit less than the rates for Africa and Asia. It is clear that these percentage changes are sensitive to the respective 1950 output bases, but even in absolute terms, Latin American manufacturing is of significant size. The total output of Latin American manufacturing in 1974 was comparable to that of the European Economic Community in 1950, and Brazil's 1974 manufacturing production was very close to that of Germany and that of France in 1950. Total Latin American manufacturing output in the mid-1970s was one and a half times that of Asia (excluding Japan) and more than five times that of Africa (excluding South Africa). The size of India's manufacturing sector (30 percent of its region's total) roughly corresponded to that of Argentina or Mexico and was considerably smaller than Brazil's. The per capita difference between Latin America and Asia was, of course, much greater.

The rates of expansion of Latin American manufacturing were uneven in a number of ways. They varied considerably over time, and the unevenness among individual nations' rates of growth was such that it is difficult to establish clear stages for the region as a whole. Uruguay's manufacturing and gross domestic product (GDP) growth was the lowest in Latin America, averaging only 2.3 percent per annum between 1950 and 1975. As we have seen in chapters 5 and 6, Uruguay was one of South America's leading industrial nations in the 1920s, but during the 1930s its industrial growth lagged far behind that of other nations on the continent (see Figure A.1). Uruguayan industrial output did demonstrate some vigor in the 1940s and early 1950s, but after 1955 it stagnated for about a decade. Between 1961 and 1975, the average annual manufacturing growth in Uruguay was but 1.8 percent, with food, beverages, tobacco, paper, and stone, glass, and cement the only industrial lines experiencing significant growth. Bolivia's industrial

TABLE 7.1
Indicators of South American Manufacturing Activity, 1960
(1960 Prices)

	Manufacturing Output				*Manufacturing Employment*			
					Factories		Artisanal	
	U.S. $1,000,000	(1940=100)	Per Capita	(1940=100)	**1,000 People**	**(1940=100)**	**1,000 People**	**(1940=100)**
Argentina	$5,804	(237)	$277.0	(160)	960	(157)	700	(114)
Bolivia	74	(93)[a]	20.1	(76)[a]	23	(153)	162	(130)
Brazil	7,145	(525)	101.6	(309)	1,600	(196)	1,250	(149)
Chile	828	(301)	108.5	(200)	240	(174)	207	(139)
Colombia	936	(437)	40.5	(256)	252	(229)	496	(146)
Ecuador	175	(299)	40.5	(171)	50	(294)	201	(127)
Paraguay	118	(101)[a]	47.1	(88)[a]	18	(300)	64	(136)
Peru	561	(194)[a]	56.1	(155)[a]	206	(316)	330	(100)
Uruguay	421	(252)	170.4	(201)	146	(185)	59	(89)
Venezuela	642	(456)	87.9	(231)	177	(334)	118	(173)
TOTAL SOUTH AMERICA					3,672	(193)	3,587	(131)
Mexico	4,036	(441)	112.1	(243)	1,000	(270)	556	(151)
TOTAL LATIN AMERICA					5,110	(212)	3,458	(135)

SOURCE: United Nations Economic Commission for Latin America, *The Industrialization Process in Latin America, Statistical Annex*, mimeo (New York: United Nations, 1966), pp. 23, 17, 18, and 20.
NOTE: [a]1950=100.

TABLE 7.2

Some Indicators of South American Industrial Growth Through the 1970s

	Manufacturing Output as % of GDP		*Per Capita GDP[a] 1961*	*Average Annual Growth, 1961-1975*		*Mftg. as a % of GDP 1975*	*Annual Growth GDP 1977*	*Per Capita GDP[a] 1977*
	1950	1960		Mftg.	GDP			
Argentina	23.2	26.3	$1,167	5.7	4.2	32.2	4.7	$1,727
Bolivia	12.4	11.6	283	6.6	5.4	13.6	4.8	478
Brazil	17.9	22.3	506	8.8	7.7	25.6	4.7	1,088
Chile	23.1	24.9	1,065	2.6	2.9	23.8	8.6	1,038
Colombia	13.7	16.4	398	6.5	5.5	18.8	5.0	607
Ecuador	17.1	17.0	310	8.6	7.2	20.3	6.4	618
Paraguay	17.8	15.2	352	6.1	5.0	17.5	11.8	538
Peru	10.9	13.3	630	8.1	5.5	18.7	0.4	889
Uruguay	23.0	24.3	1,188	1.6	1.3	25.4	3.4	1,321
Venezuela	6.9	9.2	1,377	8.7	5.6	13.4	6.8	2,063
Mexico	18.6	19.2	672	7.7	6.6	24.1	3.2	991
Latin America	19.1	20.3	653	7.1	5.9	23.9	4.5	1,063

SOURCES: United Nations Economic Commission for Latin America, *Economic Survey of Latin America, 1976* (Santiago, Chile: 1977), p. 429; Inter-American Development Bank, *Annual Report, 1978* (Washington, D.C.: 1979), pp. 90, 91.

NOTE: [a]In 1976 $ U.S. The per capita figures for the core industrial nations in the Organization for Economic Cooperation and Development (U.S., Canada, Japan, Western Europe) were 1961: $3,041; 1977: $5,081.

sector, always small and disrupted by the 1952 revolution, also grew slowly, averaging only about 3.3 percent per annum in the twenty-five years after 1950, although like several nations, its growth in the 1960s and 1970s was much higher than that of the 1940s and 1950s. Chile's industry grew fairly slowly throughout the whole period, but as we will see later in the chapter, its performance in the 1970s lowered its overall average. In contrast, Brazil's manufacturing output grew rapidly through the quarter of a century, averaging 8.7 percent per year, and its proportion of total Latin American manufacturing rose from 23.3 percent in 1950 to 35.1 percent in 1974. In 1974, Mexico and Brazil together produced 57.5 percent of the value of Latin American manufactured articles, and although Argentina's proportion of Latin American manufacturing output slipped from 29.6 percent in 1960 to 20.3 percent in 1974, in 1974 the three nations together accounted for 77.8 percent of total Latin American manufacturing output and, as Table 7.3 shows, nearly 80 percent of the total increase of that production over the twenty-five years.

Table 7.3 also shows the changing composition of manufacturing growth, and this is even more interesting. The commodities that ECLA classed as intermediate, durable consumer, and investment products were less than 35 percent of Latin American manufacturing output in 1950, but they constituted practically 60 percent of the Latin American total in 1974 and contributed almost 70 percent of the increase in that total between 1950 and 1974. Moreover, more than 80 percent of the growth of those product lines occurred in Argentina, Brazil, and Mexico and virtually 100 percent in the first seven nations listed on Table 7.3. And the fastest growing consumer durables and intermediate products were not furniture and textiles; they were those commodities I have labeled modern consumer goods and the inputs their production requires. With no significant changes in the distribution of income, the composition of demand continued to make middle- and upper-class markets the most profitable to serve.

Not all modern consumer goods are luxury goods (for example, plastic products and nylon textiles), but the upper third of income receivers, controlling between 60 and 80 percent of personal income in the more industrialized nations (see Figure A.3), consume most manufactured goods and a highly disproportionate share of modern consumer goods (U.N. ECLA, 1957, pp. 250-253; U.N. ECLA, 1966, pp. 78, 79, 81; Diaz Alejandro, 1970, pp. 122-125, 224-247, 268; Cline, 1972, pp. 211, 217). The fastest growing, most dynamic portion of manufacturing output has continued to be large-scale domestic and foreign firms producing modern consumer goods like automobiles, pharmaceuticals, refrigerators, processed foods, and television sets, and backward-linked intermediate goods like steel, glass, fuels, and chemicals. The plant scales of these manufacturing product groups go a long way toward explaining the pattern shown in Tables 7.2 and 7.3: the industrially most dynamic economies were those with the largest internal markets.

In those economies, however, this form of manufacturing growth has exacerbated the tendencies toward technological dualism discussed in chapter 6. In the

TABLE 7.3
Composition of Latin American Manufacturing Growth, 1950-1975

	% National Mftg. Output			*1950-1975*		
	1950	1960	1974	Avg. Annual Growth Rates	% National Mftg. Growth	% Latin American Mftg. Growth within each Product Group
Argentina, Brazil, Mexico						
Nondurable products	63.8	51.5	36.2	4.6	29.6	69.0
Intermediate products	23.5	28.9	35.2	8.9	38.0	81.4
Durable consumer and investment products	12.7	19.6	28.6	10.8	32.4	87.5
Total	100.0	100.0	100.0	7.1	100.0	79.0
Chile, Colombia, Peru, Venezuela						
Nondurable products	64.8	54.7	49.5	5.1	44.9	20.2
Intermediate products	28.3	30.2	33.0	6.9	34.4	14.2
Durable consumer and investment products	6.9	15.1	17.5	10.4	20.7	10.8
Total	100.0	100.0	100.0	6.3	100.0	15.2
Bolivia, Ecuador, Paraguay, Uruguay, and others						
Nondurable products	79.3	76.8	68.1	4.6	63.4	10.8
Intermediate products	14.2	16.5	23.8	7.5	27.8	4.4
Durable consumer and investment products	6.5	6.7	8.1	6.2	8.8	1.7
Total	100.0	100.0	100.0	5.2	100.0	5.7
Latin America						
Nondurable products	65.5	54.1	40.3	4.7	33.8	100.0
Intermediate products	23.3	28.2	34.1	8.6	36.8	100.0
Durable consumer and investment products	11.2	17.7	25.6	10.6	29.2	100.0
Total	100.0	100.0	100.0	6.9	100.0	100.0

SOURCE: United Nations Economic Commission for Latin America, *Economic Survey of Latin America, 1976* (Santiago, Chile: 1977), pp. 436, 442.

manufacturing activities of the most industrially advanced nations, there is an increasingly sharp dichotomy between what I will call the "monopoly" sector and the "competitive" sector. The first is made up of relatively few large, high-productivity firms directly and indirectly producing principally for the well-to-do, and the latter is made up of many small firms with low and stagnant levels of labor productivity producing mostly for the 60 percent of the population at the bottom of the income distribution. Moreover, the relative expansion of the monopoly side of the dualistic industrial structures has led to increasing the extent of centralization in manufacturing as a whole (see Table 7.4) and has also heightened backward-linkage dependence of industrial growth on imported inputs.

ECLA analysts have done considerable work on the relationships among income distribution, the mix between what they call "vegatative" and "dynamic" industries (similar to my competitive and monopoly sectors), and industrial concentration. But questions of relative firm sizes and degrees of competitiveness apparently have been of little interest to North American economists writing on the development problems of Third World nations, and there is a serious shortage of empirical and analytical works in English on the subject.[2] Substantial industrial centralization characterizes the more industrialized nations of Argentina, Brazil, Chile, Colombia, and Mexico which had quantitatively significant industrial sectors in the early twentieth century, as well as in those nations like Peru, Ecuador, and Venezuela, where for all intents and purposes the industrial sectors are only thirty to forty years old. Small-scale, diffused industry predominates only in those areas, like Central America, Bolivia, and Paraguay, with little industrial activity and that little mostly wage goods.

In the industrially more advanced areas, the few large-scale firms controlling markets in their respective product lines use sophisticated, highly capitalized production processes and appear to behave in the manner predicted by the economic theory of imperfect competition; that is, they exercise market power to maximize profits by restricting output and raising prices. While this practice allows the survival of some smaller firms on the periphery of the market, the predominant pattern in static terms is the allocative inefficiency of imperfectly competitive markets described in textbooks (for example, Schere, 1972). The logic concerning dynamic efficiency (that is, whether over an extended period of time an imperfectly competitive industrial structure will or will not promote more growth in output and productivity than firms operating in competitive markets) is the subject of considerable dispute but, in the context of South American societies, not encouraging.

A cost-saving innovation introduced by a firm selling in a competitive market will cause product price to decline. The fall in product price forces all firms producing that product to adopt the innovation in order to continue operating. Furthermore, the lower product price diffuses the benefits among all product purchasers and stimulates economic activity widely through backward, forward, and income-multiplier linkages. In a noncompetitive setting, however, cost savings in a

TABLE 7.4
Some Characteristics of Manufacturing Firms by Size: Selected Countries, 1950-1962

	Brazil (1950)	*Chile* (1957)	*Colombia* (1960)	*Venezuela* (1961)	*Central America* (1962)
Percentage of total employment by size of firm					
5-19 workers	16.4	15.4	18.7	36.6	25.5
20-99 workers	22.5	27.4	27.2	26.1	37.4
100 and more workers	61.1	57.2	54.1	37.3	37.1
Index of value added per worker by firm size					
5-19 workers	100.0	100.0	100.0	100.0	100.0
20-99 workers	114.9	124.5	169.7	146.2	207.5
100 and more workers	145.5	189.7	289.7	294.9	259.7
Index of installed horsepower per worker by firm size					
5-19 workers	100.0	100.0	100.0	100.0	
20-99 workers	109.1	141.2	153.8	212.5	
100 and more workers	150.0	229.4	315.4	818.8	

SOURCE: United Nations Economic Commission for Latin America, *The Process of Industrial Development in Latin America* (New York: United Nations, 1966), p. 63.

particular firm or set of firms tend not to be reflected in lower product prices but rather in higher profits and wages within those firms. Thus competitive market pressures do not force all firms to become more efficient, and in any case, the general economic stimulus is muted and restricted. On the other hand, the increased financial ability and incentive of a large, high-profit imperfect competitor to undertake large research programs and investment projects are considered by many economists (following the lead of Joseph Schumpeter) as more than offsetting these disadvantages and as making monopoly and oligopoly firms more likely sources of materially progressive behavior than competitive firms. But even in the United States, most research is underwritten by the state, and only a small percentage (around 11 percent in the early 1960s) of total research and development expenditures is directed toward improving production processes while the overwhelming proportion of research is essentially part of the sales effort–product designs to improve marketability (Gustafson, 1962). The manner in which monopolistic organizations affect invention and innovation in the United States is not of central importance to studying the Latin American industrial sectors, however, for irrespective of size and market position, industrial firms in Latin America do virtually no research and development work, importing their technology from the industrialized nations (see, for example, Katz, 1972). As a consequence, the South American nations are left with the disadvantages of industrial centralization–allocative inefficiency and weak mechanisms for diffusing productivity increases throughout the economy–while the major source of potential dynamism from industrial centralization is lost because of the dependent form that South American industrial growth has taken.

The issue of dependence is not something that stands apart from centralization. The pattern of industrial production, a consequence of the distribution of income, has furthered centralization through the technical conditions underlying the production of upper-class consumer goods, and these same technical conditions have fostered dependence on imported intermediate products and on imported machinery embodying a technology whose complexity reduces the step-by-step, learning-by-doing development of indigenous production techniques. Thereby, the progressive movement to more elaborate consumer goods to satisfy well-to-do consumers has offset the import-saving effects of domestic backward-linkage, input-producing firms (who in turn require imported inputs, too). So although relative to domestic industrial output, the proportions of imported inputs required may decline, the pattern of output growth requires that the absolute volume of imported inputs still rise in accompaniment.

The vulnerability of South American economies to external shocks was brutally underscored when in late 1973 the Organization of Petroleum Exporting Countries (OPEC) began to use their world market power collectively to pursue common economic and political goals. (Neither Venezuela nor Ecuador joined the oil embargo.) In the following years, petroleum prices more than quadrupled while a worldwide capitalist recession constricted South American export markets. Between 1973 and 1975, the current account deficits of all South American nations rose from U.S. $1.8 billion to U.S. $10.6 billion; Brazil, with its heavy dependence on imported oil, accounted for 57 percent of the total increase (Street, 1977; see Table A.3). The external events were not the only causes, but there is no question that they were major contributors to the slowdown of economic activity, heightened inflation, and sharp increases in foreign indebtedness that all but two or three South American economies experienced.

These short-run events had significant political implications within each nation, of course, as competing groups mobilized to prevent erosion of their economic position. Furthermore, economic dependency has long-run implications for domestic politics which, though perhaps less dramatic, are probably even more deleterious to industrial development. The increases in export earnings needed to support industrial growth means that precisely at the time of greatest industrial expansion, the economic position of export interests (under present property arrangements) is enlarged and consolidated (dos Santos, 1970; Bodenheimer, 1971). The way in which industrial progress strengthens those elements most likely to be hostile to that progress exemplifies the contradictory nature of capitalist growth in South America.

Among other concerns, the continuing dependence of the industrial sectors on imports significantly dampened ECLA's earlier optimism about import-substituting industrialization strategies.[3] From the 1960s, promotion of manufactured exports has begun to figure more importantly in ECLA work, including the attempt to establish a protected market for Latin American industrial exporters through the Latin American Free Trade Area and to open up markets in developed nations for Latin American manufactured exports through the United Nations Conference on Trade and Development (UNCTAD). In the abstract, this strategy has the attraction that the major problems are again perceived to lie in external rather than internal arrangements, and if successful, such efforts might relieve pressures from balance-of-payments deficits and along the lines of Japan and, with even stronger reservations, of South Korea, Taiwan, and Hong Kong, expand markets for industrial products without having to redistribute income internally or make other changes that are unfavorable to domestic vested interests. There are serious technical problems associated with this program (including the presence of multinational corporations discussed below), but the political problems of finding substantial markets for South American industrial exports appear even greater. Both developed and underdeveloped nations have domestic economic interests whose very existence depends on elaborate trade barriers. One distinct possibility is that one or two of the largest Latin American nations might establish essentially colonial relations with some of the smaller, less industrialized Latin American nations in order to push an export strategy. The beginnings of such a situation, known as "sub-imperialism," has been noted in Brazil's economic relations with Paraguay and in the Brazilian military government's enthusiasm in helping the U.S. to crush reform movements throughout Latin America. Although Mexican governments have at least nominally kept considerably more distance between their intra-hemisphere political stance and that of the U.S., Mexican capital could conceivably turn several of the Central American republics into economic "sub-colonies."[4]

Returning to the more internal aspects of South American industrial growth, government policies promoting industrial growth have directly supported the centralization of domestic industrial production which, with its implications for monopolistic behavior and external dependency, has such dubious implications for continuing growth. In what is still the major work on the subject, Bain (1968) lists internal (to the firm) economies of large-scale production and control over special factors of production as two of the three most important barriers to the entry of new competition into concentrated markets. Government industrial promotion policies have effectively established these conditions. High tariffs to protect and promote domestic production of manufactured goods have closed off the small domestic markets from foreign competition and enabled large-scale firms, whether foreign or domestically owned, to exercise substantial market power within the tariff walls. Similarly, raw materials and capital goods have been imported at favorable exchange rates and allocated to firms through import licenses. Whether the criterion for the licenses' distribution was economic efficiency, political influence, or outright bribery, they have ended up in the hands of the largest firms and have deterred potential rivals, particularly domestic ones, from expanding or entering the domains of the large firms. Bain regarded absolute size as the third major barrier to entry. As a new firm of efficient scale would require considerable financing, governmental allocation of subsidized credit has worked in the same ways as import licensing to discourage entry from domestic sources. So even if the relatively small markets of the more industrialized South American nations permit the establishment of new firms on an efficient scale, domestic political control over imports and credit, frequently pressured by such institutions as the International Monetary Fund, the World Bank, and the U.S. Export-Import Bank, has discouraged entry by new firms, particularly locally owned ones.

But these obstacles for domestic entrepreneurs are opportunities for foreign firms, and giant multinational corporations (MNCs) have invested heavily in the industrial sectors of the South American nations, a type of penetration which presents a new stage of capitalist expansion by the core industrialized nations. The pressure to expand abroad that was felt in the late nineteenth century in industrialized economies of Europe and, to a lesser extent, North America came from two principal needs: to utilize domestic capacity of the new capital and intermediate goods industries; and to tap foreign sources for raw materials and foodstuffs (see chapter 2). As a consequence, foreign capital (mostly British) went into export-related activities and public utilities (see chapter 4). The most important component of mid-twentieth-century MNC investment in South America, however, goes into industrial sectors (see Table 7.5). In contrast to, say, the British owners of Argentine railroads at the turn of the twentieth century who invested in

TABLE 7.5
Year-end Values of U.S. Direct Foreign Investment in Latin America, 1956 and 1975

	Total (billions of $ U.S.)	*Total %*	*Mining & Smelting*	*Petroleum*	*Manufact.*	*Pub. Util.*	*Trans. Commun. Pub. Util.*	*Trade*	*Fin. & Insur.*	*Other*
Argentina										
1956	0.46	100.0	n.a.	n.a.	53.4	14.6		9.4		6.0
1975	1.12	100.0	n.a.	12.7	65.3		0.1	7.9		5.2
Brazil										
1956	1.22	100.0		17.3	50.4	14.0		12.2		
1975	4.56	100.0	2.9	6.4	68.0		0.5	8.7	7.6	5.9
Chile										
1956	0.68	100.0	64.2		5.8			1.8		1.3
1975	0.30	100.0	4.3		16.4		43.1	9.0	1.0	
Colombia										
1956	0.30	100.0		35.9	22.4	14.4		15.1		
1975	0.65	100.0	2.5	0.7	76.6		1.1	14.6	1.8	2.7
Mexico										
1956	0.69	100.0	24.1	2.5	46.5	13.5		10.7		2.8
1975	3.18	100.0	2.5	0.7	76.6		1.1	14.6	1.8	2.7
Peru										
1956	0.34	100.0	64.4		7.6			8.7		9.6
1975	1.21	100.0	5.8	20.0	13.7			5.0	0.1	2.8
Venezuela										
1956	1.83	100.0		77.1	4.3	2.0		4.0		
1975	2.07	100.0		41.7	32.8		1.5	13.6	7.0	
ALL LATIN AMERICAN REPUBLICS										
1956	4.74	100.0	14.7	29.9	20.7	16.2		6.8		11.7
1975	22.22	100.0	6.6	15.2	38.5		2.2	10.4	20.7	6.5

SOURCE: *Survey of Current Business* 38 (September 1958), p. 18, and 56 (August 1976), p. 49.

foreign production to facilitate sales in their own domestic markets, the modern MNCs invest in foreign production for sale in those foreign markets. While the economic activity generated by nineteenth-century British investment in South America had the desirable by-product of enlarging markets for British exports of consumer goods, this new form of MNC investment replaces such exports from the core nations. As noted in the last chapter, the shift in foreign investment from export to industrial sectors began in the depression years of the 1930s, and its resurgence from the late 1950s reflects the continuation of South American import-substituting industrialization policies, the expansion of the South American domestic markets, and increasing congealing of U.S. industrial structures in *consumer* goods production. This last is the principal imperialist impulse under monopoly capitalism.[5]

One might infer from the change in sectoral composition of foreign investment that the extent and direction of foreign capital's political presence in the host nations would change significantly. For instance, the operation of a U.S. mining corporation in a South American nation requires little from the host nation beyond a particular form of political stability to protect its property and to guarantee the flow of labor into the mines and the flow of product and profits to the U.S. The General Motors or Volkswagen automobile producer in South America, of course, needs the same type of political stability for protecting its property and profits, but in addition, its profitable operations depend in a direct and immediate way on internal financial conditions, tariffs, transportation networks, and other factors affecting the expansion of domestic markets (for automobiles, in this example), while the mining corporations have little direct concern with such matters. So it would appear that the MNC would find that its interests coincide with a number of domestic political groups toward whose reformist goals the export-sector foreign investor was either indifferent or hostile. But in practice, there are debilitating contradictions in these MNCs' interests. Implementing the types of reform measures where successes, holding everything else constant, would be to the MNCs' advantage, releases additional political forces which are potentially antagonistic to holding everything else constant, threatening property in general and foreigners' property in particular. Furthermore, the market for the MNCs' products depends on an extremely unequal distribution of income, and far-reaching redistributive policies might actually contract rather than expand domestic markets for their products. As a consequence of both these factors, MNC reformist sympathies tend to remain at the level of rhetoric, as in the Alliance for Progress, and the actual political influence of the large foreign enterprises continues to be one of cautious conservatism, afraid to rock the boat.

There is a rapidly growing body of literature on the more narrowly economic effects of MNCs' operations in the Third World. Not surprisingly, MNCs do make profits, and they do repatriate them for distribution to stockholders living in the U.S., Europe, and Japan. Some of these profits are the result of slippery practices that are possible because the local firms are subsidiaries of foreign corporations.

For instance, a foreign subsidiary will often utilize machinery that had been used and fully depreciated (written off as a cost of production for tax purposes) by another subsidiary, and in doing so, be able to depreciate the machinery again. Moreover, as the machinery was bought from another subsidiary of the same corporation, the price paid for it by first subsidiary could very well be unrealistically inflated, and thus, on its books costs will be higher and profits lower, thus avoiding tax liabilities in the nation in which it is located. In effect, this subsidiary is transferring its profits to the unit from which it bought the machinery. The sale, financing, and leasing of machinery, patents, copyrights, intermediate products, and a whole range of services between subsidiaries of the same MNC are thus internal to the corporation itself in spite of the subsidiaries' location in different countries, and the prices ("transfer prices") set for the transactions can be, and apparently frequently are, manipulated so that large proportions of a MNC's overall profits can appear to be realized in those subsidiaries where tax laws, exchange regulations, or whatever are the most favorable (Seers, 1963; Lall, 1979). As a result, when transfer prices comprise a significant proportion of a subsidiary's costs, it is extremely difficult for the economist as well as the local tax collector to know just how profitable a particular subsidiary's activities are. This example illustrates the difficulty of effectively regulating a subsidiary of an MNC, and the multinational organization of the giant corporations gives them the ability to avoid or subvert a whole range of domestic economic policies, including those aimed at inducing MNCs to produce for export (U.S. Department of Commerce, 1974, pp. 25-40).

These aspects of MNC operations—repatriated profits, ability to juggle the location of realized profits, and the difficulty of effectively controlling their operations by national regulations—are the core of much of the criticism of the MNCs in South America. Added to these are the charges that the MNCs often borrow from local financial markets, their operations stunt the development of the local industrial entrepreneurship, they employ inappropriately sophisticated technology, and they produce goods which are not really needed but are profitable. Occasionally, the case against the MNCs is summed up in words to the effect that their operations are oriented toward overall profit maximization irrespective of the needs of the host nations; in other words, they are capitalist enterprises. Apologists for the MNCs, principally MNC executives, U.S. government officials, and North American economists, respond that the MNCs' investments enable host nations to have productive resources drawn from other-than-domestic savings, and even when the MNCs borrow locally, they put domestic savings to more productive uses than local entrepreneurs would have. Related to this last point, the MNCs are said to bring into a South American economy advanced industrial technology, modern organizational and managerial skills, enlightened personnel practices (including managerial and worker training programs for local people), high-paying jobs, and other good things.

Just as in the debate over the effects of foreign investment and export production in the nineteenth century reviewed in chapter 4, the terms of this debate are extremely narrow: the amounts of economic resources MNCs do or do not make available for capitalist industrial development. And within these terms, the MNCs on balance are probably a positive force (U.N. ECLA, 1972, pp. 265-308). From much of the critical literature, one would infer that Canada is poverty-stricken and economically stagnant because of massive MNC investment ravishing its resources while India is affluent and materially progressive because it has experienced such slight penetration by the MNCs. In the South American nations, both the MNCs and the domestically owned private firms are *capitalist* enterprises using similar means to pursue similar ends. This cardinal fact is obscured when the nationality of the firms occupies the center of the stage and again, as in the works mentioned in chapter 4, the "nation," be it Brazil, Argentina, or whatever, becomes a materialized abstraction that is purported to have interests, pride, aspirations, and the capacity to suffer. Actually, it is not those segments of the population who really do suffer deprivation and indignity that much of the critical literature, in effect, is trying to defend against the MNCs; rather, the concern seems to be over the welfare of the national industrial bourgeoisie, who, against logic and historical evidence, are implicitly represented as being more progressive in business affairs, more benevolent toward workers, and above all, more sensitive and responsive to general national interests than their counterparts running the MNC subsidiaries and parent corporations.[6]

Outside the narrow terms which focus on economic resource flows and encourage an empty nationalism at the expense of a critical analysis of capitalist institutions, any precise cost-benefit calculation is an illusion. The broader, more important aspects of the MNCs' role in South American industrialization must consider their positions within the particular economies, that is, their relation to the dualistic organization of industrial production. In contributions to industrial dualism, it is hard to exaggerate the importance of the MNCs. MNC subsidiaries along with state-owned firms frequently predominate in the monopoly side of the bifurcated structures, and domestic private capital is in sure control of only the smaller, less progressive firms producing in competitive markets. In spite of this role, however, the MNCs did not create the conditions of industrial dualism, with its correlaries of industrial concentration and dependence; they simply followed market opportunities which stemmed from the internal distribution of national incomes, the product of internal struggles and institutions which clearly were influenced (but not determined) by foreign interests.

The dualistic organization of the industrial sector is refelcted in the character of the industrial working class, and the tendencies among the urban workers described for the 1930s and early 1940s continued to develop through the post-World War II period. Growth of the large modern industrial firms, public and private, domestic and foreign, has not required augmenting the work force in corresponding numbers; industrial growth led by modern industry has occurred with a relative decline in the number of those workers. This phenomenon together with the conditions of their work and the profitability of the large firms (noted in the last chapter) has allowed monopoly-sector industrial, transport, and mine workers to organize into coherent unions that have been capable of protecting their members' wages and working conditions with far more success than have workers in competitive wage goods, service, and construction firms. Compared to workers in small firms, much less to the swollen ranks of the underemployed subproletariat in the urban service sector and to rural workers, those in the monopoly sector constitute a privileged and exclusive minority (Gregory, 1974; Souza, 1978). The workers in the smaller wage goods firms have grown in numbers roughly in proportion to the growth in wage goods output, and although their work frequently requires more skill in that it involves a greater variety of tasks and more responsibility for organizing and performing them, the relative weakness of their trade union organizations has meant that these workers are paid less, have less job security, and are less apt to be protected by social legislation than their counterparts in the monopoly sector.

For analytical and descriptive purposes, economists often divide a nation's economic activity into three groups: primary (agriculture, forestry, fishing); secondary (manufacturing, mining, construction); and tertiary (services). Using these categories, a stage theory of economic development that is still extremely influential was presented in the work of Colin Clark (1957). Drawing principally from the experiences of the Western European and North American industrialized nations and from the conceptions of the nineteenth-century "German historical school," he suggested that as economic growth proceeded, increases in per capita income led to a changing pattern of consumer demand that induced the bulk of a nation's work force to be successively employed in each of the three types of economic activity, service employment predominance indicating the highest, essentially post-industrial stage. It is doubtful whether the South American nations with such high proportions of their work forces in services can be usefully regarded as having achieved this favored position. While some expansion of service employment has been the consequence of industrial growth in much the same way that, say, late nineteenth- and early twentieth-century U.S. industrial growth led to the increased service employment, most of the urban service employment is the result of economic failure rather than success.

One component of increased service employment has been the result of greater geographical concentration of industrial production brought about by extending railroad lines, expanding dock facilities, and above all, building roads. The greater integration of national markets through lower transportation costs between major cities and outlying areas has led to the demise of many local firms whose markets had been protected from the competition of urban firms by high internal transportation costs. This process has even increased the centralization of wage goods industries as well as heightened the regional concentration of industrial production, thus requiring more workers in transport, handling, and distribution activities.[7] Some of these service workers are white-collar employees, some are wage workers, and some are independent proprietors of small shops and trucking firms.

Another component of service employment which has a similar range of occupational status is the people offering personal services to the better-off consumers. But in South America, domestic servants, barbers, physicians, and laundry workers are examples of service employment which reflect the composition of demand from a skewed distribution of income rather than from a general increase in per capita income as envisioned by Clark. The growth of these services, then, has the same market source as that for consumer durables.

Finally we arrive at the serious core of the urban poor who either are chronically unemployed or when they work, do so in service occupations such as self-employed street hawkers, bootblacks, car washers, petty criminals, and those who for others wait in lines at government offices. These jobs are typified by insecurity, underemployment, poverty, and virtually no opportunity for advancement, and they are responses to desperation rather than to market demand. Sometimes these people occupy positions that shade into the lower ranks of other service worker categories, and occasionally they work for small wage goods or construction firms, but unlike the reserve army of the unemployed in nineteenth-century England, they are not linked to the work force of the dynamic industries even to the degree that their presence acts as a drag on industrial wages in the monopoly sector. Competitive firms and household employers of domestic servants do benefit from these people's plight, but the major sources of accumulation and growth do not depend on their exploitation; such processes are indifferent to them. People concerned with preserving the social order, however, cannot be indifferent to the explosive potential represented by the desperately poor and unsocialized strata living on the edges of the major cities, and public expenditures for welfare and repression contribute to the fiscal strain and consequent inflationary forces which characterize the more industrialized South American nations.

Salaried white-collar employment, a category of job status which cuts across all productive activity, has also increased substantially in the post-World War II years. The numerical growth of this group has resulted from the increasing complexity of industrial production and distribution and of the surrounding social and political relationships. Thus the need for veritable armies of clerks, bookkeepers, lawyers, sales managers, media administrators, politicians, jurists, financial advisers, office supervisors, and public officials to record, coordinate, regulate, and maintain the economy and society in its myriad of detail. Although for the most part their work has little or nothing to do directly with commodity production, they perform important functions in sustaining the conditions of capitalist production, and they are duly rewarded. The volume and pattern of their consumption is a second, vital contribution these people make toward supporting production in general and the structure of production in particular. While it is not clear that white-collar workers produce, they certainly do consume, and large numbers of them consume goods produced by monopoly-sector firms.[8] In most of the largest nations of South America the middle classes have managed to legislate formal distinctions between salaried and wage workers, and salaried workers are treated preferentially by public and private provisions covering remuneration, job security, pensions, and social insurance programs (Mesa Lago, 1978). Within the middle class there exist very definite hierarchies of income and status, although considerable upward mobility is possible. But getting into positions on the lower rungs of the middle-class ladder from below is considerably more difficult, and requiring a degree from an institution of higher education for such a job, no matter how irrelevant for performing its duties, is an important mechanism for guarding the gates against mobility *into* the middle class.

This is an appropriate place to summarize and identify these features of the most advanced South American urban economies. Manufacturing is characterized by a sharp technological and organizational dualism in which the monopoly portion is populated by a few large, technologically sophisticated domestic and foreign firms, producing modern consumer goods or backward-linked inputs with a relatively well-organized and well-paid work force; the competitive, wage goods side contains many small firms engaged principally in wage goods production, using simpler, more labor-intensive techniques and operating in competitive markets with an atomized and low-wage work force. Industrial accumulation and growth are led by monopoly firms which offer few additional employment opportunities, service occupations and the state are the source of most new jobs, and large proportions of the economically active populations are salaried white-collar workers employed by public and private bureaucracies in managerial and clerical capacities. With large firms controlling markets for modern industrial products, strong unions possessing substantial bargaining power in respect to the state and the large firms, the middle class protected by social legislation covering wages, job security, and working conditions, and government regulations covering a wide range of economic activity, the competitive market as an allocating and governing mechanism is important only for the activities and products of the poorest and most economically marginal strata of the urban population. The centralized and dirigistic states' inability to collect taxes commensurate with needed expenditures to subsidize monopoly-sector accumulation and to quell social unrest breeds inflation which, in the face of structural and technological rigidities, does little to reduce high rates of unemployment; as such, South American economies have been exploring the frontiers of "stagflation" for several decades.

Looking over this list, it is clear that despite their relatively low levels of industrialization and per capita incomes, manufacturing production and urban areas of the more industrialized nations of South America, by structure and organization, are full-fledged members of the genus Monopoly Capitalism as defined in chapter 1. Accordingly, the economic models and theories formulated to study the current economic performance of the developed nations of North America and Western Europe are more useful for understanding contemporary South American industrial growth than those reflecting the competitive industrial capitalism of nineteenth-century England and the northern states of the U.S. Facile comparisons of, say, U.S. per capita income and sectoral distribution of the work force in 1854 with those of South America in the 1950s (for example, Ramos, 1970, pp. 181-213) should not mislead the study of industrialization; the organization of the industrial sector and of the society around it should be the basis of comparison and the criterion for selecting relevant theoretical frameworks. From all this, clearly the appropriate conceptual guides ought to be drawn from the imperfect competition models of monopoly and oligopoly, the Keynesian models which, based on those industrial organizations, expect that insufficient demand induces contractions of output and employment rather than of prices and wage rates, and even more to the point, those neo-Marxian works which have gone beyond the first two sets of theories from orthodox economics and attempted to present a more integrated view of the economy, society, and politics under conditions of monopoly capitalism.[9] I will return to this general argument in chapter 8, after applying a monopoly capitalist interpretive framework to some prominent cases in order to specify it more precisely and to identify some salient species differences in South American monopoly capitalism.

ARGENTINA: THE FAILURE OF REFORM AND COMPETITIVE CAPITALISM

As mentioned at the end of chapter 5, workers were the principal source of support for Perón's political ascendance between 1943 and 1946.[10] The most powerful groups of workers were those industrial monopoly-sector and transport workers organized in established unions, and Perón assiduously courted these large unions' leadership and members. But even before the 1946 election which carried him to the presidency, Perón recognized the political potential of the masses of competitive-sector workers whose plight had been for the most part ignored by established unions, and by 1949 he had systematically organized the *descamisados* of Buenos Aires, the inland cities, and the countryside into the most powerful political movement in Argentina. The personal charisma of Eva Perón was crucial in these newly politicized groups' support of Perón, but Peronist policies (in which Eva was again instrumental) did benefit the *descamisados* in tangible ways.

By direct legislation pertaining to wages and benefits (including establishing a social security system), wages and salaries rose as a proportion of total income at the expense of entrepreneurial and property incomes. Even more interesting, however, is that between 1945-1946 and 1950-1952, wages of unskilled workers rose 17 percent while those of skilled workers rose 4 percent (Diaz Alejandro, 1970, p. 124), and it is a fair inference that competitive-sector workers made greater relative gains from their work than did monopoly-sector workers, particularly when one includes the greater expanded employment opportunities for the former (see below). The promulgation and reinforcement of regulations which increased job security and improved working conditions as well as governmental construction of low-cost housing and workers' recreational, educational, and health facilities reinforced the gains by poorer strata of workers relative to those employed in the monopoly sector (U.N. ECLA, 1969, p. 150).

As Perón never made a concerted effort to change property relations, these redistributive policies raised labor costs for employers, and one might expect that the competitive-sector enterprises were hardest hit in that, relative to the monopoly sector, the increase in their labor costs was greater and labor was a higher proportion of their total cost. But Peronist policies were not exclusively class policies, and they benefited competitive-sector employers as well as workers. Subsidized public credits were made available to the private sector, and their distribution strongly favored small firms and helped them with costs (Altimir, *et al.*, 1967, pp. 719-720), and government policies strongly stimulated demand for competitive-sector products. Some of this was the response of construction firms to the government's building program mentioned earlier, but the increased demand for industrial products was not so much the result of direct governmental purchases as of induced changes in private-sector demand. The redirection of income toward lower-income recipients increased aggregate consumer demand generally by a cross-sectional Keynesian effect, that is, Argentinians with lower incomes spend a higher proportion of their income than do those with high incomes (U.N. ECLA, 1969, p. 152). Even more important, however, was the change in the *composition* of aggregate consumption demand. The rechanneling of income toward families with the lowest incomes and the resulting increase in demand for wage goods led to substantial increases in industrial output and employment by the competitive sector. The correspondence of competitive-sector production with wage goods was not exact, of course, but Table 7.6 shows that it was close enough to lead to the dramatic expansion of the output of food and beverages for domestic consumption, textiles, clothing, wood products, and leather goods—all produced by small firms and major consumption items in workers' family budgets (Diaz Alejandro, 1970, pp. 122-125, 224-247, 268; U.N. ECLA, 1966, p. 77; U.N. ECLA, 1969, p. 154). Also contributing to the demand for small firms' output were exchange controls and tariffs which gave particularly high levels of effective protection for domestic wage goods producers.

In sharp contrast to such wage goods industries and construction-linked stone-glass-ceramics, the growth of "heavier" industries like electrical machinery and appliances, vehicles and machinery, metals, petroleum refining, rubber products, and chemicals in the late 1940s lagged far behind their growth in succeeding years, and the predominance of small firms in industrial output growth caused a significant lessening of industrial concentration during these years (Goetz, 1976, pp. 519-532). It is precisely the characteristics of the competitive-sector firms leading the expansion of industrial output during the late 1940s—small, labor-intensive, and technologically backward firms—that account for the stagnation of labor productivity growth in the immediate postwar period (Diaz Alejandro, 1970, pp. 239-241; U.N. ECLA, 1957, pp. 39-41). Katz (1969, pp. 84-92) found that output growth in the late 1940s and early 1950s was attributable almost exclusively to increases in amounts of productive factors employed with static technology, and other studies have shown that there was little or no net increase in capital equipment used in manufacturing, nor in the economy as a whole during this period (Diaz Alejandro, 1970, p. 116; U.N. ECLA, 1959, p. 28).

Agricultural production, however, declined as a result of rising labor and input costs and price controls on output, dragging down forward-linked export processing (see the first row of Table 7.6). The contraction of rural production and employment heightened the flow of people from the countryside to the city where employment opportunities were growing. Cereal and livestock exports, the major foreign exchange earners, declined both because of diminished production and because of increased domestic consumption of these products, which are wage goods (Diaz Alejandro, 1970, p. 125*n*). Even though imports as a proportion of domestic production were abnormally low during these years, again consistent with the relatively low import requirements of competitive-sector production, the decline in export earnings finally did lead to a severe exchange shortage in 1949 (Diaz Alejandro, 1970, pp. 250, 228).

More important than foreign exchange availability, however, was the increasingly untenable financial position of the central government in domestic currency. Table 7.7 shows that the central government's real tax revenues rose dramatically between 1946 and 1951 and that those increased receipts were due almost exclusively to applying higher effective tax rates to an extremely slow-growing total tax base. These higher rates were achieved through strengthening direct and progressive taxation relative to indirect taxes (U.N. ECLA, 1956, pp. 115, 117, 132, 137-151). The fiscal change was another mark of the political success of Peronist policies, but the slowly growing tax base was a sign of economic weakness. Peronist policies were expensive, and for the increased tax revenues between 1946 and 1951 to have been sufficient to cover just the *increases* in government expenditures in the same period, Argentine aggregate growth would have had to be more than twice the actual average. Argentina equalled this level of economic performance in the later 1960s and 1970s; the level is only a little better than the average growth rate for the rest of Latin America in the immediate post-World War II and early Korean War years, but it was substantially greater than the competitive capitalist manufacturing, construction, and services could stimulate in Argentina. At this time, nontax government revenues were small and stable parts of total government receipts. Between 1946 and 1951, the difference between tax revenues and expenditures increased (in constant peso terms) almost 30 percent. In 1951 the difference between taxes and expenditures amounted to about 12 percent of Argentine gross domestic product. The hostility of foreign and domestic lending sources forced the government to rely on massive use of central bank loans to finance its deficits, thereby fueling domestic inflation (Diaz Alejandro, 1970, p. 364). The confluence of external and internal problems signaled that the political strategy of promoting the competitive sector had reached its economic limits, and Peronist policies from the early 1950s hesitatingly turned to the monopoly sector.

This policy direction was intensified after the fall of Perón and the military's

TABLE 7.6
Argentina: The Structure of Manufacturing at Factor Cost
(in percentages)

	1937-1939	*1948-1950*	*1963-1965*	*1974-1976*
Food, beverages, tobacco	38.0	26.1	19.3	15.8
Textiles, leather, clothing	17.0	22.3	13.3	12.4
Wood and furniture	2.1	2.1	1.7	1.2
Paper, printing, publishing	7.6	5.6	5.2	4.0
Chemicals	4.4	5.8	8.0	
Petroleum refining	4.9	5.3	8.4	19.2 (Chemicals, Petroleum refining, Rubber products combined)
Rubber products	0.8	1.0	1.4	
Stone, clay, ceramics	4.3	5.1	4.3	4.0
Basic metals	6.4	6.5	10.1	6.2
Vehicles, machinery	5.6	9.6	16.5	33.4 (Vehicles, machinery and Electrical machinery, appliances combined)
Electrical machinery, appliances	1.1	2.0	5.8	
Other manufactures, handicrafts	7.9	8.7	6.1	3.7
TOTAL	100.0	100.0	100.0	100.0

SOURCES: Carlos F. Diaz Alejandro, *Essays on the Economic History of the Argentine Republic* (New Haven, Conn.: Yale University Press, 1970), p. 224; United Nations Economic Commission for Latin America, *Economic Survey of Latin America, 1970* (New York: United Nations, 1972), p. 107; United Nations Economic Commission for Latin America, *Economic Survey of Latin America, 1976* (Santiago, Chile: United Nations, 1977), p. 33.

TABLE 7.7
Argentina: Central Government Tax Revenues
and Expenditures in Selected Years

	1946	*1951*	*1961*	*1969*	*1973*	*Average 1975-1977*
Tax revenue as % GDP	8.2	15.0	8.5	6.2	4.8	4.7
Tax revenues in 1,000,000 pesos in 1950 prices	4,625	6,928	7,798	7,678	7,021	7,184
Current and capital expenditures as % GDP	16.1	20.0	8.5	8.3	10.1	13.2
Expenditures in 1,000,000 pesos in 1950 prices	9,085	12,641	7,982	10,123	14,956	15,438

SOURCES: Derived from Carlos F. Diaz Alejandro, *Essays on the Economic History of the Argentine Republic* (New Haven, Conn.: Yale University Press, 1970), pp. 398, 408, 490, 528; Inter-American Development Bank, *Economic and Social Progress in Latin America* (Washington, D.C., 1973), pp. 346, 367, 368, 369; Ibid., 1974, pp. 459, 461; Ibid., 1976, pp. 396, 408, 409; United Nations Economic Commission for Latin America, *Economic Survey of Latin America, 1955* (New York: United Nations, 1956), pp. 115, 117, 132.

assumption of political power in 1955. Public policy from this point on redistributed money income from the bottom to the top (U.N. ECLA, 1969, pp. 135, 184-185, 150)–thus enlarging domestic markets for such monopoly-sector products as consumer durables and their inputs and increasing private savings and investment. Such policies also favored larger enterprises with public credit, encouraged foreign investment, and changed the tariff structure to benefit monopoly-sector producers (Diaz Alejandro, 1970, pp. 260-262; Randall, 1977). Production tied to mass consumption and housing construction stagnated or declined in the post-1950 years, and highly concentrated industries such as vehicles, basic metals, petroleum refining, and electrical appliances expanded markedly (see Table 7.6). This pattern of monopoly-sector expansion had a series of predictable consequences: economic growth was accompanied by significant increases in capital accumulation, technological change, labor productivity, industrial concentration, and corporate profits as a percentage of GDP (Diaz Alejandro, 1970, pp. 116, 240-241; Katz, 1969, pp. 93-96, 158-161); unemployment began to be a problem (Diaz Alejandro, 1970, p. 239); labor's income share declined and property's share rose (U.N. ECLA, 1969, pp. 184-185; Carlos de Pablo, 1977); the Argentine economy became increasingly dependent on the importation of capital and intermediate goods (Diaz Alejandro, 1970, p. 517); and the only gains relative to total income made by wage and salary earners between 1953 and 1965 were by those employed in mining, industry, and public utilities, and these gains accrued principally to those in the upper levels of wage and salary earners (U.N. ECLA, 1969, pp. 118-121, 135).

The efforts by post-Peronist governments to promote accumulation and economic growth by encouraging monopoly-sector production and profits achieved some material success, but the decades of political turmoil and stop-go economic growth are measures of the strains inherent in the program. Nurturing monopoly-sector expansion, even with high rates of foreign investment, required substantial state expenditures (including tax revenues foregone as incentives) to establish the economic conditions for profitable activity by monopoly-sector firms. In addition, expenditures oriented toward the competitive sector continued to be necessary for maintaining the political legitimacy for such policies. The balance between these competing demands could be struck only as long as economic growth yielded sufficient state revenues to cover the costs of sustaining the economic and political conditions of that growth.

While GDP in constant prices more than doubled in the twenty years from the mid-1950s to the 1970s, Table 7.7 shows that tax revenues of the central government declined not only relative to GDP but even in terms of the absolute volume of financial resources available to the central government. A large part of the shrinkage in the government's tax yields stemmed from the drastic weakening of direct taxation (especially income taxes) and the resulting tax relief to upper-income taxpayers (U.N. ECLA, 1969, p. 143)–a component of the effort to encourage monopoly-sector expansion and gain political support. But although the governments relied increasingly on indirect taxes, the degree of regressiveness was virtually unchanged as successive governments were politically unable to shift the tax burden to lower-income recipients (U.N. ECLA, 1956, pp. 138; 1969, 143; 1972, 54-55). Effective tax rates and tax revenues both shrank.

Central government expenditures relative to GDP also declined somewhat after the early 1950s, but from the mid-1960s they have increased steadily in absolute and relative terms until the budgetary deficit in 1975-1977 was, as a proportion of GDP, the largest in South America by a significant margin (see Table A.2). The expenditure requirements for supporting monopoly-sector expansion were not offset by massive reductions in competitive-sector expenditures. Between 1953 and 1961, increases in transfer payments were of greatest benefit to income recipients in the sixth through ninth deciles—presumably lowering labor costs for their monopoly-sector employers—but not at the expense of diminished benefits to those in the lower deciles. The importance of education and public health expenditures to the incomes of poor families increased slightly; moreover, the social security system established by Perón was not dismantled but in fact represented increased proportions of poor families' incomes as more people became eligible for its benefits. Related to these figures, support for competitive-sector production, where poorer workers were employed, was not completely abandoned even though it was reduced (U.N. ECLA, 1969, p. 150).

The inability of the Argentine government to shift the tax burden and curtail social welfare expenditures was the consequence of irresistible political pressure from the workers—monopoly and competitive, urban and rural—and from small-scale entrepreneurs. The political mobilization of the Argentine masses, *not* technical errors in economic policy, is the legacy of Perón which has worked against sustained capitalist growth in the post-Perón years. In spite of continuing efforts to suppress and depoliticize the population, successive military and civilian governments have experienced profound difficulty in maintaining the economic and political conditions necessary for monopoly capitalist industrialization.

BRAZIL: THE MONOPOLY CAPITALIST MIRACLE

The changes of political and economic direction in Argentina highlight the difficulties involved in bringing about monopoly capitalist industrial growth, but the "Brazilian economic miracle" shows that considerable industrial dynamism can be achieved when popular forces are weak and state policy is ruthless and intelligent. The military coup which deposed President João Goulart in 1964 was principally a reaction to the apparent threat from Goulart's attempts to mobilize urban and rural workers as a basis of support for his efforts to promote reform and growth. The domestic waves of strikes in response to a proposed wage freeze in the early 1960s, however, was yet another reminder that it is extremely difficult to keep workers enthusiastic about liberal reforms when it is clear they will bear the cost (Mendes de Almeida and Lowry, 1976), and the military intervention was initially a relief to many liberals as well as to the possessing classes.

Continuing from Vargas's initiatives in the late 1930s and early 1940s, the top down, corporatist form of labor organization reflected the manipulative intent of presidential populism, and the unions' limited autonomy and poorly developed organization at the level of the work site, along with the segmentation of the industrial work force, undermined workers' ability to mount any concerted resistance to the military.

While continuing to crush brutally any opposition, the military vigorously implemented an ambitious and coherent industrialization program. The planning was done by the officers in power (the Superior War College teaches more than marching and ideology), an able group of Brazilian economists, and personnel from the Agency for International Development, University of California, Ford Foundation, and elsewhere. The major elements of the program were reducing real wages, lifting restrictions on profits of domestic and foreign enterprises, encouraging industrial centralization, subsidizing exports, expanding state infrastructural investment, increasing public enterprises' production of goods and services complementary to private production, reorganizing capital markets, and developing an extensive consumer credit system to enable purchase of consumer durables by middle-class families.[11] From the end of 1965 to the beginning of 1975, manufacturing production grew at an annual rate of around 11 percent and GDP at an annual average of 9 percent (6 percent per capita). As Table 7.8 shows, the industry groups leading this growth were chemicals, machinery and metallurgy, electrical and communication equipment, and transportation equipment, while not surprisingly, wage goods lagged far behind. Direct government purchases, subsidized exports, and middle-class credit buying reinforced the pattern of consumer demand set principally by upper-income receivers. Table 7.9 shows the important contribution the state and foreign investors made to Brazil's industrial growth.

In other aspects of the industrialization effort, the military governments have encouraged increased production in other, complementary activities like mining, construction, agriculture, and transportation, which supply necessary inputs to industrial production. Agriculture is especially important, because it must produce food for the urban population at prices low enough to allow other purchases from consumer budgets, and agricultural exports earn most of the foreign exchange needed to import industrial inputs. But as already noted in the case of Germany, this supporting role is qualitatively different from that of English agriculture in eighteenth- and nineteenth-century competitive industrial development. In nineteenth-century Germany and twentieth-century Brazil, the agricultural sector's most important role in industrialization is supplying agricultural commodities, and this function can be performed even if agriculture is noncapitalist and stagnant in output and labor productivity. Table 7.10 illustrates these differences from competitive capitalist industrialization by contrasting the relative productivity of Brazilian agriculture with that of manufacturing, and reproducing the corresponding figures for the United Kingdom and Germany from Table 2.6 for comparative purposes.

Another vitally important policy effort was reforming the state's fiscal affairs.

TABLE 7.8
Brazil: The Structure of Manufacturing Value Added

	1950	1970	1974	*Average Annual Growth Rates* 1975	1976	1977
Food products, beverages, tobacco	25.5	17.1	15.1	1.4	12.0	
Textiles, clothing, shoes, textile and leather products	25.7	13.2	11.1	3.4	7.2	
Timber and furniture	5.6	4.6				
Paper and paper products	2.1	2.6	2.7	−14.6	20.8	2.5
Printing and publishing	4.2	3.7				
Rubber products	2.1	2.0	2.7	4.7	11.2	−2.0
Chemicals, plastics, pharmaceuticals, cosmetics	9.4	16.7	21.1	3.0	17.8	6.5
Nonmetallic minerals	7.4	6.9	7.2	9.0	12.0	8.3
Metallurgy	7.4	11.6	10.2	9.2	13.5	7.2
Machinery and electrical equipment	3.9	12.5	17.2	7.2	11.6	
Transportation equipment	2.3	8.0	12.8	0.5	7.2	−2.6
Miscellaneous	1.9	2.1				
TOTAL	100.0	100.0	100.0	3.8	10.5	2.3

SOURCES: W. Baer, *Industrialization and Economic Development in Brazil* (Homewood, Ill.: Irwin, 1965), p. 269; *Anuário Estatística do Brasil, 1976* (Rio de Janeiro: Fundacao Instituto do Geografia e Estástistica) Vol. 37, pp. 179, 201; W. Baer, *The Brazilian Economy: Its Growth and Development* (Columbus, Ohio: Grid Publishing Co., 1979), p. 96.

TABLE 7.9
Brazil: Sectoral Distribution of Net Assets of 5,113 Largest Firms (percentage distribution, 1974)

	Total	*State Enterprise*	*Multi-national*	*Private Domestic*
Mining	100	62	12	26
Manufacturing				
1. Food products	100	1	31	68
2. Beverages	100	.....	14	86
3. Tobacco	100	.....	99	1
4. Textiles	100	.....	13	87
5. Leather and goods	100	.....	11	89
6. Wood and products	100	.....	9	91
7. Furniture	100	.....	.....	100
8. Printing and publishing	100	.....	2	98
9. Chemicals and petroleum	100	55	23	22
10. Rubber	100	6	61	33
11. Nonmetallic minerals	100	2	35	63
12. Metal products	100	34	12	54
13. Machinery	100	1	46	53
14. Electrical machinery	100	.....	61	39
15. Transport materials	100	4	63	33
16. Miscellaneous	100	.....	47	53
Agriculture	100	1	3	96
Construction and engineering	100	15	3	82
Public utilities	100	88	7	6
Commerce	100	.....	5	95
Services	100	27	4	69
Total	100	37	15	48

SOURCE: Werner Baer, *The Brazilian Economy: Its Growth and Development* (Columbus, Ohio: Grid Publishing Co., 1979), p. 150.

TABLE 7.10
Relative Productivity of Labor in Agriculture and Industry

	% Total Production in Sector Divided by % Total Employment in Sector					
	Brazil		Germany		United Kingdom	
	1940	**1970**	**1882**	**1907**	**1801**	**1851**
Agriculture	0.53	0.40	0.78	0.71	0.91	0.94
Industry	1.24	1.35	0.84	1.32	0.79	0.80

SOURCES: Werner Baer, *Industrialization and Economic Development in Brazil* (Columbus, Ohio: Grid Publishing Co., 1979), pp. 18, 27; James R. Wilkie and P. Turovsky (eds.), *Statistical Abstract of Latin America,* Vol. 17 (Los Angeles: UCLA Latin American Center Publications, 1976), pp. 33, 135; Table 9.

The tax structure was changed so that receipts rose at least as fast as nominal output, and enforcement mechanisms were greatly tightened. Table A.2 shows how effective the state has been in obtaining the resources to finance its programs. This is crucial not only because the state has an active role in promoting and monitoring production, but as Argentina's experience demonstrates, the state must also maintain the market conditions for modern consumer goods and at the same time guarantee social peace. In the early 1960s, Brazilian per capita income was less than half that of Argentina, Chile, Uruguay, and of course Venezuela; hence a distribution of income especially skewed toward the top income receivers was necessary for expanding markets for the modern consumer goods and backward-linked inputs produced by the leading industrial firms.[12] The centralization of property ownership in the Brazilian economy is such to ensure that economic growth, whether from modern industry or staple exports, generates even more unequally distributed incomes. Similarly, power among contending groups is such that inflation also contributes to the skewed distribution of income. But there is no strong natural or automatic mechanism that can be relied upon, and maintaining and reproducing the market conditions for monopoly capitalist industrial development requires a powerful and vigilant state. This is a different and more formidable task than that faced by the state in late nineteenth-century Germany or in the mid-twentieth-century U.S. German industrial growth was not highly sensitive to patterns of consumer demand, and in the U.S., high per capita income, cultural homogeneity, and a more equitable distribution of income allow concessions to working and lower classes in the form of income redistribution and income maintenance policies which contribute both to market demand for modern consumer goods and to social peace. In Brazil, on the other hand, even a modest redistribution of income from the top to the bottom can curtail demand for modern consumer goods and related economic growth, and Table 7.11 shows that this certainly has been avoided. As a consequence, the state engages in outright repression rather than welfare as the more effective device to promote industrial growth and political stability, but even with considerable help from the U.S., the inability of the regime and the social order it represents to legitimate itself in the eyes of the poorest half of the population through income redistribution policies places great strains on political institutions.

Even though repression might work, at least in the short run, to neutralize dissent from the poorest and least organized, the regime must draw positive support from some important parts of Brazilian society; the entire society is not run at gunpoint. The industrial propertied classes do provide some support, but as Table 7.9 suggests, the substantial presence of multinational corporations and state firms in the most progressive product lines and financial institutions restricts the political influence of the domestic industrial bourgeoisie. This class is not strong numerically or economically, and furthermore, important political divisions exist among even its most powerful members. Brazilian industralists continue to protest vigorously against the rise in effective taxation, foreign investment, and the unparalleled expansion of public enterprises (Mendonca de Barros and Graham, 1978). These charges are not without justification—see Tables 7.9 and A.2. It is difficult to know how pervasive anti-statism is among Brazilian industrialists and MNC managers, but at the very least, their support of the regime and its policies is qualified in important ways.

So how can we explain the political support underlying Brazilian state policies? We could continue to go down the list of classes and their place in political life, but the most important bases of political support for the Brazilian military government and its policies can be more readily understood by looking at income-receiving *strata* rather than at roles in the process of production. It is the higher-income receivers, being in a position to purchase modern consumer goods, who are the major pillars of support for the Brazilian state and social order. This group, of course, includes the entire propertied class (as consumers), but numerically and politically more important are, again, the veritable armies of clerks, bookkeepers, lawyers, sales managers, media administrators, teachers, jurists, financial advisers, brokers, office managers, and public officials needed to record, regulate, coordinate, and justify the economy and society in its myriad of detail. In addition to protecting the privileges and incomes of the people in the modern middle class, the post-1964 Brazilian regime has consolidated its political support by creating an imaginative set of consumer credit arrangements, and the upper stratum of the sharply segmented working class is also susceptible to being brought into the fold by this means (Souza, 1978). The ideology of this powerful group is adequately expressed by the rubric "consumerism," and these people's allegiance to the regime depends principally on its ability to deliver the goods.

From this brief discussion, one can see that there are at least three important ways in which consistent economic growth is vital for sustaining the social and political order underlying Brazilian monopoly capitalist industrial development:

TABLE 7.11
Brazil: Size Distribution of Income and Purchasing Power of Income-Receiving Groups

	% of Economically Active Population					*Gini Coefficient*
	0-60	61-80	81-90	91-95	96-100	
Proportion of income						
1960	22.7	20.4	16.4	11.6	28.9	0.57[a]
1970	16.5	16.9	15.0	13.0	38.6	0.64[a]
Purchasing power of income in 1960 prices (100 = 1960 per capita income)						
1960	37.8	102.0	164.0	232.0	578.0	
1970	36.4	112.0	200.0	344.6	1023.1	

SOURCE: Derived from Richard Weisskopf and Adolfo Figueroa, "Traversing the Social Pyramid: A Comparative Review of Income Distribution," *Latin American Research Review* 11, no. 2 (1976), p. 91.
NOTE: [a]Calculated from seven categories.

political support from upper-income receivers and consumers; financial and technical support by foreign interests; and sufficient revenues through the fiscal system for the state to promote the economy and suppress and divide the lower and working classes.

The economic slowdown that began in the mid-1970s has indeed threatened these conditions and starkly illustrates the need for steady growth. The sharp economic slump of 1974-1975 was followed by a partial comeback in 1976, but GDP growth fell to 4.7 percent in 1977 (see Table 7.2)—only 2.3 percent for manufacturing. It rose slightly again in 1978, and the preliminary figures on 1979 growth are very close to the rates of 1977. (See recent issues of *Latin American Economic Report* and *Latin American Political Report* for intelligent and current reporting.) Brazil's strong dependence on imported oil (see Table A.3—it is estimated that oil accounted for about half of the value of Brazilian imports in the last half of 1979) has been a continuing problem, contributing to the economic decline. These economic setbacks have led to the partial unraveling of Brazilian monopoly capitalism. The government has reduced foreign borrowing and cut back expenditures as tax receipts have fallen (see Table A.2), inflation has risen to around 30 percent per annum, industrialists' criticism of the government has increased in volume and stidency, and white- and blue-collar workers have escalated strike activity in order to protect their income positions.

The government's response has been to change personnel in the economic ministries and generally take a hard line toward public expressions of dissatisfaction. There is a definite potential for political change, but with the exception of heightened working-class organization and militancy among the urban poor, there is not much indication that these potential changes are likely to take either democratic or egalitarian directions. There is evident confusion and consternation among top economic planners and politicians, who are desperately trying to get Brazil back on a 7 or 8 percent growth trajectory. If they succeed quickly enough, the resumption of this rate of expansion may give the regime the breathing space it needs to reduce its dependence on imported oil by developing domestic sources of petroleum, hydroelectric, and nuclear power, to pay off some of its massive public foreign debt, to receive some benefits from recent investment projects, to bring down the rate of inflation, and to buy off dissidents. That is, the economic growth, if it can be resumed, may enable the regime to ameliorate Brazil's political and social problems with technical solutions, but clearly this task is not going to be easy.

CHILE: BEYOND MONOPOLY CAPITALISM?

The model of monopoly capitalism also sheds light on the rise and fall of the "Chilean Road to Socialism" and on the subsequent disasters. Throughout the country's history, the possessing classes in Chile have probably been the most unified and flexible in Latin America (Pike, 1963), and in the twentieth century, the Chilean working class has been politically influential and well organized, although highly segmented (Angell, 1972). The large middle class has acted as political broker between the two powerful classes, and the result was a relatively open political process, low and erratic rates of industrial growth, a high degree of import dependence, and persistent inflation.

Salvador Allende, the candidate of various coalitions of left-wing parties, made very strong showings in presidential elections during the 1950s and 1960s. In 1970, with the backing of Socialist, Communist, and other radical parties, he was elected president with (as usual) a plurality of votes, a rather general socialist platform, and a commitment to respect constitutional procedures. Although candidates of his coalition party (Popular Unity) made gains in elections held between 1970 and 1973, Popular Unity never had the confidence of a firm majority backing. As a consequence, Allende was forced throughout his presidency to balance the sometimes conflicting interests of his core constituency of urban and rural workers with the need to attract new sources of political support; the process of building socialism in Chile thus proceeded too slowly (for workers who spontaneously occupied factories and farms) and too quickly (for potential supporters who were frightened by the rapidity of change).[13]

Unlike the Popular Unity government, neither U.S. nor domestic opponents felt any obligation to restrict themselves to legal tactics, and a heavily financed and well-coordinated attack was launched to create chaos in Chile and discredit the Allende regime. Local groups were subverted and subsidized by foreign and domestic opponents, but this by itself is inadequate to explain why those counter-revolutionary efforts were successful when, for instance, these kinds of tactics (and eventually much harsher, more direct ones) were unable to crush socialism in Vietnam. The explanation lies in the extent to which Chilean society conformed to the South American model of monopoly capitalism.

First and most obviously, Chile's economic dependence enabled the U.S. government and corporations to wreak considerable economic damage through international commodity and capital markets. In Chile, the industrial bourgeoisie, while retaining control over the centralized industrial sector, was able to sabotage key areas of production. But even after its control was diluted, the highly developed division of labor and economic interdependence within Chile enabled small trucking firms to paralyze the economy by shutdowns. Within the working class, the strength of economism in the labor elite was revealed by El Teniente copper miners who struck for higher wages at a critical time (Roxborough, *et al.*, 1977, pp. 208-210). By late 1972 the economic squeeze was intense, and some important political support, particularly from white-collar workers (whose number practically equal wage-earning production workers), was withdrawn. In many respects, this period was the finest hour of the attempt to build socialism in Chile; as the Allende government was undecided about whether to go forward or to retreat, the initiative passed to the hands of workers who took charge of affairs at local levels and began the "People's Power" phase of constructing socialism.

But these workers, without sufficient cohesion, arms, or strong allies, were simply not strong enough to withstand the combined forces of the military and reactionary classes; in September 1973 the military took power in a bloodbath without precedent in Chilean history, and the middle-class parties applauded. The military and secret police systematically murdered, imprisoned, tortured, and exiled tens of thousands of Chileans to restore "order."

Then began another large-scale social experiment. The military government circulated translations of Milton Friedman's *Capitalism and Freedom* (1962) and with the advice of Friedman and other University of Chicago economists (including Chileans), tried to force a free-market solution to Chile's economic and social problems.[14] This was economic freedom in a police state where economic power was highly centralized in private and public hands and where all labor organizations were disbanded and their leaders persecuted. Nevertheless, by 1975 great strides had been made in returning nationalized firms and lands to private (including MNC) ownership, there was significant economic decontrolling, the government budget ran a surplus, payments to foreign creditors were resumed, and the World Bank, which had lent nothing to Chile between 1970 and 1973, was pumping in tens of millions of dollars. Also in 1975, real industrial output had fallen to a level below that of 1965, per capita GDP approximated that of 1962, the official reported unemployment rate in Santiago during the last quarter was 16.5 percent, and inflation hovered around the 400 percent mark (IDB, 1976, pp. 186-188). Beginning in 1976, there has been some economic recovery as the military government reluctantly began to intervene more directly in the economy, and modern consumer goods led manufacturing expansion. But the middle class is still not getting many of these goods, the middle-class political parties remain outlawed, and although still suppressed by draconian measures, the working and lower classes show signs of resistance. As a consequence of the last, the government has grudgingly instituted some social welfare measures. In that the state is centralized and harsh, one political condition for a monopoly capitalist development model exists, but to establish its full conditions will apparently require large-scale changes in perceptions among those in political control and much more passivity on the part of the Chilean working class than they have shown in the past. Time is likely to run out.

The analytical framework of monopoly capitalism helps, then, to identify the obstacles to building a politically successful socialism or an economically successful capitalism by the means used in Chile during the 1970s. But such an approach does not help in seeing the significance of Chilean socialism for the future of South America. In aggregate economic terms, the three years of socialist construction were neither a disaster nor an unqualified success. When one looks at social indicators, such as the decline in general mortalitv and infant mortality during these years, one is getting much closer to the importance of the Allende years to the people of Chile. But radical redistributions of wealth, income, and power are not unknown in history; what is especially significant about the Chilean effort was that along with redistribution, an organization of production was beginning to emerge which was consonant with the social goals. With too few exceptions (two, three?), where socialism has been politically successful, the economic need to produce and reproduce the material conditions of a humane society has led to authoritarian hierarchies and stultifying divisions of labor in the work place. These capitalist forms of work organization (discussed in chapters 2 and 5) are incompatible with socialist goals, and the historical achievement of the Chilean people in those turbulent years was to show that a democratic, participatory system of work organization could further socialism by supplying the goods and by reaffirming egalitarian social relationships in a South American nation which had experienced substantial capitalist industrialization. Espinoza and Zimbalist (1978) documents this process, and it should be read by all concerned with these issues.

NOTES

1. Quintana (1970) is an edited collection of some of the most important ECLA documents on theory and policy, and the introduction by Quintana is an excellent (though uncritical) survey of the salients of the ECLA analyses. Baer (1962), Cardoso (1977), Flanders and Baer (1964), and Hirschman (1961) are more balanced assessments of ECLA prescriptions of import-substituting industrialization.

2. For good general discussions of the relationship between economic centralization and growth in underdeveloped areas, see Merhav (1969) and White (1974). Bain (1966) is a comparative, empirical study which includes some Third World nations and contains numerous insights. Also see Bottomley (1965), Lagos E. (1966), and Leff (1974) for some specifically Latin American studies.

Economic centralization translates into concentrations of wealth and power. Lagos E. (1962) and Zeitlin, *et al.* (1974) are "power elite" studies of pre-Allende Chile, and de Imaz (1970) is a corresponding study of Argentina. Lustig (1980) lists and describes the major ECLA theorists' work on income distribution and composition of industrial growth.

3. For the disillusionment with import-substituting industrialization and the shift of emphasis by ECLA in the 1960s, see Quintana (1970, pp. xlii-xlvii, 257-278), Cardoso (1977), Baer (1963), Felix (1968), and Robock (1970).

4. Marini (1972), dos Santos (1974, pp. 471-480), and Martins (1974, pp. 274-284) discuss Brazilian "sub-imperialism." Pellicer (1974) is a good treatment of Mexican foreign policy.

5. Much of the best work on the roots of MNC expansion is based on Hymer (1960), published by the Massachusetts Institute of Technology Press in 1976. Hymer's later works and Vernon (1966), Caves (1971), and Moran (1973) are some of the most suggestive works on this phase of capitalist expansion. Wilkins (1974) is an extremely useful compilation of U.S. foreign investment, company by company, in the twentieth century.

6. Good analyses on the effect of MNC penetration in the Third World are scarce. Barnett and Muller (1974) and Quijano Obregon (1973) represent different styles in this mediocre literature. Chilcote and Edelstein (1974, pp. 60-63) focuses narrowly on the flow of economic resources in discussing the effects of the MNCs and has a good bibliography of similar works. Emmanuel (1974 and 1976) are sensible discussions of these issues; Caves (1974) surveys and tests some propositions of MNC activities; and Ingles and Fairchild (1977) offers empirical support for my argument presented in the text.

7. Perloff and Wingo (1961) is a compact survey of the spatial patterns of U.S. growth. For Latin America, see Blakemore and Smith (1971), Gilbert (1974), and Odell and Preston (1973). Weaver (1970) is an empirical study of regional changes in the Chilean economy between 1950 and 1964, illustrating some of these forces.

8. The distinction between productive and unproductive labor is very old, but it has fallen into disrepute among orthodox economists in the last century. A clear statement of one distinction between these two types of labor is in Adam Smith (1776, pp. 314-315); for comparisons of Marx's and Smith's differences on this subject, see Horvat (1969, pp. 122-186) and Gough (1973). Nicolaus (1967) is a useful application of Smith's distinction (although he uses Marxian language), and Baumol (1967) is extremely suggestive even though his analysis is couched in terms of orthodox economic theory.

9. Among the best of the broader works (not all neo-Marxist) are Baran and Sweezy (1966) and Menshikov (1969) for the character of the large corporations and the circulation process; Averitt (1962) and O'Connor (1973) for technological dualism and state policy; Gordon (1972), Silverman and Yanowitch (1974), Braverman (1974) and Edwards (1979) for the organization of the labor force and

the work process; and Bowles and Gintis (1976) and Collins (1971) on the role of education.

10. I am grateful to Julia Coan Allen for help in formulating this interpretation of post-World War II Argentina. Throughout this section, all references to Perón and Peronist policies are to refer to Perón's first presidency, 1946-1955.

11. For a range of interpretations and evidence about the Brazilian miracle, see Baer (1979), Erickson (1977), Dye and de Souza e Silva (1979), Furtado (1973), Stepan (1973, pp. 60-141), Evans (1974), Flynn (1974), Tyler (1976), Leeds (1977), and Mendonca de Barros and Graham (1978).

12. A 1972 input-output study by Francisco Lopes concludes that a redistribution on income from the top to the bottom in Brazil would severely curtail demand for transportation equipment, petroleum products, rubber, and electrical equipment and would substantially increase markets for wage goods, including food, textiles, apparel, leather goods, beverages, tobacco, and commerce (Tyler, 1976, pp. 874-875).

13. Roxborough, *et al.* (1977) is an excellent, comprehensive treatment of the Allende years and immediate aftermath. *Latin American Perspectives* (1974; 1975, pp. 69-106; 1976, pp. 19-97; and 1977, pp. 83-113, 121-125) have good analyses of particular facets. Spence (1978), Nunn (1979), and Loveman (1979) review the voluminous literature on the Allende years and their aftermath.

14. The term "Chicago boys" refers to the University of Chicago-trained Chilean economists (mostly at the Catholic University of Santiago) who have been working closely with the military, perhaps since 1971 or so. See Letelier (1976), Roxborough (1977, pp. 187-277) and IDB (1974 and 1975) for the personnel and policies of the Chilean junta.

8

CONCLUSIONS

In the last chapter, after delineating some of the general features of monopoly capitalism in South America, the outlines of post-World War II Argentina, Brazil, and Chile gave three angles of vision on the character and implications of this form of industrial expansion. This final chapter continues the discussion of contemporary industrial growth but at the more general, methodological level of chapter 1.

The last section of chapter 2 listed some of the general principles which have been distilled from competitive capitalist industrial development. One which I found acceptable was that real gains in the productivity of human labor could be achieved in manufacturing. An extension of this principle is that capitalist industrial development is predicated principally on increasing the productivity of human labor, and that the most interesting questions concern the receipt and use of this increased product, rather than the receipt and use of product which simply reflects a corresponding loss by others (in other words, questions about relative surplus value rather than absolute surplus value). The failure to recognize the materially progressive nature of capitalist industrial growth underlies the contention by some scholars (for example, those working in the more extreme forms of dependency theory as well as some identified with the "modern world-system" approach of Immanuel Wallerstein, 1974 and 1979) that the industrial advance of the core nations was possible principally through the extraction of economic resources from peripheral regions, a proposition ably criticized by Brenner (1977).

In that same section, I also identified from competitive capitalist industrial development a series of generalizations which I argued were not warranted, since they are specific to that particular, historically bound phase of industrialization. This argument required distinguishing more systematically the major features of competitive capitalist and finance capitalist industrial development, and I summarized the major differences in Table 2.4. These differences are more dramatic than those between financial and monopoly capitalist industrialization, but recognizing the distinction between the last two phases is still vital. For instance, in monopoly capitalist development (relative to finance capitalism) the domestic industrial bourgeoisie play a less significant economic and political role, and a powerful central state that gives a great deal of direction is the source of more initiation and control. These differences are matters of degree, but when embedded in the respective contexts of the nature of the leading product lines, we see the emergence of a qualitatively different form of industrial growth. In all three phases of industrial development, those benefiting from the production of leading categories of industrial goods could be counted on to support industrial expansion, although the political significance of that support declines in each successive phase. In place of producers promoting competitive capitalist industrial growth in the late eighteenth and early nineteenth centuries, we see the rise in political importance of those *using* industrial products in both finance and monopoly capitalism. Yet, as Russian history suggests, finance capitalist industrial development without a powerful industrial bourgeoisie is severely handicapped, while in modern Brazil, monopoly capitalist industrialization does not appear to be seriously damaged by this weakness. That is, in monopoly capitalism the shift in necessary political support from the propertied classes involved in the production of the leading product lines to those using the product is closer to completion, and the historical transition from finance capitalism, led by intermediate and capital goods, to monopoly capitalism, with modern consumer goods, signified qualitative changes in who, as the user, has a stake in industrial growth and the political influence to promote it. I have characterized the corresponding ideological difference as being that of a militaristic nationalism as opposed to that of consumerism. As described in chapters 6 and 7, these labels imply profound differences in the social and cultural milieu appropriate for industrial growth as well as significant differences in the type of policies required to promote growth. Table 8.1 summarizes the differences among the three historically successive types of industrial development.

Throughout this book, I have insisted on the fundamentally important differences in the evolving phases of capitalist industrial development, starting with wage goods as the locus of principal dynamism in competitive capitalism, that locus moving to backward-linked lines of production in finance capitalism, and in monopoly capitalism its returning to consumer goods, but as a set of consumer goods in which the process of production and often the character of the product had been transformed. The implications of these differences, as shown by Table 8.1, are far-reaching, but they are either ignored completely or subordinated to insignificance by stage theories of economic growth, sociological "modernization" theory, and any other attempts to derive lessons from history by analogy or by use of universalistic theories emphasizing similarities of industrial development. There is another important approach which is clearly related to those mentioned above: Gerschenkron (1966) and Moore (1966) give considerable emphasis to

TABLE 8.1
Competitive, Finance, and Monopoly Capitalist Industrial Development: Characteristics, Conditions, and Mechanisms

	Competitive	*Finance Capitalist*	*Monopoly Capitalist*
Characteristics of leading product lines			
Type of product	Wage goods	Intermediate and capital goods	Modern consumer goods
Production processes and industrial structure	Labor-intensive technology; many small firms	Capital-intensive technology; few large firms	Capital-intensive technology; a few large firms
Necessary conditions for growth of leading product lines			
Factor mobilization	Need for large numbers of aggressive entrepreneurs and availability of massive labor and modest capital inputs	Need for some entrepreneurs sensitive to social and political parameters and availability of modest labor and massive capital inputs	Need for some technically competent managers and availability of modest labor and massive capital inputs
Product markets	Wage workers, domestic and foreign	State, other productive enterprises, and foreign investment	Modern middle class, other high income receivers, and state
Social and Cultural order	Unrestricted geographical and sectoral mobility of productive factors	Unrestricted geographical and sectoral mobility for *industrial and urban* productive factors	Unrestricted geographical and sectoral mobility *for industrial and urban* productive factors
	Considerable occupational and social mobility	Some limited opportunities for occupational and social mobility	Some limited opportunities for occupational and social mobility, principally within the middle class
	Status derived largely from position in private production process	Some status from control over large-scale productive assets, although other factors may continue to exert decisive influence	Status largely determined by position in private and public bureaucracies, linked to income levels and consumption patterns

	Ideology of aggressive, competitive individualism; industrial bourgeoisie's drive to accumulate productive assets unencumbered by government regulations and cultural restraints of social responsibility or "irrationality"	Ideology of nationalism, which may mitigate industrial bourgeoisie's drive for private accumulation	Ideology of consumerism, pervasive even among the high-level bureaucrats in charge of leading production lines
Political order	Decisive political influence exerted by industrial bourgeoisie as a class, expressing its economic power, supported at crucial junctures by working class	Considerable political influence wielded by owners of large scale industry, and the conflicts within the propertied class (e.g. agriculture vs. industry) both require and are a source of significant independent political power vested in central state	Political power centralized in state, and the most substantial influence from outside the political apparatus is exercised by the literate, articulate, modern middle class with organizational skills
Mechanisms			
Coordination of economic activity	Decentralized market system	Cartels and state	State planning
Principal agents of social and cultural change	Industrial bourgeoisie	Industrial bourgeoisie and state, the latter able to negotiate the minimum changes necessary to accommodate industrial growth without destroying the pre-industrial social and cultural order	State regulates and monitors slight changes needed
Social control	Industrial bourgeoisie at production sites and liberal ideology; state enforces private, "free" contracts	Industrial bourgeoisie and nationalist ideology; state redistributes income for social and political stability, not economic stimulus, and uses police powers when necessary	Consumerism; state assumes principal responsibility for social control by use of police power and by distributing income and subsidizing firms so that certain groups receive increasing amounts of modern consumer goods

national developmental differences, but they attribute these observed differences to the historical particularities of each nation (that is, "degree of backwardness," and the organization of the countryside) and still regard industrialization as an essentially unchanging process. When looked at in this way, the differences between Gerschenkron and Rostow are matters of rather unimportant degree.

Ahistorical conceptions of capitalist industrial development are not limited to liberal scholarship. The predominant school in current European Marxist thought argues trenchantly that the essence of capitalism has not changed since Marx wrote and that with minor emendations, his analyses of competitive capitalism remain fully adequate to comprehend the central forces of contemporary capitalism.[1]

These conflicting opinions about whether or not capitalism has changed are extremely important, and a key element of this importance is that they embody diverse perceptions of the nature and likelihood of industrial growth. Both neoclassical economic theory and Marx's own analyses lead one to expect industrial capitalism to be inherently dynamic, propelled by the competition among individual capitals which tend to receive the prevailing average rate of profit. But in the advanced nations of South America, although labor power and the means of production overwhelmingly have assumed commodity form, rates of industrial growth do not necessarily demonstrate the compulsively expansionary impulse expected nor in any meaningful sense can one say that there is a single prevailing rate of profit ruling the returns to all enterprises. These expectations are based on the logic of *competitive* capitalism, and it is a mistake to identify capitalism, as an analytical category, only with its historically transient form of competitive capitalism. Doing so leads some Marxist scholars, especially those using multiple "modes of production" categories, to assert that "real capitalism" does not exist in these nations, although they do not seem interested in comparing the social relations of production of, say, Argentina in 1975 with those of Germany in 1875 (see Foster-Carter, 1978). Others recognize that the more economically advanced nations of South America are indeed capitalist, but then, because of their identification of capitalism with its competitive phase, they feel the need to devise special, ad hoc explanations for sluggish economic growth. In these explanations, even Marxists frequently eschew class analysis and apply frameworks like dependency theory, which focus on commodity relations and circulation spheres.

The confusion between capitalism and competitive capitalism has led liberal scholars into a similar analytical quandry, and the "obstacles to growth" literature is one of the consequences. International economic relationships still rank as the favorite obstacle, but population growth and agricultural stagnation also figure prominently in such works. Population growth is an area of study that lends itself to especially general and ahistorical treatments.[2] An example of this tendency is the abstract, arithmetic approach which simply says that population growth, as the denominator of the per capita income ratio (GNP/population), drags down possible gains in that ratio. But this Malthusian formula obscures the fact that people are producers as well as consumers, and as such contribute to increases in the numerator, too. So, why have more people not actually generated substantially more output? One argument is that in the face of rapid population growth, the proportion of the population under, say, fourteen years of age grows rapidly, increasing the dependency rate (the number of nonworkers per worker) and lowering the proportion of the population that is economically active. But again, this approach avoids the stark fact that even of those economically active in South America, only a small proportion is able to find productive employment. In chapter 2, we saw that population growth in England made important contributions to industrialization, but even in the later nineteenth-century industrializations of Germany and Russia, the functional role of population growth to industrialization was already in question. In twentieth-century South America, the ability of population growth to stimulate industrial growth is even more dubious. To understand these economies' inability to employ additional people productively, one must directly confront the institutions of monopoly capitalism, including the technical conditions of production, centralization of capital, and the segmentation of the labor force.

The organization and sluggish performance of South American agriculture is another common explanation for the uneven growth record of the South American industrial sectors. The agricultural sector has retarded industrial growth, according to these studies, by not supplying the produce, markets, labor, and capital necessary to support continuing industrial expansion.[3] The most extreme form of this argument is to formulate a "dual economy" argument in which a potentially progressive urban industrial capitalism, described in very general terms, is depicted as being retarded by agrarian "feudalism." This type of argument, of course, has considerable appeal to liberals, because through this perception, capitalism as a set of social and economic relationships can still be portrayed as essentially progressive, enlightened, and liberating, and the empirical record can be dismissed as the consequence of being shackled by precapitalist forms rooted in "tradition" or "the colonial heritage."[4] Again referring to chapter 2, the experience of Germany (in contrast to England) indicates that modern industrialization can proceed even though the agricultural sector is noncapitalist in organization and is virtually stagnant in output and labor productivity. The industrial capitalism forthcoming from such conditions is not *liberal* industrial capitalism (compare Moore, 1966), but agricultural development, as it is commonly understood, does not appear to have been necessary to support industrial development in the multifaceted ways which characterized English competitive capitalism. Drawing from German and Russian industrial history, what does appear vital is effective political control over the agricultural producers, be they tenants, peasant proprietors, wage laborers, or whatever, to ensure the supply of agricultural commodities in sufficient quantities to feed the urban populace, to pay for imports of machinery and intermediate products through agricultural exports, and so on. Of course, the more agricultural produce per rural inhabitant, the less harsh, efficient, and costly the political controls need to be, but one cannot rely on historical support when arguing that industrial growth requires the transformation of the countryside so that it becomes like the city in organization, culture, or prosperity.[5]

My intention here is not to diminish the importance of population growth and agricultural stagnation for industrial development; these are prominent features in the distinctive South American social formations. But I am arguing that their status as problems, obstacles, impediments, or whatever for industrial growth is defined by the particular institutional forms and logic of modern industrial production, and without an understanding of the internal character of the current monopoly phase of industrial capitalism, only very vague and uncertain meanings can be attached to these processes. Of course, this is just as true for other aspects of South American economic life like dependence, MNCs, balance-of-payments deficits, unemployment, education ("human capital"), income distribution, patterns of government policies, inflation, and technological dualism, none of which can be fruitfully studied in isolation from the others. The status of these conditions as problems is not due to the magnitude of each and even of their sum; their importance is that together they form a system which frequently is not materially progressive.

Industrial growth under monopoly capitalist conditions depends on the monopoly-sector firms which, with noncompetitive markets, concentrated economic power, machine-using technology, and administered prices, simply do not contain an internal, self-reinforcing expansionary dynamic. Without strong monitoring from extra-market sources and conscious coordination from centralized institutions, monopoly capitalism chronically tends toward stagnation and retrogression whether located in North America, Western Europe, or South America. Moreover, economic stability is constantly threatened when mistakes or problems in a few key firms can seriously affect the functioning of the whole economy. The need for centralized direction is so strong that, as in the case of late nineteenth-century Britain, a liberal heritage was already a marked drawback under finance capitalist conditions; the social and political decentralization crucial for economic growth in earlier, competitive capitalism became inappropriate for material advance when the orgnaization of economic life changed. The superior post-World War II economic performance of German and Japanese monopoly capitalism compared to that of the U.S. and Great Britain is a further illustration of this point. Wartime destruction of old plant and equipment and Marshall Plan-financed reconstruction with modern productive techniques do not adequately explain the economic buoyancy of the defeated fascist powers. The vital element missing in such conventional explanations is that the centralized social and political institutions of Germany and Japan have been better able to exert the type of control, coordination, and judicious subsidization consonant with the requirements of monopoly capitalism than their liberal competitors' more decentralized institutions. This is what underlay the impressive record of these nations' economic growth, which did not even need the prop of massive armaments expenditures.

To promote capitalist accumulation and industrial growth, South American governments must subsidize monopoly production through cheap credit, grants, tax breaks, below-cost pricing of publicly produced inputs, and the supply of some goods and services for monopoly-sector workers to reduce wage bills. In addition, the state must maintain social peace and expand markets for modern consumer goods and intermediate products manufactured by monopoly-sector firms, which are the principal source of industrial expansion. These functions are like those of the state in the U.S. and accordingly are subject to the same contradictions: the costs of monopoly-sector production are increasingly socialized, but profits continue to be privately appropriated. Thus the state expenditures required to maintain the conditions for economic growth chronically outrun available revenues, and the state is plagued by recurring fiscal and political crises and inflation.[6] These symptoms are obvious in South America, but their severity reflects the presence of a policy constraint which does not exist in the U.S., where concessions to working and lower classes in the form of income redistribution and income maintenance policies can contribute to both social peace and market demand for monopoly-sector products. In South America, on the other hand, even a modest redistribution of income from the top to the bottom can curtail demand for the products of the monopoly sector and slow economic growth. The crucial link between income distribution and growth-inducing demand is badly blurred when the discussion is cast in the overly aggregated terms of Keynes' effective demand or Marx's surplus realization; what is at issue in these nations is not the general question of sufficient demand or realized surplus but rather the specific conditions for the sufficiency of a particular pattern of demand and the realizaiton of particular firms' surpluses, which, in the context of low per capita incomes, depends on highly inequitable distributions of income. As a consequence of these pressures and constraints, outright repression rather than welfare is more effective in promoting industrial growth. Even with U.S. help, however, such policies are expensive and uncertain, and the situation encourages the formation of praetorian governments over which even the wealthiest may have little influence.

These are some of the difficulties which monopoly capitalist industrial development entails, but I do not mean to exaggerate the bleakness of prospects for such development in South America. As stated in chapter 1, this book has been organized along the lines of dual historical movements. I have used the first side of this historical duality—the historically changing character of capitalist industrial development—as a guide for presenting the evolution of South American social formations—the second side of the duality. The social and political configurations of the South American nations did not lend themselves to competitive or finance capitalist industrial development, but the beginnings of strong central states and sizable urban middle classes in the 1920s and 1930s and the continued suppression of the working and lower classes are examples of processes which appear much more consonant with the conditions for monopoly capitalist industrial development in several nations in the last quarter of the twentieth century. That is, the peculiar character of monopoly capitalist industrial development could very well breathe new life into social configurations which appeared archaic and incapable of economic vitality when judged by the standards of competitive and finance capitalism. Only a historically informed analysis of industrial development, combined with the specifics of South American social formations (that is, dependency, powerful rural elites, population growth, and so on), can provide adequate conceptual guides for understanding the aspirations of the Peruvian military junta, the economic failure and political turmoil of Uruguay, the need for the Colombian state and "progressive" bourgeoisie to shake off the influence of rural possessing classes and rural and urban workers, and the precarious nature of economic and political balance in Venezuela.

It is monopoly capitalism, complete with its extravagant use of natural resources, political authoritarianism, social hierarchies, cultural flattening, and ecological damage, which holds the economic promise of capitalism in South America.

NOTES

1. Mosely (1979) is a good expression of this position. In chapter 1, I quoted Marx's well-known statement: "The country that is more developed industrially only shows, to the less developed, the image of its own future" (Marx, 1867, pp. 8-9). Whether or not the viewpoint expressed by this sentence was belied by Marx's own historical and theoretical writings, it should be clear by now that my own conception of historical change implies the converse position: the less industrially developed (but developing) nations show the more developed some indication of their futures. The features of late nineteenth-century German industrial growth were apparent as strong tendencies in England and the United States at the same time; the first section of chapter 6 notes that many of the South American economies were characterized by high rates of unemployment concurrent with high rates of inflation before "stagflation" became a serious problem in the United States and Western Europe, with the attendant crisis in Keynesian theory; and despite the differences in analysis and language, the conclusions of a study for the international corporate elite's Trilateral Commission by Crozier, *et al.* (1975) is consistent with what I say about Brazil in respect to the incompatabilities between monopoly capitalist economic growth and liberal freedoms.

2. The economic literature on population growth in Latin America is voluminous. Gonzalez (1974) is an example of its dubious analytical quality, Sanchez-Albornoz (1974) is an extremely useful compilation of Latin American population history, Cassen (1976) is a competent review of orthodox work, and *Latin American Perspectives* (1977, pp. 2-41) applies Marxian theory to Latin American population issues.

3. Johnston (1970) and Johnston and Kilby (1975) are excellent sources for conventional views on the contribution of agricultural growth to general economic expansion. The earlier attention to the necessity of releasing agricultural labor for urban industrial employment has diminished as scholars have finally begun to

notice the severity of unemployment and underemployment in Third World cities.

4. Lewis (1954), drawing from Ricardo, was the inspiration for subsequent work on the "dual economy" (in sharp constrast to my "industrial dualism"). Fei and Ranis (1964) and Kelley *et al.* (1972) are prominent examples of the narrowing of Lewis's work down to conform to the scope of neoclassical economic theory, thus enabling considerably more rigorous treatment of essentially trivial issues. Furtado (1976), Lambert (1967), and Stein and Stein (1970) apply broader versions of the dual economy approach to Latin America.

5. The revolution in the Bolivian countryside beginning in 1952 dramatically demonstrated that when severe oppression of rural workers is the basis of agricultural organization and production, even a temporary relaxation of pressure can be exceedingly dangerous. Also, Bolivia's experience conforms to the generalization of Barrington Moore (1966, p. 480): "The peasants have provided the dynamite to bring down the old building. To the subsequent work of reconstruction they have brought nothing. . . ." Malloy (1970), Malloy and Thorn (1971), Volk (1975), and Mayoraga (1978) are good studies of the background and consequences of the Bolivian revolution.

6. See O'Connor (1973) and Davis (1963) for the roots of "political inflation," a conception which, interestingly enough, is closer to that of the conservative monetarists than to the liberal reformism of the structuralists. Baer and Kerstenetzky (1964), Thorp (1971), Wachter (1976), and Thorp and Whitehead (1979) are good surveys of the standard debates on the sources and effects of South American inflation. As indicated by my discussion of petroleum prices, internal political struggle is not the only source of inflation.

APPENDIX

TABLE A.1
Population, Population Growth, and Urbanization in Latin America, 1850-1970
(millions of persons)

	ca. 1850	*ca. 1900*			*1930*	*1940*				*1950*	
			Percentage in Cities				Average Growth/	Percentage in Cities			Average Growth/
	Pop.	Pop.	Over 10,000	Over 100,000	Pop.	Pop.	year 1930-1940	Over 20,000	Over 100,000	Pop.	year 1940-1850
Mexico	7.7	13.6	12.7	3.3	16.6	19.8	1.8	17.7	11.1	26.6	2.9
Guatemala	.9	1.4	16.9	0.0	1.8	2.2	2.1	11.1	11.1	3.0	3.2
El Salvador	.4	.9	15.4	0.0	1.4	1.6	1.6	12.5	0.0	1.9	1.6
Honduras	.4	.4	8.4	0.0	.9	1.1	2.1	9.1	0.0	1.4	2.1
Nicaragua	.3	.4	n.a.	n.a.	.7	.9	1.8	11.1	0.0	1.1	2.4
Costa Rica	.1	.3	28.4	0.0	.5	.6	2.1	16.7	16.7	.8	3.1
Panama	.....	.....	.....	.....	.5	.6	1.7	33.3	16.7	.8	2.5
Argentina	1.1	4.7	27.1	16.8	11.9	14.2	1.7	40.8	29.6	17.1	1.9
Bolivia	1.4	1.7	8.0	0.0	2.2	2.5	1.5	16.0	8.0	3.0	1.9
Brazil	7.2	17.3	10.9	5.8	33.6	41.2	2.3	16.0	11.7	52.3	2.6
Chile	1.3	2.9	21.8	14.1	4.4	5.1	1.5	35.3	23.5	6.1	1.6
Colombia	2.2	3.8	9.4	2.9	7.4	9.1	2.1	14.3	8.8	11.6	2.5
Ecuador	.8	1.4	12.3	0.0	2.2	2.6	1.8	15.4	11.5	3.2	2.2
Paraguay	.5	.4	16.5	0.0	.9	1.1	2.3	9.1	9.1	2.2	1.9
Peru	1.9	3.8	7.4	3.9	5.7	6.7	1.6	13.4	9.0	8.0	1.6
Uruguay	.1	.9	30.0	28.7	1.7	1.9	1.3	42.1	31.6	2.2	1.2
Venezuela	1.5	2.3	22.8	0.0	3.0	3.7	2.3	18.9	10.8	5.3	2.6

TABLE A.1—Continued
Population, Population Growth, and Urbanization in Latin America, 1850-1970
(millions of persons)

	1960				*1970*		*1977*		
	Pop.	Average Growth/ year 1950-1960	Percentage in cities Over 20,000	Over 100,000	Pop.	Average Growth/ year 1960-1970	Pop.	Average Growth/ year 1970-1977	Average Urban Growth/year 1970-1977
Mexico	36.0	3.0	33.9	23.1	50.7	3.4	64.4	3.5	5.0
Guatemala	4.0	2.7	15.0	10.0	5.3	2.8	6.2	2.8	2.2
El Salvador	2.5	2.7	16.0	8.0	3.4	3.2	4.3	3.1	3.8
Honduras	1.8	2.8	11.1	0.0	2.6	2.3	2.9	2.7	4.6
Nicaragua	1.5	2.8	20.0	13.3	2.0	2.9	2.3	3.2	5.1
Costa Rica	1.2	3.6	25.0	16.7	1.7	3.3	2.1	2.9	4.9
Panama	1.0	2.9	40.0	30.0	1.4	2.9	1.8	3.1	4.4
Argentina	20.9	2.0	54.5	42.6	24.4	1.5	26.1	1.7	2.3
Bolivia	3.7	2.0	21.6	16.2	4.7	2.3	4.8	2.3	3.1
Brazil	70.3	2.9	28.9	19.3	93.2	2.8	113.2	2.8	4.8
Chile	7.7	2.4	51.9	31.2	9.7	2.3	10.7	1.9	2.9
Colombia	15.9	3.1	30.2	21.4	22.2	3.3	24.8	2.7	5.1
Ecuador	4.3	2.9	25.6	18.6	6.0	3.3	7.1	2.9	4.6
Paraguay	2.5	2.1	16.0	16.0	2.9	1.8	2.8	3.4	3.1
Peru	10.0	2.3	26.0	17.0	13.6	3.0	16.4	2.9	5.2
Uruguay	2.5	1.4	56.0	40.0	2.9	1.4	2.8	0.9	0.8
Venezuela	7.7	3.7	42.9	28.6	10.8	3.2	12.7	3.1	4.1

SOURCES: Nicolás Sánchez-Abornez, *The Population of Latin America* (Berkeley: University of California Press, 1974), pp. 169, 184, 185, 178, 179, 245; Inter-American Development Bank, *Economic and Social Progress in Latin America, 1977 Report*, p. 390.

NOTE: n.a. = not available.

TABLE A.2
Central Government Finances
(% GDP)

	Tax Revenues						*Total Expenditures*				*Budgetary Balances*[a]			
	1961	1963-1965	1966-1969	1969-1971	1971-1974	1975-1977	1961	1969-1971	1972-1974	1975-1977	1961	1969-1971	1972-1974	1975-1977
Argentina	8.5	5.5	7.1	6.1	4.9	4.7	8.6	8.6	10.5	13.2	−0.2	−1.8	−5.1	−8.1
Bolivia	6.5	7.7	8.1	7.8	10.1	10.1	8.9	11.0	14.4	17.7	−1.7	−2.3	−2.6	−1.3
Brazil	6.9	7.9	10.0	10.3	11.5	9.8	11.6	10.3	10.8	10.1	−2.0	−0.4	−0.2	0.0
Chile	15.9	15.6	18.6	19.3	16.6	20.1	19.4	22.7	26.6	21.9	−2.7	−3.1	−8.4	−0.6
Colombia	6.7	7.1	8.5	8.7	7.9	8.5	10.5	10.1	9.7	8.4	−0.1	−1.1	−1.4	−0.3
Ecuador	9.1	8.6	8.7	9.2	11.3	14.6	12.5	13.4	12.4	16.7	−2.3	−2.7	−0.5	−1.6
Paraguay	8.0	8.1	9.5	10.3	8.4	8.3	8.5	11.7	9.6	10.3	−0.1	−0.3	0.0	−0.9
Peru	14.4	15.7	15.8	14.2	13.3	12.7	15.5	18.7	18.9	19.9	−3.6	−1.4	−3.7	−5.9
Uruguay	10.3	12.6	12.2	11.7	13.1	12.9	19.3	16.5	16.6	16.2	−0.5	−3.4	−2.8	−2.7
Venezuela	14.7	12.4	12.6	13.1	18.2	22.1	23.2	20.6	24.0	30.6	−4.7	−0.9	0.6	−1.4

SOURCE: Inter-American Development Bank, *Economic and Social Progress in Latin America: 1970 Report*, p. 52; *1973 Report*, pp. 367-370; *1974 Report*, p. 459; *1976 Report*, pp. 409, 411; *1977 Report*, pp. 406, 407, 409.

NOTE: [a]The net difference between total expenditures and total receipts; taxes make up from 75% to 95% of total receipts.

TABLE A.3
Net Exports of Crude Oil and Refined Petroleum Products
(1,000 barrels)

	1960		*1977*[a]	
	Crude	Refined	Crude	Refined
Argentina	−22.9	−12.2	−21.5	−12.9
Bolivia	1.1	0.0	4.5	−0.2
Brazil	−37.9	−31.9	−307.4	20.2
Chile	−3.7	0.1	0.0	−26.5
Colombia	31.3	3.5	−9.0	6.4
Ecuador	−1.6	0.0	45.3	−0.5
Paraguay	0.0	2.5	−2.0	−0.4
Peru	2.9	−0.8	−14.1	−1.1
Uruguay	−9.1	−1.8	−13.2	−1.1
Venezuela	731.0	250.0	744.0	278.7

SOURCE: Inter-American Development Bank, *Economic and Social Progress in Latin America, 1977 Report,* pp. 448, 449.
NOTE: [a]Preliminary Data indicates net imports.

FIGURE A.1
Latin America: Indicators of Long-term Trends in the Volume of Manufacturing Output, 1900-1963

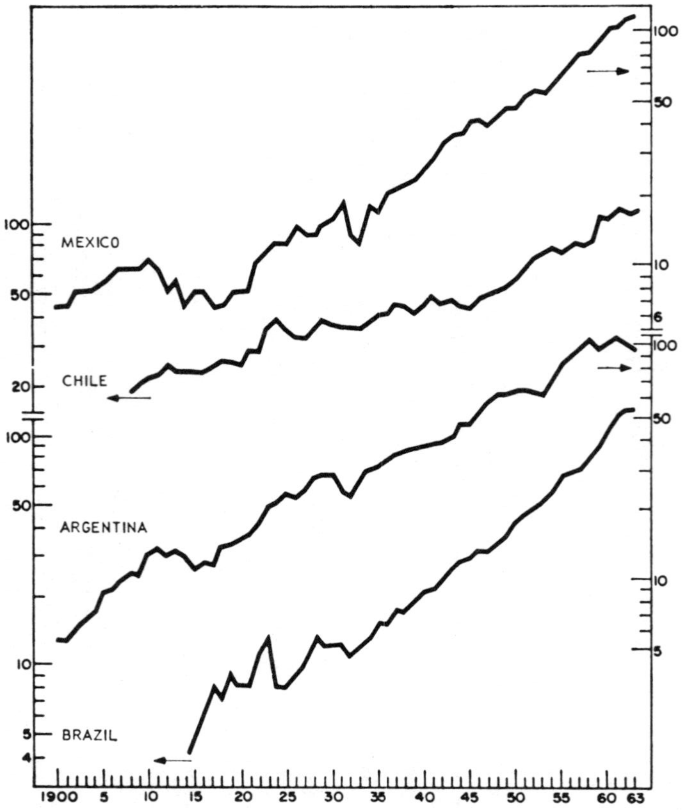

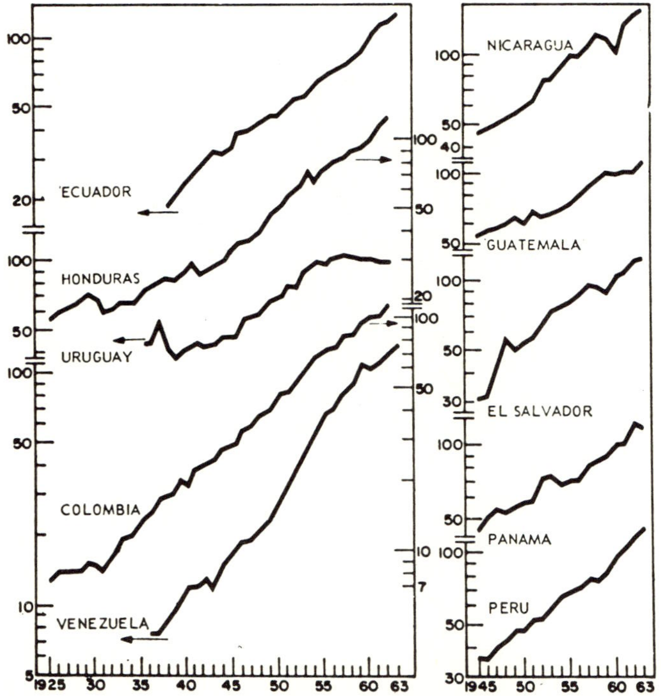

SOURCE: U.N. ECLA, *The Process of Industrial Development in Latin America* (New York: United Nations, 1966), p. 10.

FIGURE A.2
Latin America: Share of Manufacturing Sector in Total Production, 1899-1963

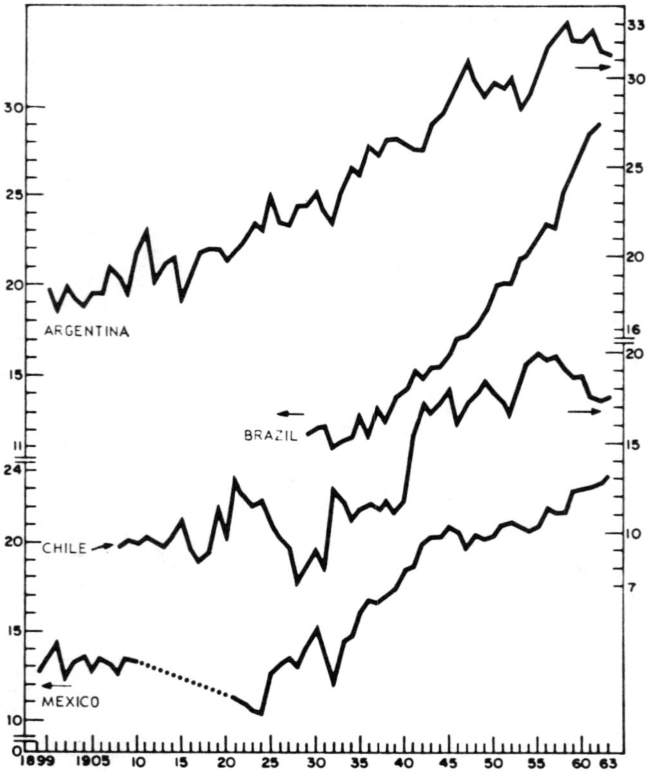

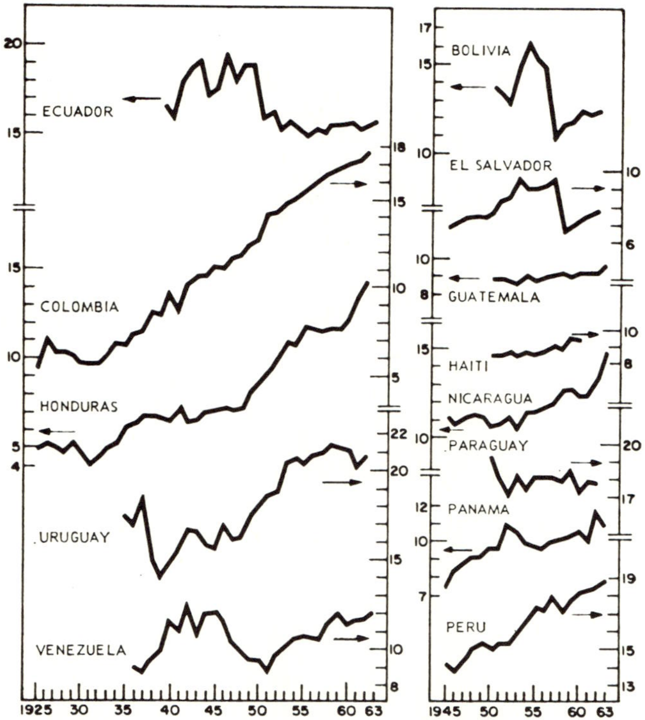

SOURCE: U.N. ECLA, *The Process of Industrial Development in Latin America* (New York: United Nations, 1966), p. 13.

FIGURE A.3
Income Distribution by Groups, Early 1960s

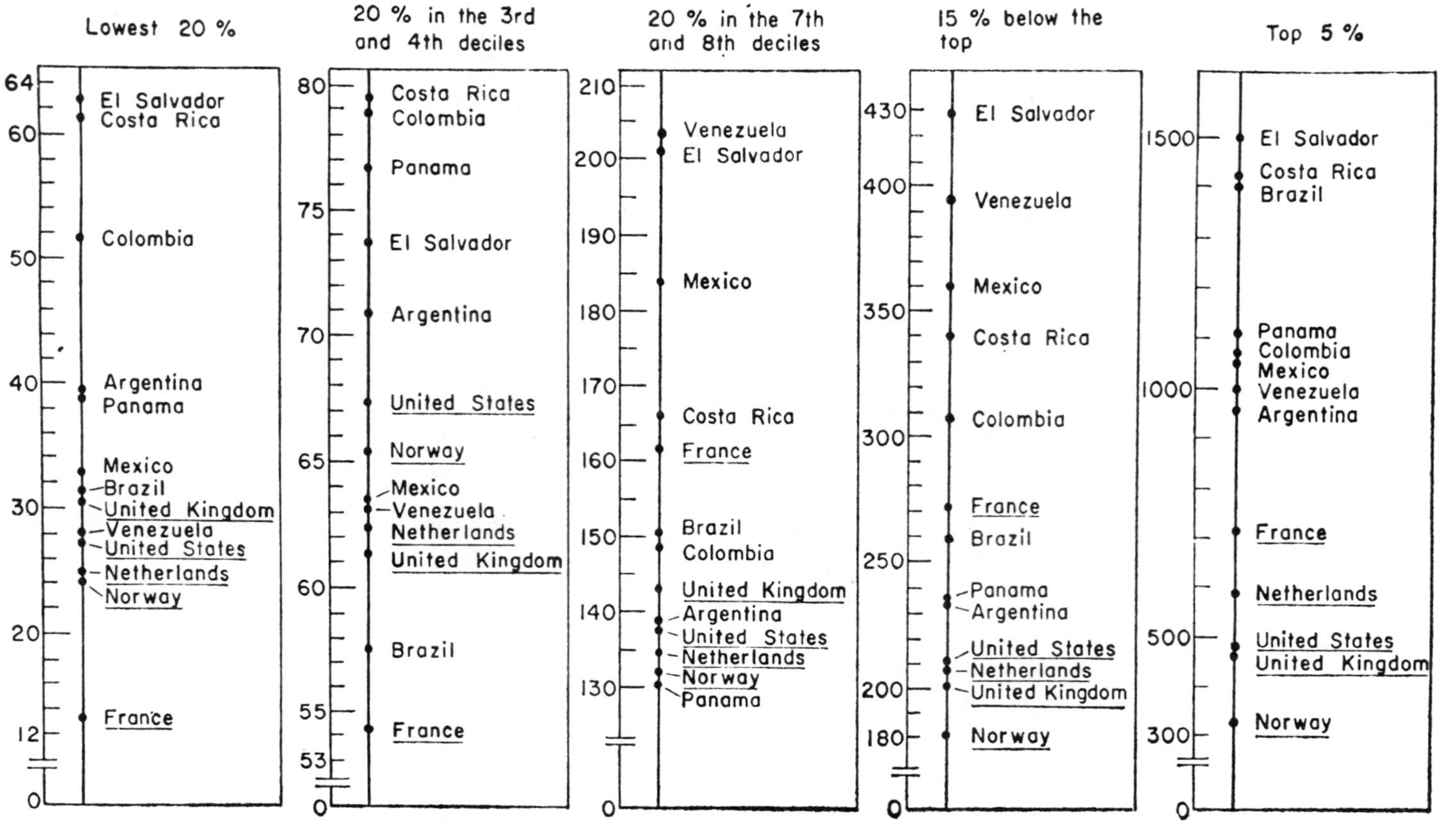

SOURCE: U.N. ECLA, *Income Distribution in Latin America* (New York: United Nations, 1971), p. 15.

BIBLIOGRAPHY

CHAPTER 1. INTRODUCTION: MODELS, METHODS, AND HISTORICAL STUDY

Adelman, Irma
1961 *Theories of Economic Growth.* Stanford, Calif.: Stanford University Press.

Ames, Edward & Rosenberg, Nathan
1965 "The Progressive Division and Specialization of Industries," *Journal of Development Studies* 1: 363-383.

Ashcraft, Richard
1972 "Marx and Weber on Liberalism as Bourgeois Ideology," *Comparative Studies in Society and History* 14: 130-168.

Averitt, Robert T.
1962 *The Dual Economy.* New York: Norton.

Baldwin, Robert E.
1966 *Economic Development and Growth.* New York: Wiley.

Baran, Paul & Sweezy, Paul
1966 *Monopoly Capital.* New York: Monthly Review Press.

Baumol, William J.
1967 "Macroeconomics of Unbalanced Growth: The Anatomy of Urban Crisis," *American Economic Review* 57: 415-426.

Bendix, Reinhard
1967 "Tradition and Modernity Reconsidered," *Comparative Studies in Society and History* 9: 292-346.

Benton, Ted
1977 *The Philosophical Foundations of the Three Sociologies.* London: Routledge & Kegan Paul.

Braverman, Harry
1974 *Labor and Monopoly Capital: The Degradation of Work in the Twentieth Century.* New York: Monthly Review.

Brenner, Robert
1977 "The Origin of Capitalist Development: A Critique of Neo-Smithian Marxism," *New Left Review* no. 104: 25-92.
Chandler, Alfred D., Jr.
1977 *The Visible Hand: The Managerial Revolution in American Business.* Cambridge, Mass.: Belknap Press of Harvard University Press.
1978 "The United States: Evolution of Enterprise," in Peter Mathias and M. M. Postan (eds.), *The Cambridge Economic History of Europe,* vol. 7, Pt. 2. Cambridge: Cambridge University Press.
Chenery, Hollis B. and Syrquin, Moises
1975 *Patterns of Development 1950-1970.* London: Oxford University Press.
Cortes Conde, Roberto and Stein, Stanley
1977 *Latin America: A Guide to Economic History, 1830-1930.* Berkeley: University of California Press.
Davis, Lance, *et al.*
1972 *American Economic Growth.* New York: Harper & Row.
Desai, Maghnad
1974 *Marxian Economic Theory.* London: Gray-Mills.
Dobb, Maurice
1955 "Historical Materialism and the Economic Factor," in his *On Economic Theory and Socialism: Collected Papers.* New York: International Publishers.
Dowd, Douglas
1974 *The Twisted Dream: Capitalist Development in the United States Since 1776.* Boston: Winthrop.
Edwards, Richard C.
1979 *Contested Terrain: The Transformation of the Workplace in the Twentieth Century.* New York: Basic Books.
Engels, Friedrich
1878 *Anti-Duhring.* Reprint ed., Moscow: Foreign Languages Publishing House, 1959.
1890 Letter to Conrad Schmidt (August 5), in Marx and Engels, *Selected Works in Two Volumes,* vol. 2. Moscow: Foreign Languages Publishing House, 1958.
1890/a, 1893, 1894 Letters to Schmidt, Bloch, Schmidt (1890); Mehring (1893); "Starkenburg" (1894), in Marx and Engels, *Selected Works in Two Volumes.* Moscow: Foreign Languages Publishing House.
Fogel, Robert W. & Engerman, Stanley
1975 *Time on the Cross,* 2 vols. Boston: Little, Brown.
Frank, Andre Gunder
1969 "Sociology of Development and the Underdevelopment of Sociology," in his *Latin America: Underdevelopment or Revolution.* New York: Monthly Review Press.
Friedman, Milton
1966 "The Methodology of Positive Economics," in his *Essays in Positive Economics.* Chicago: University of Chicago Press.

Furtado, Celso
1967 *Development and Underdevelopment.* Berkeley: University of California Press.
Genovese, Eugene D.
1968 "Marxian Interpretations of the Slave South," in B. J. Bernstein (ed.), *Towards a New Past: Dissenting Essays in American History.* New York: Pantheon Books.
Gordon, David M.
1972 *Theories of Poverty and Underemployment: Orthodix, Radical, and Dual Labor Market Perspectives.* Lexington, Mass.: D.C. Heath.
Harcourt, G. C.
1972 *Some Cambridge Controversies in the Theory of Capital.* Cambridge: Cambridge University Press.
Higgins, Benjamin
1968 *Economic Development.* New York: Norton.
Hirschman, Albert O.
1965 "Obstacles to Development: A Classification and Quasi-Vanishing Act," *Economic Development and Cultural Change* 13: 385-393.
1978 *The Strategy of Economic Development.* New York: Norton.
Hoselitz, Bert F.
1960 "Theories of Stages of Economic Growth," in B. Hoselitz, *et al.* (eds.), *Theories of Economic Growth.* New York: The Free Press.
Kemp, Tom
1978 *Historical Patterns of Industrialization.* New York: Longmans.
Kolko, Gabriel
1967 *Triumph of Conservatism: A Reinterpretation of American History, 1900-1916.* New York: Quadrangle Books.
Levine, David P.
1975 "The Theory of the Growth of the Capitalist Economy," *Economic Development and Cultural Change* 24: 47-74.
Lewis, W. Arthur
1954 "Economic Development with Unlimited Supplies of Labor," *Manchester School of Economic and Social Studies* 22: 139-191.
McCloskey, Donald N.
1978 "The Achievements of the Cliometric School," *Journal of Economic History* 38: 13-28.
McMurty, John
1978 *The Structure of Marx's World View.* Princeton, N.J.: Princeton University Press.
Marcuse, Herbert
1967 *One-Dimensional Man.* Boston: Beacon Press.
Marx, Karl
1848 "The Bourgeoisie and the Counter-Revolution," in Marx & Engels, *Selected Works in Two Volumes,* vol. 1. Moscow: Foreign Languages Publishing House, 1958.
1852 "The Eighteenth Brumaire of Louis Bonaparte," in Marx and Engels, *Selected Works in Two Volumes,* vol. 1. Moscow: Foreign

Languages Publishing House, 1958.
1857-1858 *Pre-Capitalist Economic Formations,* ed. E. J. Hobsbawm. New York: International Publishers, 1965.
1859 Preface to *A Contribution to the Critique of Political Economy,* in Marx & Engels, *Selected Works in Two Volumes,* vol. 1. Moscow: Foreign Languages Publishing House, 1958.
1867 *Capital,* vol. 1. Reprint ed., Moscow: Progress Publishers, 1965.
1894 *Capital,* vol. 3. Reprint ed., Moscow: Progress Publishers, 1965.

Marx, Karl & Engels, Friedrich
1846 *The German Ideology.* New York: International Publishers, 1966.

Meier, Gerald M. (ed.)
1964 *Leading Issues in Development Economics.* New York: Oxford University Press.
1970 *Leading Issues in Development Economics,* 2d ed. New York: Oxford University Press.

Miernyk, William H.
1965 *Elements of Input-Output Analysis.* New York: Random House.

Myint, Hla
1958 "The 'Classical Theory' of International Trade and the Underdeveloped Countries," *Economic Journal* 68: 317-338.

Nafziger, E. Wayne
1976 "A Critique of Development Economics in the U.S.," *Journal of Development Studies* 13, 18-34.

Nell, Edward J.
1967 "Theories of Growth and Theories of Value," *Economic Development and Cultural Change* 16: 15-26.
1972 "Property and the Means of Production: A Primer on the Cambridge Controversy," *Review of Radical Political Economics* 4: 1-27.
1972a "Two Books on the Theory of Income Distribution," *Journal Economic Literature* 10: 442-453.

North, Douglass
1965 "Industrialization in the United States," in H. J. Habbakuk and M. M. Postan (eds.), *The Cambridge Economic History of Europe,* vol. 6, Pt. 2. Cambridge: Cambridge University Press.
1978 "Structure and Performance: The Tasks of Economic History," *Journal of Economic Literature* 16: 963-978.

North, Douglass and Thomas, Robert P.
1970 "An Economic Theory of the Growth of the Western World," *Economic History Review* 23: 1-17.

Nutter, G. Warren and Einhorn, Henry A.
1969 *Enterprise Monopoly in the United States 1899-1958.* New York: Colombia University Press.

O'Conner, James
1973 *The Fiscal Crisis of the State.* New York: St. Martin's.

Okun, B. and Richardson, R. W.
1961 *Studies in Economic Development.* New York: Holt, Rinehart, & Winston.
Redlich, Fritz " 'New' and Traidtional Approaches to Economic History and
1965 Their Interdependence," *Journal of Economic History* 25: 430-495.
Rosenberg, Nathan
1963 "Capital Goods, Technology, and Economic Growth," *Oxford Economic Papers,* new series 15: 217-227.
1963a "Technological Change in the Machine Tool Industry, 1840-1910," *Journal of Economic History* 23: 414-443.
Rostow, Walter W.
1960 *The Stages of Economic Growth.* Cambridge: Cambridge University Press.
Solow, Robert and Temin, Peter
1978 "Introduction: The Inputs to Growth," in Peter Mathias and M. M. Postan (eds.), *The Cambridge Economic History of Europe,* vol. 7, Pt. 1, Cambridge: Cambridge University Press.
Stone, Lawrence
1977 "History and the Social Sciences in the Twentieth Century," in C. F. Delzell (ed.), *The Future of History.* Nashville, Tenn.: Vanderbilt University Press.
Supple, Barry
1963 "Introduction: Economic History, Economic Theory, and Economic Growth," in B. Supple (ed.), *The Experience of Economic Growth.* New York: Random House.
Survey of Current Business
1974 "The Input-Output Structure of the U.S. Economy, 1967," 54, 2, 24-56.
Sutcliffe, R. B.
1971 *Industry and Underdevelopment.* London: Addison-Wesley.
Sweezy, Paul
1964 *The Theory of Capitalist Development.* New York: Monthly Review Press.
Swingewood, Alan
1975 *Marx and Modern Social Theory.* New York: Halsted Press.
Tipps, Dean
1973 "Modernization Theory and the Study of National Societies: A Critical Perspective," *Comparative Studies in Society and History* 15: 199-226.
Trotsky, Leon
1932 *The History of the Russian Revolution,* vol. 1. New York: Simon & Schuster.
Toulmin, Stephen
1961 *Foresight and Understanding: An Enquiry into the Aims of Science.* New York and Evanston, Ill.: Harper & Row.

U.S. Department of Commerce
1975 *Historical Statistics of the United States, Colonial Times to 1970,* Part 2. Washington, D.C.: Government Printing Office.
Vatter, Harold
1967 "Has There Been a Twentieth-Century Consumer Durables Revolution?" *Journal of Economic History* 27: 1-16.
1978 *The Drive to Industrial Maturity.* Westport, Conn.: Greenwood Press.
Weaver, Frederick Stirton
1978 "*Cui Bono?* and the Economic Function of Racism," *Review of Black Political Economy* 8, no. 3: 302-313.
Weinstein, James
1968 *The Corporate Ideal in the Liberal State: 1900-1918.* Boston: Beacon Press.
Wolman, Leo
1924 *The Growth of American Trade Unions, 1880-1923.* New York: National Bureau of Economic Research.
Yan, Chiou-shuang
1969 *Introduction to Input-Output Economics.* New York: Holt, Rinehart, & Winston.
Yotopoulos, Pan and Nugent, Jeffrey B.
1976 *Economics of Development: Empirical Investigations.* New York: Harper & Row.

CHAPTER 2. THE DYNAMICS OF CAPITALIST INDUSTRIAL DEVELOPMENT, 1750-1914

Abegglen, James C.
1958 *The Japanese Factory: Aspects of its Social Organization.* Glencoe, Ill.: Free Press.
Ashworth, William W.
1960 *An Economic History of England, 1870-1939.* New York: Barnes & Noble.
1962 *A Short History of the International Economy Since 1850,* 2d ed. London: Longmans.
Bairoch, Paul
1973 "Agriculture and the Industrial Revolution 1700 - 1914," in C. Cipolla (ed.), *The Fontana Economic History of Europe,* Vol. 3. London: Fontana Books.
Barkin, Kenneth D.
1970 *The Controversy Over German Industrialization, 1890-1902.* Chicago: University of Chicago Press.
Barratt Brown, Michael
1974 *The Economics of Imperialism.* Baltimore: Penguin Books.
Bergier, J. F.
1973 "The Industrial Bourgeoisie and the Rise of the Working Class,

1700-1914," in C. Cipolla (ed.), *The Fontana Economic History of Europe,* Vol. 3. London: Fontana Books.

Borchadt, Knut
1973 "Germany 1700-1914," in C. Cipolla (ed.), *The Fontana Economic History of Europe,* Vol. 4, pt. 1. London: Fontana Books.

Brenner, Robert
1977 "The Origin of Capitalist Development: A Critique of Neo-Smithian Marxism," *New Left Review* no. 104: 116-192.

Brutzkus, Boris
1966 "The Historical Peculiarities of the Social and Economic Development of Russia," in R. Bendix & S. M. Lipset (eds.), *Class, Status, and Power.* New York: Free Press.

Crisp, Olga
1967 "Russia, 1860-1914," in R. Cameron *et al., Banking in The Early Stages of Industrialization,* London: Oxford University Press.
1978 "Labour and Industrialization in Russia," in Peter Mathias and M. M. Postan (eds.), *The Cambridge Economic History of Europe,* Vol. 7, pt. 2. Cambridge: Cambridge University Press.

Crouzet, F.
1972 *Capital Formation in the Industrial Revolution.* New York: Barnes & Noble.

Dahrendorf, Ralf
1969 *Society and Democracy in Germany.* Garden City, N.Y.: Anchor Books.

Deane, Phyllis
1967 *The First Industrial Revolution,* 2d ed. Cambridge: Cambridge University Press.

Deane, Phyllis and Cole, W. A.
1969 *British Economic Growth, 1688-1959.* Cambridge: Cambridge University Press.

Feis, Herbert
1930 *Europe: The World's Banker, 1870-1914.* Reprint ed., New York: W. W. Norton, 1965.

Gatrell, V. A. C.
1977 "Labour, Power, and the Size of Firms in Lancashire Cotton in the Second Quarter of the Nineteenth Century," *Economic History Review* 30, no. 1 (February): 95-139.

Geertz, Clifford
1963 *Peddlers and Princes.* Chicago: University of Chicago Press.

Gerschenkron, Alexander
1943 *Bread and Democracy in Germany.* Berkeley: University of California Press.
1965 "Agrarian Policies and Industrialization, Russia, 1861-1914," in H. J. Habbakuk and M. M. Postan (eds.), *Cambridge Economic History of Europe,* Vol. 6, Part 2, Cambridge: Cambridge University Press.

1966 *Economic Backwardness in Historical Perspective,* Cambridge, Mass.: Harvard University Press.

Gillis, John R.
1965 "Aristocracy and Bureaucracy in Nineteenth-Century Prussia," *Past and Present* 41 (November): 105-129.

Goldsmith, Raymond W.
1961 "The Economic Growth of Tsarist Russia, 1860-1913," *Economic Development and Cultural Change* 9: 441-475.

Kaser, M. C.
1978 "Russian Entrepreneurship," in Peter Mathias and M. M. Postan (eds.), *The Cambridge Economic History of Europe,* Vol. 7, pt. 2. Cambridge: Cambridge University Press.

Kemp, Tom
1967 *Theories of Imperialism.* London: Dobson.

Kent, George O.
1978 *Bismarck and His Times.* Carbondale, Ill.: Southern Illinois University Press.

Kocka, Jurgen
1978 "Entrepreneurs and Managers in German Industrialization," in Peter Mathias and M. M. Postan (eds.), *The Cambridge Economic History of Europe,* vol. 7, pt. 1. Cambridge: Cambridge University Press.

Komlos, John
1978 "The Kreditbanken and German Growth: A Postscript," *Journal of Economic History* 38: 476-479.

Landes, David S.
1965 "Japan and Europe: Contrasts in Industrialization," in W. W. Lockwood (ed.), *State and Economic Enterprise in Japan.* Princeton, N.J.: Princeton University Press.
1966 "The Structure of Enterprise in the Nineteenth Century: The Case of Britain and Germany." Reprinted in D. S. Landes (ed.), *The Rise of Capitalism.* New York: Macmillan.
1969 *The Unbound Prometheus.* Cambridge: Cambridge University Press.

Lazonick, William
1974 "Karl Marx and Enclosures in England," *Review of Radical Political Economy* 6, no. 2: 1-59.

Lebovics, Herman
1967 " 'Agrarians' vs. 'Industrializers', Social Conservative Resistance to Industrialism and Capitalism in Late Nineteenth Century Germany," *International Review of Social History* 12: 31-65.

Haimson, Leopold
1964 and 1965 "The Problem of Social Stability in Urban Russia," pts. 1 and 2, *Slavic Review* 23 and 24, 619-642 and 1-23.

Hamerow, Theodore S.
1958 *Restoration, Revolution, Reaction: Economics and Politics in Germany, 1815-1871.* Princeton, N.J.: Princeton University Press.
1969 *The Social Foundations of German Unification, 1858-1871.* Princeton, N.J.: Princeton University Press.

Henderson, W. O.
1954 *Britain and Industrial Europe, 1750-1870.* Liverpool: Liverpool University Press.
1975 *The Rise of German Industrial Power, 1834-1914.* Berkeley: University of California Press.
Hobsbawm, Eric J.
1964 "The Labour Aristocracy in Nineteenth Century Britain," in his *Labouring Men: Studies in the History of Labour.* London: Weidenfeld & Hicolson.
Hobsbawm, Eric J. and Hartwell, R. M.
1963 "The Standard of Living During the Industrial Revolution: A Discussion," *Economic History Review* 16: 119-146.
Hobson, John A.
1902 *Imperialism: A Study.* Reprint ed., Ann Arbor, Mich.: University of Michigan Press, 1965.
Hoffman, Walther G.
1965 *Das Wachstum der Deutschen Wirtschaft Seit der Mitte des 19.* Jahrhunderts. Berlin: Springer-Verlag.
Jones, E. L.
1975 *Agriculture and the Industrial Revolution.* New York: Halstead Press.
Kahan, Arcadius
1967 "Government Policies and the Industrialization of Russia," *Journal of Economic History* 27: 460-477.
1968 "Nineteenth Century European Experience with Policies of Economic Nationalism," in H. G. Johnson (ed)., *Economic Nationalism in Old and New States.* London: George Allen Unwin.
Lenin, V. I.
1917 *Imperialism, The Highest Stage of Capitalism.* Reprint ed., Peking: Foreign Languages Press, 1965.
Luxemburg, Rosa
1913 *The Accumulation of Capital.* Reprint ed., New York: Monthly Review Press, 1964.
Lyaschchenko, P.
1949 *The History of the National Economy of Russia to the 1917 Revolution.* New York: Macmillan.
MacDonough, Oliver
1977 *Early Victorian Government, 1830-1870.* New York: Holmes & Meier.
McKay, John P.
1970 *Pioneers for Profit: Foreign Entrepreneurship in Russian Industrialization, 1885-1913.* Chicago: University of Chicago Press.
Mantoux, Paul
1961 *The Industrial Revolution in the Eighteenth Century,* Rev. ed. New York: Harper & Row.
Marglin, Stephen A.
1974 "What Do Bosses Do? The Origins and Functions of Hierarchy in

Capitalist Production," *Review of Radical Political Economics* 6, no. 2: 60-112.

Marx, Karl
1848 "The Bourgeoisie and the Counter-Revolution," in Marx and Engels, *Selected Works in Two Volumes.* Moscow: Foreign Languages Publishing House, 1958.
1857-1858 *Grundrisse.* Reprint ed.: New York: Vintage, 1973.
1867 *Capital,* Vol. 1. Reprint ed., Moscow: Progress Publishers, 1965.

Maschke, E.
1969 "Outline of the History of German Cartels, 1873 to 1914." Reprinted in F. Crouzet, W. H. Chaioner, & W. M. Stern (eds.), *Essays in European Economic History, 1789-1914.* London: St. Martin's Press.

Milward, Alan S. and Saul, S. B.
1977 *The Development of the Economies of Continental Europe, 1840-1914.* Cambridge, Mass.: Harvard University Press.

Mitrany, David
1961 *Marx Against the Peasant.* New York: Collier Books.

Moore, Barrington
1966 *Social Origins of Dictatorship and Democracy.* Boston: Beacon Press.

Owen, Roger and Sutcliffe, Bob (eds.)
1972 *Studies in the Theory of Imperialism.* London: Longman.

Pollard, Sidney
1968 *The Genesis of Modern Management.* Baltimore, Md.: Penguin.
1978 "Labour in Great Britain," in Peter Mathias and M. M. Postan (eds.), *The Cambridge Economic History of Europe,* Vol. 7, pt. 1. Cambridge: Cambridge University Press.

Portal, Roger
1965 "The Industrialization of Russia," in H. J. Habbakuk and M. M. Postan (eds.), *The Cambridge Economic History of Europe,* Vol. 6, pt. 2. Cambridge: Cambridge University Press.

Rimlinger, Gaston V.
1960 "Autocracy and the Factory Order in Early Russian Industrialization," *Journal of Economic History* 20: 67-92.
1971 *Welfare Policy and Industrialization in Europe, America, and Russia.* New York: Wiley.

Robinson, Geroid T.
1932 *Rural Russia Under the Old Regime.* London: Longmans, Green.

Rogger, Hans
1961-1962 "Nationalism and the State: A Russian Dilemma," *Comparative Studies in Society and History* 4: 253-264.

Sagarra, Eda
1977 *A Social History of Germany, 1648-1914.* New York: Holmes & Meier.

Semmel, Bernard
1970 *The Rise of Free Trade Imperialism: Classical Political Economy, the Empire of Free Trade and Imperialism, 1750-1850.* Cambridge: Cambridge University Press.

Stolper, Gustav, *et al.*
1967 *The German Economy, 1870 to the Present.* New York: Harcourt, Brace, & World.

Szeftel, Marc
1963 "The Form of Government of the Russian Empire Prior to the Constitutional Reforms of 1905-1906," in J. S. Curtiss (ed.), *Essays in Russian and Soviet History in Honor of Geroid Tanquery Robinson.* New York: Columbia University Press.

Thompson, Edward P.
1963 *The Making of the English Working Class.* New York: Vintage.

Tilly, Richard
1956 "The Political Economy of Public Finance and the Industrialization of Prussia, 1815-1866," *Journal of Economic History* 26: 484-497.
1967 "Germany: 1815-1870," in Rondo Cameron, *et al., Banking in the Early Stages of Industrialization.* London: Oxford University Press.

von Laue, Theodore H.
1960-1961 "Imperial Russia at the Turn of the Century: The Cultural Slope and the Revolution from Without," *Comparative Studies in Society and History* 3: 352-367.
1963 "On the Crises of the Russian Polity," in J. S. Curtiss (ed.), *Essays in Russian and Soviet History in Honor of Geroid Tanquery Robinson.* New York: Colombia University Press.

von Tunzelmann, G. N.
1979 "Trends in Real Wages, 1750-1850, Revisited," *Economic History Review* 32: 33-49.

Weaver, Frederick Stirton
1976 "Capitalist Development, Empire, and Latin American Underdevelopment, An Interpretive Essay on Historical Changes," *Latin American Perspectives* 3, no. 4 (Fall): 17-53.
1978 "*Cui Bono?* and the Economic Function of Racism," *Review of Black Political Economy* 8, no. 3 (Spring): 302-313.

Wehler, Hans-Ulrich
1969 *Bismarck und der Imperialismus.* Cologne: Kiepenheuer U. Witsch.
1970 "Bismarck's Imperialism, 1862-1890," *Past and Present* 48: 119-155.

Wilson, Charles H.
1967 "Trade, Society, and the State," in E. E. Rich and C. H. Wilson (eds.), *The Cambridge Economic History of Europe,* Vol. 4. Cambridge: Cambridge University Press.

Wunderlich, Frieda
1961 *Farm Labor in Germany 1810-1945: Its Historical Development Within the Framework of Agricultural and Social Policy.* Princeton, N.J.: Princeton University Press.
Yamey, George L.
1965 "Social Stability in Pre-Revolutionary Russia: A Critical Note," *Slavic Review* 24: 521-527.

CHAPTER 3. POLITICAL INDEPENDENCE IN LATIN AMERICA, 1750-1860

Ashcraft, Richard
1972 "Marx and Weber on Liberalism as Bourgeois Ideology," *Comparative Studies in Society and History* 14: 130-168.
Aubrey, H. B.
1949 "Deliberate Industrialization," *Social Research* 16: 158-182.
Barbier, Jacques A.
1977 "The Culmination of the Bourbon Reforms, 1787-1792," *Hispanic American Historical Review* 57: 51-68.
Bauer, Arnold
1971 "The Church and Spanish American Agrarian Structure: 1765-1865," *The Americas* 28: 78-99.
Bowser, F. P.
1972 "The African in Colonial Spanish America: Reflection on Research Achievements and Priorities," *Latin American Research Review* 7: 77-94.
Brading, Donald A.
1971 *Miners and Merchants in Colonial Mexico, 1763-1810.* Cambridge: Cambridge University Press.
1973 "Government and Elite in Late Colonial Mexico," *Hispanic American Historical Review* 53: 389-415.
Burgin, Myron
1946 *The Economic Aspects of Argentine Federalism, 1820-1852.* Cambridge, Mass.: Harvard University Press.
Bushnell, David
1956 "Two Stages in Colombian Tariff Policy: The Radical Era and the Return to Protection (1861-1885)," *Inter-American Economic Affairs* 9: 3-23.
Campbell, Leon G.
1979 "Recent Research on Andean Peasant Revolts, 1750-1820," *Latin American Research Review* 14: 3-50.
Cooney, John Hoyt
1972 "Paraguayan Isolation under Dr. Francia: A Reëvaluation," *HAHR* 52: 102-122.
Dean, Warren
1971 "Latifundia and Land Policy in Nineteenth Century Brazil," *HAHR* 51: 606-625.

di Tella, Tocuato S.
1973 "The Dangerous Classes in Early Nineteenth Century Mexico," *Journal of Latin American Studies* 5: 79-105.
Emmanuel, Arghiri
1972 *Unequal Exchange: A Study of the Imperialism of Trade.* New York: Monthly Review Press.
Engels, Friedrich
1884 "The Origin of the Family, Private Property, and the State," in Marx and Engels, *Selected Works in Two Volumes,* Vol. 2. Moscow: Foreign Languages Publishing House, 1958.
Ferrer, Aldo
1967 *The Argentine Economy: An Economic History of Argentina.* Berkeley: University of California Press.
Foster, George
1960 *Culture and Conquest: America's Spanish Heritage.* New York: Quadrangle Books.
Frank, Andre Gunder
1972 *Lumpenbourgeoisie: Lumpendevelopment.* New York: Monthly Review Press.
Furtado, Celso
1963 *The Economic Growth of Brazil,* Berkeley: University of California Press.
1976 *Economic Development of Latin America,* 2d ed. Cambridge: Cambridge University Press.
Galloway, J. H.
1971 "The Last Years of Slavery on the Sugar Plantations of Northeastern Brazil," *HAHR* 51: 586-605.
Gibson, Charles C.
1966 *Spain in America.* New York: Harper & Row.
Graham, Richard
1972 *Independence in Latin America: A Comparative Approach.* New York: Knopf.
Griffin, Charles C.
1949 "Economic and Social Aspects of the Era of Spanish American Independence," *HAHR* 29: 170-187.
Hale, Charles A.
1973 "The Reconstruction of Nineteenth Century Politics in Spanish America: A Case for the History of Ideas," *Latin American Research Review* 8: 53-73.
Halperin-Donghi, Tulio
1973 *The Aftermath of Revolution in Latin America.* New York: Harper & Row.
Hamnett, Brian R.
1969 "The Appropriation of Mexican Church Wealth by the Spanish Bourbon Government: 'The Consolidación de Vales Reales', 1805-1809," *Journal of Latin American Studies* 1: 85-113.
1971 *Politics and Trade in Southern Mexico, 1750-1821.* Cambridge:

Cambridge University Press.

Haring, Clarence H.
1963 *The Spanish Empire in America.* New York: Harcourt, Brace, Jovanovich.

Harrison, John P.
1952 "The Evolution of the Colombian Tobacco Trade to 1875," *HAHR* 32: 163-174.

Humphreys, Robin A. and Lynch, John
1965 "Introduction" to Humphreys and Lynch (eds.), *Origins of the Latin American Revolutions, 1808-1826.* New York: Borzoi Books.

Johnson, John J.
1958 *Political Change in Latin America.* Stanford, Calif.: Stanford University Press.
1964 *Military and Society in Latin America.* Stanford, Calif.: Stanford University Press.

Keith, Robert G.
1971 "Encomienda, Hacienda and Corregimiento in Spanish America: A Structural Analysis," *HAHR* 51: 431-446.

Lockhart, James
1968 *Spanish Peru, 1532-1560.* Madison, Wisc.: University of Wisconsin Press.
1972 "The Social History of Colonial Spanish America," *Latin American Research Review* 7: 6-45.

Luxemburg, Rosa
1913 *The Accumulation of Capital.* Reprint ed., New York: Monthly Review Press, 1964.

Lynch, John
1973 *The Spanish American Revolution, 1808-1826.* New York: W. W. Norton.

Marx, Karl
1852 "The Eighteenth Brumaire of Louis Bonaparte," in Marx and Engels, *Selected Works in Two Volumes,* Vol. 1. Moscow: Foreign Languages Publishing House.

Marx, Karl & Engels, Friedrich
1846 *The German Ideology.* Reprint ed., New York: International Publishers, 1966.

Meade, Teresa
1978 "The Transition to Capitalism in Brazil: Notes on a Third Road," *Latin American Perspectives* 5: 7-26.

Mitrany, David
1930 *The Land and the Peasant in Rumania.* Reprint ed., New York: Greenwood Press, 1968.

Moore, Barrington
1966 *Social Origins of Dictatorship and Democracy.* Boston: Beacon Press.

Mörner, Magnus
1967 *Race Mixture in the History of Latin America.* Boston: Little, Brown.

1973 "The Spanish American Hacienda: A Survey of Recent Research and Debate," *HAHR* 53: 183-216.

Morse, Richard M.
1954 "Toward a Theory of Spanish American Government," *Journal of the History of Ideas* 15: 71-93.
1964 "The Heritage of Latin America," in L. Hartz (ed.), *The Founding of New Societies.* New York: Harcourt, Brace & World.

Mosk, Sanford
1948 "Latin America and the World Economy, 1850-1914," *Inter-American Economic Affairs* 2: 53-82.

Parry, John H.
1971 *The Spanish Seaborne Empire.* New York: Knopf.

Phelan, J. H.
1960 "Authority and Flexibility in the Spanish Imperial Bureaucracy," *Administrative Science Quarterly* 5: 47-65.
1978 *The People and the King: The Comunero Revolution in Colombia, 1781,* Madison, Wisc.: University of Wisconsin Press.

Platt, D. C. M.
1968 *Finance, Trade, and Politics in British Foreign Policy, 1815-1914.* London: Oxford University Press.

Potash, Robert A.
1959 *El Banco de Avío de México: el fomento de la indústria, 1821-1846.* Mexico City: Fondo de Cultura Económica.

Rippy, J. Fred
1959 *British Investments in Latin America, 1822-1949,* Minneapolis, Minn.: University of Minnesota Press.

Rowe, John H.
1957 "The Incas Under Spanish Colonial Institutions," *HAHR* 37: 155-199.

Safford, Frank
1965 "Foreign and National Enterprise in Nineteenth Century Colombia," *The Business History Review* 39: 503-526.
1972 "Social Aspects of Politics in Nineteenth-Century Latin America: New Granada, 1825-1850," *Journal of Social History* 5: 344-370.

Seckinger, Ron L.
1977 "Interpreting Brazilian Independence," *Latin American Research Review* 12: 228-231.

Service, E. R.
1955 "Indian-European Relations in Colonial Latin America," *American Anthropologist* 57: 411-425.

Smith, Peter
Politics and Beef in Argentina: Patterns of Conflict and Change. New York: Columbia University Press.

Spalding, Karen
1972 "The Colonial Indian: Past and Future Research Perspectives," *Latin American Research Review* 7: 47-76.

Stein, Stanley J. & Stein, Barbara
1970 *The Colonial Heritage of Latin America: Essays on Economic*

Dependence in Perspective. New York: Oxford University Press.

Toulmin, Stephen
1961 *Foresight and Understanding: An Enquiry into the Aims of Science.* New York: Harper & Row.

Urrutia, Miguel
1969 *The Development of the Colombian Labor Movement.* New Haven, Conn.: Yale University Press.

Vicens Vives, Jaime
1969 *An Economic History of Spain.* Princeton, N.J.: Princeton University Press.

Weaver, Frederick Stirton
1976 "Capitalist Development, Empire, and Latin American Underdevelopment: An Interpretive Essay on Historical Change," *Latin American Perspectives* 3: 17-53.

Wilson, Charles H.
1967 "Trade, Society and the State," in E. E. Rich & C. H. Wilson (eds.), *Cambridge Economic History of Europe,* Vol. 4. Cambridge: Cambridge University Press.

Wolf, Eric
1959 *Sons of the Shaking Earth.* Chicago: University of Chicago Press.

CHAPTER 4. LATIN AMERICA IN THE INTERNATIONAL DIVISION OF LABOR, 1840-1914

Amin, Samir
1974 *Accumulation on a World Scale: A Critique of the Theory of Underdevelopment.* New York: Monthly Review Press.

Baldwin, Robert E.
1956 "Patterns of Development in Newly Settled Regions," *Manchester School of Economic and Social Studies* 24: 161-179.
1963 "Export Technology and Development from a Subsistence Level," *Economic Journal* 73: 80-92.
1966 *Economic Development and Export Growth: A Study of Northern Rhodesia, 1920-1960.* Berkeley: University of California Press.

Baran, Paul
1952 "On the Political Economy of Backwardness," *The Manchester School of Economic and Social Studies* 20: 66-84.
1962 *The Political Economy of Growth.* New York: Monthly Review Press.

Bath, C. Richard and James, Kilmus D.
1976 "Dependency Analysis of Latin America," *Latin American Research Review* 11: 3-54.

Bauer, Arnold
1971 "Chilean Rural Labor in the Nineteenth Century," *American Historical Review* 76: 1059-1083.

Berg, Ronald and Weaver, Frederick S.
1978 "Towards a Reinterpretation of Political Change in Peru During

the First Century of Independence," *Journal of Inter-American Studies and World Affairs* 20: 69-84.

Berquist, Charles
1978 *Coffee and Conflict in Colombia, 1886-1910.* Durham, N.C.: Duke University Press.

Bertram, Gordon W.
1959 "Economic Growth in Canadian Industry, 1879-1915: The Staple Model and the Take-off Hypothesis," *Canadian Journal of Economics and Political Science* 29: 393-414.

Blakemore, Harold
1965 "The Chilean Revolution of 1891 and its Historiography," *HAHR* 45: 393-422.

Buckley, Kenneth
1958 "The Role of Staple Industries in Canada's Economic Development," *Journal of Economic History* 18: 439-450.

Cairncross, A. K.
1961 "International Trade and Economic Development," *Economica,* new series, 28: 235-251.

Cardoso, Fernando H.
1977 "The Consumption of Dependency Theory in the U.S.," *Latin American Research Review* 12: 7-24.

Cardoso, Fernando H. and Faletto, Enzo
1979 *Dependency and Development in Latin America.* Berkeley: University of California Press.

Caves, Richard E.
1965 " 'Vent for Surplus' Models of Trade and Growth," in R. E. Baldwin, *et al.* (eds.), *Trade, Growth and Balance of Payments.* Chicago: Rand McNally.
1971 "The Export-Led Growth Model as a Research Tool in Economic History," in J. Bhagwati *et al.* (eds.), *Trade, Balance of Payments and Growth.* Amsterdam: North Holland.

Caves, Richard E. and Holton, R. H.
1959 *The Canadian Economy.* Cambridge, Mass.: Harvard University Press.

Caves, Richard E. and Johnson, Harry G. (eds.)
1968 *Readings in International Economics.* Homewood, Ill.: R. D. Irwin for the American Economics Association.

Chenery, Hollis and Strout, A. M.
1966 "Foreign Assistance and Economic Development," *American Economic Review* 57: 701-729.

Chilcote, R. H. and Edelstein, J. C. (eds.)
1974 *Latin America: The Struggle with Dependency and Beyond.* Cambridge, Mass.: Schenken.

Corradi, Juan E.
1974 "Argentina," in R. H. Chilcote & J. C. Edelstein (eds.) *Latin America.* Cambridge, Mass.: Schenken.

Cueva, Augustin
1976 "A Summary of 'Problems and Perspectives on Dependency Theory,' " *Latin American Perspectives* 3: 12-16.
Dean, Warren
1969 *The Industrialization of São Paulo, 1880-1945.* Austin, Tex.: University of Texas Press.
Diaz Alejandro, Carlos F.
1970 *Essays on the Economic History of the Argentine Republic.* New Haven, Conn.: Yale University Press.
Dowd, Douglas F.
1956 "A Comparative Analysis of Economic Development in the American West and South," *Journal of Economic History* 16: 558-574.
Emmanuel, Arghiri
1972 *Unequal Exchange: A Study of the Imperialism of Trade.* New York: Monthly Review Press.
Fagen, Richard M.
1977 "Studying Latin American Politics: Some Implications of a *Dependencia* Approach," *Latin American Research Review* 12: 3-26.
Ferns, H. S.
1960 *Britain and Argentina in the Nineteenth Century.* Oxford: Clarendon Press.
Ferrer, Aldo
1967 *The Argentine Economy.* Berkeley: University of California Press.
Findlay, R. E.
1973 *International Trade and Development Theory.* New York: Columbia University Press.
Flanders, M. June
1964 "Prebisch on Protectionism: An Evaluation," *Economic Journal* 74: 305-326.
Frank, Andre Gunder
1964 "On the Mechanics of Imperialism: The Case of Brazil," *Monthly Review* 16: 284-297.
1967 "Capitalist Development of Underdevelopment in Chile," in his *Capitalism and Underdevelopment in Latin America.* New York: Monthly Review Press.
Furtado, Celso
1965 *The Economic Growth of Brazil.* Berkeley: University of California Press.
1976 *Economic Development of Latin America,* 2d ed. Cambridge: Cambridge University Press.
Gallagher, John and Robinson, Ronald
1953 "The Imperialism of Free Trade," *The Economic History Review,* 2d series , 6: 1-15.
Geertz, Clifford
1963 *Agricultural Involution.* Berkeley: University of California Press.

Genovese, Eugene
1967 *The Political Economy of Slavery.* New York: Vintage Books.
Goodrich, Carter
1964-1965 "Argentina as a New Country," *Comparative Studies in Society and History* 7: 70-88.
Greenhill, R. G. and Miller, R. M.
1973 "The Peruvian Government and the Nitrate Trade, 1873-1879," *Journal of Latin American Studies* 5: 107-131.
Haberler, Gottfried
1959 *International Trade and Economic Development.* Cairo: National Bank of Egypt.
Hanke, Lewis (ed.)
1964 *Do the Americas Have a Common History? A Critique of the Bolton Thesis.* New York: Borzoi Books.
Hanson, Simon
1938 *Argentine Meat and the British Market.* Stanford, Calif.: Stanford University Press.
Hartz, Louis
1964 "United States History in a New Perspective," in his *The Founding of New Societies.* New York: Harcourt.
Helleiner, G. K.
1972 *International Trade and Economic Development.* London: Penguin Books.
Hicks, John R.
1959 *Essays in World Economics.* Oxford: Clarendon Press.
Hirschman, Albert O.
1958 *The Strategy of Economic Development.* New Haven, Conn.: Yale University Press.
1977 "A Generalized Linkage Approach to Development, With Special Reference to Staples," in M. Nash (ed.), *Essays on Economic Development and Cultural Change, in Honor of Bert F. Hoselitz.* Chicago: University of Chicago Press.
Hymer, Steven H. and Resnick, Steven A.
1971 "International Trade and Uneven Development," in J. Bhagwati (ed.), *Trade, Balance of Payments and Growth.* Amsterdam: North Holland.
Jalee, Pierre
1969 *The Pillage of the Third World.* New York: Monthly Review Press.
Johnson, Harry G.
1962 *Money, Trade, and Economic Growth.* Cambridge, Mass.: Harvard University Press.
Keith, Robert G.
1977 *Haciendas and Plantations in Latin American History.* New York: Holmes & Meier.
Kindleberger, Charles P.
1951 "Group Behavior and International Trade," *Journal of Political Economy* 59: 30-47.

Kirsch, Henry W.
1977 *Industrial Development in a Traditional Society: The Conflict of Entrepreneurship and Modernization in Chile.* Gainsville, Fla.: University of Florida Press.

Kuhn, Thomas S.
1962 *The Structure of Scientific Revolutions.* Chicago: University of Chicago Press.

Levin, Jonathan V.
1960 *The Export Economies: Their Pattern of Development in Historical Perspective.* Cambridge, Mass.: Harvard University Press.

McGreevy, William P.
1971 *An Economic History of Colombia, 1845-1930.* Cambridge: Cambridge University Press.

Mamalakis, Markos
1971 "The Chilean Nitrate Sector, 1880-1930," in G. Ranis (ed.), *Government and Economic Development.* New Haven, Conn.: Yale University Press.
1976 *The Growth and Structure of the Chilean Economy: From Independence to Allende.* New Haven, Conn.: Yale University Press.

Marx, Karl
1867 *Capital,* Vol. 1. Reprint ed., Moscow: Progress Publishers, 1967.

Mathew, William M.
1970 "Peru and the British Guano Market, 1840-1870," *The Economic History Review,* 2d series, 23: 112-128.
1973 "Foreign Contractors and the Peruvian Government at the Outset of the Guano Trade," HAHR 52: 598-620.

Meier, Gerald M.
1968 *International Trade and Economic Development.* New York: Harper & Row.

Myint, Hla
1954-1955 "The Gains from International Trade and the Backward Countries," *The Review of Economic Studies* 22: 129-142.
1959 "The 'Classical Theory' of International Trade and the Underdeveloped Countries," *Economic Journal* 68: 317-337.

Nisbet, C. T.
1970 "Transferring Wealth from Underdeveloped to Developed Countries via Foreign Investment: A Marxist Claim Reconsidered," *Southern Economic Journal* 37: 93-96.
1971 "Reply," *Southern Economic Journal,* 38: 121-124.

North, Douglass C.
1961 *The Economic Growth of the United States, 1790 to 1860.* Englewood Cliffs, N.J.: Prentice-Hall.

Ortiz Fernández, Fernando
1947 *Cuban Counterpoint: Tobacco and Sugar.* New York: Knopf.

Perloff, Harvey and Wingo, Lowden
1961 "Natural Resource Endowment and Regional Economic Growth,"

in J. J. Spengler (ed.), *Natural Resources and Economic Growth.* Washington, D.C.: Resources for the Future.

Piel, J.
1970 "The Place of the Peasantry in the National Life of Peru in the Nineteenth Century," *Past & Present* 46: 108-133.

Pike, Frederick B.
1963 "Aspects of Class Relations in Chile, 1850-1960," *HAHR* 43: 14-43.
1963a *Chile and the United States, 1880-1962.* Notre Dame, Ind.: University of Notre Dame Press.
1967 *The Modern History of Peru.* New York: Praeger.

Powelson, John P.
1977 "The Strange Persistence of the 'Terms of Trade,' " *Inter-American Economic Affairs* 30: 17-28.

Pregger Román, Charles G.
1979 "Economic Interest Groups Within the Chilean Government, 1851-1891: Continuity and Discontinuity in Economic and Political Evolution," *Science and Society* 43: 202-332.

Quintana, Carlos (ed.)
1970 *Development Problems in Latin America.* Austin, Tex.: University of Texas Press.

Randall, Laura
1977 *An Economic History of Argentina in the Twentieth Century.* New York: Columbia University Press.

Ray, David
1973 "The Dependency Model of Latin American Underdevelopment: Three Basic Fallacies," *Journal of Inter-American Studies and World Affairs* 15: 4-20.

Ridings, Eugene W.
1978 "Class Sector Unity in an Export Economy: The Case of Nineteenth-Century Brazil," *HAHR* 58: 432-450.

Roemer, Michael
1970 *Fishing for Growth: Export-Led Development in Peru, 1950-1967.* Cambridge, Mass.: Harvard University Press.

Romero, Emilio
1967 *Historia económica del Perú,* 2d edition, Vol. 2. Lima: Editorial Universo.

Romero, Jose Luis
1963 *A History of Argentine Political Thought.* Stanford, Calif.: Stanford University Press.

Rubin, Vera (ed.)
1959 *Plantation Systems of the New World* (Seminar on Plantation Systems in the New World, San Juan, P.R., 1957). Washington, D.C.: Pan American Union.

Scobie, James R.
1964 *Revolution on the Pampas.* Austin, Tex.: University of Texas Press.
1971 *Argentina: A City and a Nation,* 2d edition. New York: Oxford

University Press.

Singer, Hans W.
1950 "The Distribution of Gains Between Investing and Borrowing Countries," *American Economic Review–Papers and Proceedings* 40: 473-485.

Smith, Peter
1969 *Politics and Beef in Argentina: Patterns of Conflict and Change.* New York: Columbia University Press.

Stein, Stanley J. and Stein, Barbara
1970 *The Colonial Heritage of Latin America: Essays on Economic Dependence in Perspective.* New York: Oxford University Press.

Sweezy, Paul
1967 "Obstacles to Economic Development," in C. Feinstein (ed.), *Socialism, Capitalism, and Economic Growth.* Cambridge: Cambridge University Press.

Thorp, Rosemary and Bertram, Geoffrey
1978 *Peru 1890-1977. Growth and Politics in an Open Economy.* New York: Columbia University Press.

Touraine, Alain and Pecaut, Daniel
1967-1968 "Working-Class Consciousness and Economic Development in Latin America," *Studies in Comparative International Development* 3. Reprinted in I. L. Horowitz (ed.), *Masses in Latin America.* New York: Oxford University Press, 1970.

Urrutia, Miguel
1969 *The Development of the Colombian Labor Movement.* New Haven, Conn.: Yale University Press.

Watkins, Melvin H.
1963 "A Staple Theory of Economic Growth," *Canadian Journal of Economics and Political Science* 29: 141-158.

Youngson, A. J.
1959 *Possibilities of Economic Progress.* Cambridge: Cambridge University Press.

CHAPTER 5. THE BEGINNINGS OF INDUSTRIAL GROWTH IN SOUTH AMERICA, 1900-1930

Alba, Victor
1968 *Politics and the Labor Movement in Latin America.* Stanford, Calif.: Stanford University Press.

Alexander, Robert J.
1962 *Labor Relations in Argentina, Brazil, and Chile.* New York: McGraw-Hill.
1965 *Organized Labor in Latin America.* New York: The Free Press.

Alonso, William
1964 "Location Theory," in J. Friedman & W. Alonso (eds.), *Regional Development and Planning.* Cambridge, Mass.: M.I.T. Press.

Ames, Edward and Rosenberg, Nathan
1965 "The Progressive Division and Specialization of Industries", *Journal of Development Studies* 1: 363-383.
Angell, Alan
1972 *Politics and the Labour Movement in Chile.* London: Oxford University Press.
Ashby, Joe C.
1967 *Organized Labor and the Mexican Revolution Under Lazaro Cardenas.* Chapel Hill, N.C.: University of North Carolina Press.
Baer, Werner
1965 *Industrialization and Economic Development in Brazil.* Homewood, Ill.: R. D. Irwin.
1979 *The Brazilian Economy: Its Growth and Development.* Columbus, Ohio: Grid Publishing Co.
Baerrenson, D. W., Carnoy, M., and Grunwald, J.
1965 *Latin American Trade Patterns.* Washington, D.C.: Brookings Institution.
Bailey, David C.
1978 "Revisionism and Recent Historiography of the Mexican Revolution," *HAHR* 58: 62-79.
Baily, Samuel L.
1967 *Labor, Nationalism, and Politics in Argentina.* New Brunswick, N.J.: Rutgers University Press.
Ballasteros, Martos and Davis, Tom E.
1963 "The Growth of Output and Employment in Basic Sectors of the Chilean Economy, 1908-1957," *Economic Development and Cultural Change* 11: 152-176.
Bauer, Arnold J.
1979 "Rural Workers in Spanish America: Problems of Peonage and Oppression," *HAHR* 59: 34-63.
Benvenuto, Luis C.
1967 *Breve historia del Uruguay: Economía y sociedad.* Buenos Aires: Eudeba Editorial Universitaria.
Blakemore, Harold and Smith, Clifford T.
1974 *Latin America: Geographical Perspectives.* London: Methuen.
Cardoso, Fernando H. and Faletto, Enzo
1979 *Dependency and Development in Latin America.* Berkeley: University of California Press.
Cavarozzi, Marcelo J. and Petras, James F.
1974 "Chile," in R. Chilcote & J. Edelstein (eds.), *Latin America: The Struggle with Dependency and Beyond.* New York: Schenkman.
Chevalier, Francois
1967 "The *Ejido* and Political Stability in Mexico," in C. Veliz (ed.), *The Politics of Conformity in Latin America.* London: Oxford University Press.
Cornblit, Oscar
1967 "European Immigrants in Argentine Industry and Politics," in

C. Veliz (ed.), *The Politics of Conformity in Latin America.* New York: Oxford University Press.

Cosio Villegas, Daniel (ed.)
1965 *Historia moderna de Mexico,* Vol. 7, pt. 1 and 2, *El porfiriato: La Vida económica.* Mexico, D.F.: Editorial Hermes.

Crevenna, Theodore (ed.)
1951 *Materiales para el estudio de la clase media en la América Latina,* 6 vols. Washington, D.C.: Pan American Union.

Cumberland, Charles C.
1968 *Mexico: The Struggle for Modernity.* New York: Oxford University Press.

Dean, Warren
1969 *The Industrialization of São Paulo, 1880-1945.* Austin, Tex.: University of Texas Press.

Diaz Alejandro, Carlos F.
1970 *Essays on the Economic History of the Argentine Republic.* New Haven, Conn.: Yale University Press.

Dulles, John W.
1974 *Anarchists and Communists in Brazil, 1900-1935.* Austin, Texas: University of Texas Press.

Dunn, John
1972 *Modern Revolutions.* Cambridge: Cambridge University Press.

Erickson, K. P., Peppe, P. V., Spalding, H. A.
1974 "Research on the Urban Working Class and Organized Labor in Argentina, Brazil, and Chile: What Is Left to Be Done?", *Latin American Research Review* 9: 115-142.

Ferrer, Aldo
1967 *The Argentine Economy.* Berkeley: University of California Press.

Furtado, Celso
1965 *Economic Growth of Brazil.* Berkeley: University of California Press.
1976 *Economic Development of Latin America,* 2d ed. Cambridge: Cambridge University Press.

Germani, Gino
1965 "The Transition to a Mass Democracy in Argentina," in D. B. Heath & R. N. Adams (eds.), *Contemporary Cultures and Societies of Latin America.* New York: Random House.
1968 "Transformation of the Social and Political Structure," in J. R. Barager (ed.), *Why Peron Came to Power.* New York: Knopf.

Glade, William P.
1969 *The Latin American Economies.* New York: Van Nostrand.

Goldfrank, Walter
1975 "World System, State Structure, and the Onset of the Mexican Revolution," *Politics and Society* 5: 417-439.
1976 "Inequality and Revolution in Rural Mexico," *Social and Economic Studies* 25: 397-410.

Gonzalez Casanova, Pablo
1970 *Democracy in Mexico,* 2d ed. New York.
Hansen, Roger D.
1971 *The Politics of Mexican Development.* Baltimore: Johns Hopkins University Press.
Hanson, Simon
1938 *Utopia in Uruguay.* New York: Oxford University Press.
Haring, Clarence H.
1931 "Chilean Politics, 1920-1928," *HAHR* 11: 1-26.
Hicks, John R.
1959 *Essays in World Economics.* Oxford: Clarendon Press.
Hill, T. P.
1964 "Growth and Investment According to International Comparisons," *Economic Journal* 74.
Hirschman, Albert O.
1968 "The Political Economy of Import-Substituting Industrialization in Latin America," *Quarterly Journal of Economics* 82: 2-32.
Hoselitz, Bert F.
1955 "Generative and Parasitic Cities," *Economic Development and Cultural Change.*
Johnson, Harry G.
1967 *Economic Policies Toward Less Developed Countries.* Washington, D.C.: Brookings Institution.
Johnson, John J.
1958 *Political Change in Latin America: The Emergence of the Middle Sectors.* Stanford, Calif.: Stanford University Press.
Kerr, C., Dunlop, J. T., Harbison, F. H., and Myers, C. A.
1960 *Industrialism and Industrial Man.* Cambridge, Mass.: Harvard University Press.
Kirsch, Henry W.
1977 *Industrial Development in a Traditional Society: The Conflict of Entrepreneurship and Modernization in Chile.* Gainsville, Fla.: University of Florida Press.
Latin American Perspectives
1975 "Mexico: The Limits of State Capitalism," Vol. 2, 2.
Leff, Nathaniel
1968 *Brazilian Capital Goods Industry, 1929-1964.* Cambridge, Mass.: Harvard University Press.
Lindahl, Goran G.
1962 *Uruguay's New Path: A Study in Politics during the First Colegiado, 1919-33.* Stockholm:
Lowe, Adolph
1952 "A Structural Model of Production," *Social Research,* 135-176.
1955 "Structural Analysis of Real Capital Formation," in National Bureau of Economic Research, *Capital Formation and Economic Growth.* Princeton, N.J.: Princeton University Press.

McGreevy, William P.
1971 *An Economic History of Colombia, 1845-1930.* Cambridge: Cambridge University Press.
Mamalakis, Markos
1976 *The Growth and Structure of the Chilean Economy: From Independence to Allende.* New Haven, Conn.: Yale University Press.
Marx, Karl
1848 "The Bourgeoisie and the Counter-Revolution," in Marx and Engels, *Selected Works in Two Volumes.* Moscow: Foreign Languages Printing House, 1958.
1852 "The Eighteenth Brumaire of Louis Bonaparte," in Marx and Engels, *Selected Works in Two Volumes.* Moscow: Foreign Languages Printing House, 1958.
1857-1858 *Grundrisse,* ed. and trs. M. Nicolaus. New York: McGraw-Hill.
1867 *Capital,* Vol. 1. Reprint ed., Moscow: Progress Publishers, 1965.
1894 *Capital,* Vol. 3. Reprint ed., Moscow: Progress Publishers, 1965.
Mattoon, Robert H., Jr.
1977 "Railroads, Coffee, and the Growth of Big Business in São Paulo, Brazil," *HAHR* 57: 273-296.
Merhav, Meir
1969 *Technological Dependence, Monopoly, and Growth.* Oxford: Pergamon Press.
Miliband, Ralph
1969 *The State in Capitalist Society.* New York: Basic Books.
Mills, C. Wright
1953 *White Collar.* New York: Oxford University Press.
Moneta, Carmellah
1959 "The Estimation of Transportation Costs in International Trade," *Journal of Political Economy* 47.
Morris, James O.
1966 *Elites, Intellectuals and Consensus, A Study of the Social Question and the Industrial Relations System in Chile.* Ithaca, N.Y.: N.Y. State School of Industrial and Labor Relations, Cornell University.
Morse, Richard M.
1971 "Trends and Issues in Latin American Urban Research, 1965-1970," *Latin American Research Review* 6: Part 1 in no. 1 (Spring), 3-52; Part 2 in no. 2 (Summer), 19-75.
Muñoz, Oscar E.
1968 "An Essay on the Process of Industrialization in Chile Since 1914," *Yale Economic Essays* 8: 135-184.
Nachman, Robert S.
1977 "Positivism, Modernization, and the Middle Class in Brazil," *HAHR* 57: 1-23.
North, Douglass
1955 "Location Theory and Regional Economic Growth," *Journal of Political Economy* 63, reprinted in J. Friedman & W. Alonso (eds.),

Regional Development and Planning. Cambridge, Mass.: M.I.T. Press, 1964.

Nun, Jose
1968 "A Latin American Phenomenon: The Middle-Class Military Coup," in J. Petras & M. Zeitlin (eds.), Greenwich, Conn.: Fawcett.

Nunn, Frederick M.
1970 *Chilean Politics, 1920-1931: The Honorable Mission of the Armed Forces.* Albuquerque, N.M.: University of New Mexico Press.

Payne, James L.
1965 *Labor and Politics in Peru.* New Haven, Conn.: Yale University Press.

Petras, James
1969 *Politics and Social Forces in Chilean Development.* Berkeley: University of California Press.
1970 "The Middle Class in Latin America," in his *Politics and Social Structure in Latin America.* New York: Monthly Review Press.

Pike, Frederick B.
1963 *Chile and the United States, 1880-1962.* South Bend, Ind.: University of Notre Dame Press.

Pinto Santa Cruz, Aníbal
1962 *Chile, un caso de desarrollo frustrado.* Santiago: Editorial Universitaria.

Poblete Tronosco, Moíses and Burnett, Ben G.
1960 *The Rise of the Latin American Labor Movement.* New York: Bookman Associates.

Randall, Laura
1977 *An Economic History of Argentina in the Twentieth Century.* New York: Columbia University Press.

Reynolds, Clark W.
1970 *The Mexican Economy: Twentieth Century Structure and Growth.* New Haven, Conn.: Yale University Press.

Rippy, J. Fred
1931 *The Capitalists and Colombia.* New York: Vanguard Press.

Romero, Emilio
1967 *Historia Económica del Perú,* 2d ed., Vol. 2. Lima: Editorial Universo.

Romero, Jose L.
1963 *A History of Argentine Political Thought.* Stanford, Calif.: Stanford University Press.

Rosenberg, Nathan
1963a "Capital Goods, Technology, and Economic Growth," *Oxford Economic Papers,* new series, 15: 217-227.
1963b "Technological Change in the Machine Tool Industry, 1840-1910," *Journal of Economic History* 23.
1972 *Technology and American Economic Growth.* New York: Harper & Row.

Ross, Stanley R. (ed.)
1966 *Is the Mexican Revolution Dead?* New York: Knopf.
Scobie, James
1971 *Argentina: A City and a Nation,* 2d ed. New York: Oxford University Press.
Smith, Robert F.
1972 *The United States and Revolutionary Nationalism in Mexico, 1916-1932.* Chicago: University of Chicago Press.
Spalding, Hobart
1977 *Organized Labor in Latin America.* New York: New York University Press.
Stein, Stanley J.
1957 *The Brazilian Cotton Manufacture; Textile Enterprise in an Underdeveloped Area, 1850-1950.* Cambridge, Mass.: Harvard University Press.
Stigler, George
1951 "Specialization is Limited by the Extent of the Market," *Journal of Political Economy,* 185-193.
Teixeira Vieira, Dorival
1951 "The Industrialization of Brazil," in T. L. Smith & A. Morchant (eds.), *Brazil: Portrait of Half a Continent.* New York: Dryden Press.
Thorp, Rosemary and Bertram, Geoffrey
1978 *Peru 1890-1977: Growth and Politics in an Open Economy.* New York: Columbia University Press.
United Nations Economic Commission for Latin America
1966 *The Process of Industrial Development in Latin America.* New York: United Nations.
Urrutia, Miguel
1969 *The Development of the Colombian Labor Movement.* New Haven, Conn.: Yale University Press.
Veliz, Claudio
1965 "Introduction", in C. Veliz (ed.), *Obstacles to Change in Latin America.* London: Oxford University Press for the Royal Institute of International Affairs.
Wolf, Eric
1969 *Peasant Wars of the Twentieth Century.* New York: Harper & Row.
Womack, John
1969 *Zapata and the Mexican Revolution.* New York: Knopf.
Wythe, George
1949 *Industry in Latin America.* 2d ed. New York: Columbia University Press.

CHAPTER 6. DEPRESSION, WAR, AND INDUSTRIAL EXPANSION, 1930-1945

Alexander, Robert J.
1962 *Labor Relations in Argentina, Brazil, and Chile.* New York: McGraw-Hill.

Angell, Alan
1972 *Politics and the Labour Movement in Chile.* London: Oxford University Press.

Baer, Werner
1979 *The Brazilian Economy: Its Growth and Development.* Columbus, Ohio: Grid Publishing Co.

Baily, Samuel L.
1967 *Labor, Nationalism, and Politics in Argentina.* New Brunswick, N.J.: Rutgers University Press.

Ballasteros, Martos and Davis, Tom E.
1963 "The Growth of Output and Employment in Basic Sectors of the Chilean Economy, 1908-1957," *Economic Development and Cultural Change* 11: 152-176.

Barager, Joseph R. (ed.)
1968 *Why Perón Came to Power: The Background to Peronism in Latin America.* New York: Borzoi.

Benvenuto, Luis C.
1967 *Breve historia del Uruguay: Economía y sociedad.* Buenos Aires: Eudeba Editorial Universitaria.

Bonilla, Frank
1964 "The Urban Worker," in J. J. Johnson (ed.), *Continuity and Change in Latin America.* Stanford, Calif.: Stanford University Press.

Braverman, Harry
1974 *Labor and Monopoly Capital: The Degradation of Work in the Twentieth Century.* New York: Monthly Review Press.

Cavarozzi, Marcelo J. and Petras, James F.
1974 "Chile," in *Latin America: The Struggle with Dependency and Beyond.* Cambridge, Mass.: Schenkman.

Ciria, Alberto
1974 *Parties and Power in Modern Argentina, 1930-1946.* Albany, N.Y.: State University of New York Press.

Cline, William R.
1972 *Potential Effects of Income Redistribution on Economic Growth: Latin American Cases.* New York: Praeger.

Corradi, Juan E.
1974 "Argentina," in *Latin America: The Struggle with Dependency and Beyond.* Cambridge, Mass.: Schenkman.

Dean, Warren
1969 *The Industrialization of São Paulo, 1880-1945.* Austin, Tex.: University of Texas Press.

Diaz Alejandro, Carlos F.
1970 *Essays on the Economic History of the Argentine Republic.* New Haven, Conn.: Yale University Press.

dos Santos, Theotonio
1974 "Brazil," in *Latin America: The Struggle with Dependency and Beyond.* Cambridge, Mass.: Schenkman.

Duggert, M.
1975 "Marx on Peasants," *Journal of Peasant Studies* 2: 159-182.
Edwards, Richard C.
1979 *Contested Terrain: The Transformation of the Workplace in the Twentieth Century*. New York: Basic Books.
Ellsworth, P. T.
1945 *Chile: An Economy in Transition*. New York: Macmillan.
Erickson, Kenneth P.
1977 *The Brazilian Corporative State and Working Class Politics*. Berkeley: University of California Press.
Erickson, K. P., Peppe, P. V., and Spalding, H. A.
1974 "Research on the Urban Working Class and Organized Labor in Argentina, Brazil, and Chile: What is Left to be Done?", *Latin American Research Review* 9: 115-142.
Felix, David
1974 "Technological Dualism in Late Industrializers: On Theory, History, and Policy," *Journal of Economic History* 34: 194-238.
Ferrer, Aldo
1967 *The Argentine Economy*. Berkeley: University of California Press.
Fluharty, Vernon Lee
1957 *Dance of the Millions, Military Rule and the Social Revolution in Colombia, 1930-1956*. Pittsburgh, Pa.: University of Pittsburgh Press.
Furtado, Celso
1965 *The Economic Growth of Brazil*, Berkeley: University of California Press.
1976 *Economic Development of Latin America*, 2d ed. Cambridge: Cambridge University Press.
Glade, William P.
1969 *The Latin American Economies*. New York: Van Nostrand.
Gordon, David M.
1972 *Theories of Poverty and Underemployment: Orthodox, Radical, and Dual Labor Market Perspectives*. Lexington, Mass.: D. C. Heath.
Gorz, Andre
1972 "Technical Intelligence and the Capitalist Division of Labor," *Telos* 12: 27-41.
Graham, Richard (ed.)
1969 *A Century of Brazilian History Since 1865: Issues and Problems*. New York: Borzoi.
Hanson, Simon
1938 *Utopia in Uruguay*. New York: Oxford University Press.
Harcourt, G. C.
1972 *Some Cambridge Controversies in the Theory of Capital*. Cambridge: Cambridge University Press.
Hobsbawm, Eric J.
1964 "The Labour Aristocracy in Nineteenth Century Britain," in his *Labouring Men: Studies in the History of Labour*. London: Weidenfeld & Nicolson.

International Bank for Reconstruction and Development
1950 *The Basis of a Development Program for Colombia.* Baltimore: The Johns Hopkins University Press for the IBRD.
Kenworthy, Eldon
1967 "Argentina: The Politics of Late Industrialization," *Foreign Affairs* 45: 463-476.
Kerr, C., Dunlop, J. T., Harbison, F. H., and Myers, C. A.
1960 *Industrialism and Industrial Man.* Cambridge, Mass.: Harvard University Press.
Keynes, John Maynard
1936 *The General Theory of Employment, Interest and Money.* Reprint ed., New York: Harcourt, Brace, 1965.
Kindleberger, Charles
1973 *The World in Depression, 1929-1933.* Berkeley: University of California Press.
Landsberger, Henry A.
1967 "The Labor Elite: Is It Revolutionary?", in S. Lipset and A. Solari (eds.), *Elites in Latin America.* New York: Oxford University Press.
Latin American Perspectives
1974 "Argentina: Peronism and Crisis," 1, no. 3.
League of Nations
1945 *Industrialization and Foreign Trade.* New York: League of Nations.
Leff, Nathaniel
1968 *Brazilian Capital Goods Industry, 1929-1964.* Cambridge, Mass.: Harvard University Press.
Lenin, V. I.
1917 *Imperialism, The Highest Stage of Capitalism.* Reprint ed., Peking: Foreign Languages Press, 1965.
Lewis, W. Arthur
1949 *Economic Survey, 1919-1939.* London: Allen & Unwin.
Lindahl, Goran G.
1962 *Uruguay's New Path: A Study in Politics during the First Cologiado, 1919-33.* Stockholm: Library and Institute of Ibero-American Studies.
Loeb, G. F.
1957 *Industrialization and Balanced Growth: With Special Reference to Brazil.* Groningen, Netherlands: J. B. Wolters.
Lukacs, Georg
1971 "Class Consciousness," in his *History and Class Consciousness: Studies in Marxist Dialectics.* London: Merlin Press.
Mamalakis, Markos
1976 *The Growth and Structure of the Chilean Economy: From Independence to Allende.* New Haven, Conn.: Yale University Press.
Marglin, Stephen A.
1974 "What Do Bosses Do? The Origins and Functions of Hierarchy in Capitalist Production," *Review of Radical Political Economy* 6: 60-112.

Mariátegui, Jose C.
1928 *Seven Interpretive Essays on Peruvian Reality.* Reprint ed., Austin, Tex.: University of Texas Press, 1971.

Meier, Gerald M.
1968 *International Trade and Economic Development,* 2d ed. New York: Harper & Row.

Merhav, Meir
1969 *Technological Dependence, Monopoly, and Growth.* Oxford: Pergamon Press.

Mitrany, David
1961 *Marx Against the Peasant.* New York: Collier Books.

Muñoz, Oscar E.
1968 "An Essay on the Process of Industrialization in Chile Since 1914," *Yale Economic Essays* 8: 135-184.

Nell, Edward J.
1972 "Property and the Means of Production: A Primer on the Cambridge Controversy," *Review of Radical Political Economy* 4: 1-27.

Payne, James L.
1965 *Labor and Politics in Peru.* New Haven, Conn.: Yale University Press.

Pinto Santa Cruz, Aníbal
1962 *Chile, un caso de desarrollo frustrado.* Santiago: Editorial Universitaria.

Potash, Robert A.
1969 *The Army and Politics in Argentina, 1928-1945. Yrigoyen to Perón,* Stanford, Calif.: Stanford University Press.

Randall, Laura
1977 *An Economic History of Argentina in the Twentieth Century.* New York: Columbia University Press.

Romero, Jose L.
1963 *A History of Argentine Political Thought,* Stanford, Calif.: Stanford University Press.

Rosenberg, Nathan
1969 "The Direction of Technological Change: Inducement Mechanisms and Focusing Devices," *Economic Development and Cultural Change* 18: 1-24.

Saul, John S.
1973 "International Corporations, Labor Aristocracies, and Economic Development in Tropical Africa," in G. Arrighi and J. S. Saul (eds.), *Essays on the Political Economy of Africa.* New York: Monthly review Press.

Scherer, F. M.
1970 *Industrial Market Structure and Economic Performance.* Chicago: Rand-McNally.

Scobie, James R.
1971 *Argentina, A City and a Nation,* 2d ed. New York: Oxford University Press.
Silverman, Bertram
1968-1969 "Labor Ideology and Economic Development in the Peronist Epoch," *Studies in Comparative International Development* 4.
Silverman, Bertram and Yanowitch, Murray (eds.)
1974 *The Workers in "Post-Industrial" Capitalism.* New York: Free Press.
Skidmore, Thomas
1967 *Politics in Brazil, 1930-1964.* New York: Oxford University Press.
Spalding, Hobart
1977 *Organized Labor in Latin America.* New York: New York University Press.
Sweezy, Paul
1942 *The Theory of Capitalist Development.* Reprint ed., New York: Monthly Review Press, 1967.
Thorp, Rosemary and Bertram, Geoffrey
1978 *Peru 1890-1970: Growth and Politics in an Open Economy.* New York: Columbia University Press.
Touraine, Alain and Pecaut, Daniel
1970 "Working-class Consciousness and Economic Development in Latin America," in I. L. Horowitz (ed.), *Masses in Latin America.* New York: Oxford University Press.
United Nations Department of Economic and Social Affairs
1955 *Foreign Capital in Latin America.* New York: United Nations.
United Nations Economic Commission for Latin America
1951 *Economic Survey of Latin America, 1949.* New York: United Nations.
1965 *External Financing in Latin America.* New York: United Nations.
1968 *Economic Development and Income Distribution in Argentina.* New York: United Nations.
Urrutia, Miguel
1969 *The Development of the Colombian Labor Movement.* New Haven, Conn.: Yale University Press.
Weeks, John
1972 "Employment, Growth, and Foreign Domination in Underdeveloped Countries," *Review of Radical Political Economy,* 4: 59-70.
White, Lawrence
1978 "The Evidence on Appropriate Factor Proportions for Manufacturing in Less Developed Countries: A Survey," *Economic Development and Cultural Change* 27: 27-59.
Wilkins, Mira
1974 *The Maturing of Multinational Enterprise.* Cambridge, Mass.: Harvard University Press.
Wirth, John D.
1970 *The Politics of Brazilian Development 1930-1954.* Stanford, Calif.: Stanford University Press.

CHAPTER 7. THE GROWTH AND STRUCTURE OF SOUTH AMERICAN INDUSTRY, 1945 TO THE PRESENT

Altimir, O., Santamaría, H., Sourrouille, J.
1967 "Los instrumentos de promoción industrial en la postguerra," *Desarrollo económico* 6: 709-734.

Angell, Alan
1972 *Politics and the Labor Movement in Chile.* London: Oxford University Press.

Averitt, Robert T.
1962 *The Dual Economy.* New York: Norton.

Baer, Werner
1962 "The Economics of Prebisch and ECLA," *Economic Development and Cultural Change* 10: 169-182.
1979 *The Brazilian Economy: Its Growth and Development.* Columbus, Ohio: Grid Publishing Co.

Bain, Joe S.
1966 *International Differences in Industrial Structure.* New Haven, Conn.: Yale University Press.
1968 *Industrial Organization,* second edition. New York: Wiley.

Baran, Paul and Sweezy, Paul
1966 *Monopoly Capital.* New York: Monthly Review Press.

Barnett, Richard J. and Muller, Ronald E.
1974 *Global Reach: The Power of the Multinational Corporations.* New York: Simon & Schuster.

Baumol, William J.
1967 "Macroeconomics of Unbalanced Growth: The Anatomy of Urban Crisis," *American Economic Review* 57: 415-426.

Blakemore, Harold and Smith, Clifford T.
1971 *Latin America: Geographical Perspectives.* London: Methuen.

Bodenheimer, Suzanne
1971 "Dependency and Imperialism: The Roots of Latin American Underdevelopment," *Politics and Society* 1: 327-357.

Bottomley, Anthony
1965 "Imperfect Competition in the Industrialization of Ecuador," *Inter-American Economic Affairs* 19: 83-94.

Bowles, Samuel and Gintis, Herbert
1976 *Schooling in Capitalist America: Educational Reform and the Contradictions of Economic Life.* New York: Basic Books.

Braverman, Harry
1974 *Labor and Monopoly Capital: The Degradation of Work in the Twentieth Century.* New York: Monthly Review Press.

Cardoso, Fernando H.
1977 "The Originality of a Copy: CEPAL and the Idea of Development," *CEPAL Review,* second half: 7-40.

Carlos de Pablo, Juan
1977 "Un analisis sectorial de la distribución funcional del ingreso," *Desarrollo económico* 16: 555-570.

Caves, Richard E.
1971 "International Corporations: The Industrial Economics of Foreign Investment," *Economica* 38: 1-27.
1974 "Multinational Firms, Competition, and Productivity in Host-Country Markets," *Economica* 41: 176-193.

Chilcote, Ronald and Edelstein, Joel
1974 "Introduction", in Chilcote and Edelstein (eds.), *Latin America: The Struggle with Dependency and Beyond.* New York: Schenkman.

Clark, Colin
1957 *The Conditions of Economic Progress,* second edition. London: Macmillan.

Cline, William R.
1972 *Potential Effects of Income Redistribution on Economic Growth: Latin American Cases.* New York: Praeger Publishers.

Collins, Randall
1971 "Functional and Conflict Theories of Educational Stratification," *American Sociological Review* 36: 1002-1019.

Crozier, Michel; Huntington, Samuel P.; Watanuki, Joji
1975 *The Crisis of Democracy, Report on the Governability of Democracies to the Trilateral Commission.* New York: New York University Press.

de Imaz, Jose L.
1970 *Los Que Mandan (Those Who Rule).* Albany, N.Y.: State University of New York Press.

Diaz Alejando, Carlos F.
1970 *Essays on the Economic History of the Argentine Republic.* New Haven, Conn.: Yale University Press.

dos Santos, Theotonio
1970 "The Structure of Dependency," *American Economic Review, Papers and Proceedings* 60: 231-236.
1974 "Brazil", in R. Chilcote and J. Edelstein (eds.), *Latin America: The Struggle with Dependency and Beyond.* New York: Schenkman.

Dye, David R. and de Souza e Silva, Carlos Eduardo
1979 "A Perspective on the Brazilian State," *Latin American Research Review* 14: 81-98.

Edwards, Richard
1979 *Contested Terrain: The Transformation of the Workplace in the Twentieth Century.* New York: Basic Books.

Emmanuel, Arghiri
1974 "Myths of Development and Myths of Underdevelopment," *New Left Review* 85: 61-82.
1976 "The Multinational Corporations and Inequality of Development," *International Social Science Journal* 28: 754-772.

Erickson, Kenneth P.
1977 *The Brazilian Corporative State and Working Class Politics.* Berkeley: University of California Press.
Espinoza, John G. and Zimbalist, Andrew S.
1978 *Economic Democracy: Workers' Participation in Chilean Industry.* New York: Academic Press.
Evans, Peter
1974 "The Military, the Multinationals, and the 'Miracle': the Political Economy of the 'Brazilian Model' of Development," *Studies in Comparative International Development* 9: 26-45.
Felix, David
1968 "The Dilemma of Import Substitution–Argentina", in G. Ranis (ed.), *Development Policy–Theory and Practice.* Cambridge, Mass.: Harvard University Press.
Flanders, M. June
1964 "Prebisch on Protectionism: An Evaluation," *Economic Journal* 74: 305-326.
Flanders, M. June and Baer, Werner
1964 "The Economics of Prebisch and ECLA: an Exchange," *Economic Development and Cultural Change* 12: 312-315.
Flynn, Peter
1974 "Brazil: Authoritarian and Class Control," *Journal of Latin American Studies* 6: 315-333.
Frank, Andre G.
1969a *Capitalism and Underdevelopment in Latin America.* New York: Monthly Review Press.
1969b *Latin America: Underdevelopment or Revolution.* New York: Monthly Review Press.
Friedman, Milton
1962 *Capitalism and Freedom.* Chicago: University of Chicago Press.
Furtado, Celso
1973 "The Post-1964 Brazilian 'Model' of Development," *Studies in Comparative International Development* 8: 115-127.
Gall, Norman
1977 "The Rise of Brazil," *Commentary* 63: 45-55.
Georgescu-Roegen, Nicholas
1970 "Structural Inflation-Lock and Balanced Growth," *Economies et Sociétés* 4: 557-605.
Gilbert, Alan
1974 *Latin America: A Geographical Perspective.* Baltimore: Penguin Books.
Goetz, Arturo Luis
1976 "Concentración y desconcentración en la indústria argentina desde la década de 1930 a la de 1960," *Desarrolla econòmico* 15: 507-548.
Gordon, David M.
1972 *Theories of Poverty and Underemployment: Orthodox, Radical, and Dual Labor Market Perspectives.* Lexington, Mass.: D. C. Heath.

Gough, Ian
1973 "Marx's Theory of Productive and Unproductive Labor," *New Left Review* 79: 47-72.

Gregory, Peter
1974 "Wage Structures in Latin America," *Journal of Developing Areas* 8: 557-579.

Gustafson, W. Eric
1962 "Research and Development, New Products and Productivity Change," *American Economic Review* 52.

Hirschman, Albert O.
1961 "Ideologies of Economic Development in Latin America," Reprinted in his *Bias for Hope: Essays on Development and Latin America.* New Haven, Conn.: Yale University Press, 1971.
1968 "The Political Economy of Import-Substituting Industrialization in Latin America," Reprinted in his *Bias for Hope.* New Haven, Conn.: Yale University Press, 1971.

Horvat, Branco
1969 *An Essay on Yugoslav Society.* White Plains, N.Y.: International Arts and Science Press.

Hymer, Stephen H.
1960 *"International Operations of National Firms—A Study of Direct Foreign Investment."* Ph.D. dissertation, Massachusetts Institute of Technology.

Ingles, Jerry L. and Fairchild, Loretta
1977 "Evaluating the Impact of Foreign Investment: Methodology and the Evidence from Mexico, Colombia, and Brazil," *Latin American Research Review* 12: 57-70.

Interamerican Development Bank
1974 *Economic and Social Progress in Latin America, 1974 Report.* Washington, D.C.
1975 *Economic and Social Progress in Latin America, 1975 Report.* Washington, D.C.
1976 *Economic and Social Progress in Latin America, 1976 Report.* Washington, D.C.

Katz, Jorge M.
1969 *Production Functions, Foreign Investment, and Growth.* Amsterdam: North Holland Publishing Co.
1972 *Importación de tecnología, Aprendizaje Local e Industriatigación Dependiente.* Buenos Aires: Institute Torcuato di Tella.

Lagos E., Ricardo
1962 *La concentración del poder económico. Su Teoría. Su Realidad Chilena.* Santiago del Chile: Editorial del Pacífico.
1966 "Industry in Chile: Some Structural Factors," Ph.D. dissertation, Duke University.

Lall, Sanjaya
1979 "Transfer Pricing and Developing Countries: Some Problems of Investigation," *World Development* 7: 59-71.

Latin American Perspectives
1974 "Chile: Blood on the Peaceful Road," 1, no. 2.
1975 "Confronting Theory and Practice," 2, no. 1.
1976 "Imperialism and the Working Class in Latin America," 3, no. 1.
1977 "Population and Imperialism; Women in Revolution," 4, no. 4.

Leeds, Anthony
1977 "Brazil as a System," University of Massachusetts, Amherst, Program in Latin American Studies, Occasional Papers Series No. 5.

Leff, Nathaniel H.
1974 "El espíritu de empresa y la organización industrial en los países menos desarrollados: los 'Grupos'," *Trimestre económico* 41: 521-541.

Letelier, Orlando
1976 "Economic 'Freedom's' Awful Toll: The 'Chicago Boys' in Chile," *Review of Radical Political Economics* 8: 44-52.

Loveman, Brian
1979 "Chile After 1970," *Latin American Research Review* 14: 284-286.

Lustig, Nora
1980 "Underconsumption in Latin American Thought: Some Considera tions," *Review of Radical Political Economy* 12: 35-42.

Marini, Rui Mauro
1972 "Brazilian Subimperialism," *Monthly Review* 23: 14-24.

Martins, Carlos E.
1974 "Brazil and the U.S. from the 1960s to the 1970s," in J. Cotler & R. Fagen (eds.), *Latin America and the U.S.: Changing Political Realities.* Stanford, Calif.: Stanford University Press.

Marx, Karl
1852 *The Eighteenth Brumaire of Louis Bonaparte.* Reprint ed., New York: International Publishers, 1963.

Mendes de Almeida, Angela and Lowry, Michael
1976 "Union Structure and Labor Organizations in Contemporary Brazil," *Latin American Perspectives* 3: 98-119.

Mendonca de Barros, Jose R. and Graham, Douglas H.
1978 "The Brazilian Economic Miracle Revisited: Private and Public Sector Initiative in a Market Economy," *Latin American Research Review* 13: 5-38.

Menshikov, S.
1969 *Millionaires and Managers.* Moscow: Progress Publishers.

Merhav, Meir
1969 *Technological Dependence, Monopoly, and Growth.* Oxford: Pergamon Press.

Mesa Lago, Carmelo
1978 *Social Security in Latin America: Pressure Groups, Stratification, and Inequality.* Pittsburgh, Pa.: University of Pittsburgh Press.

Moran, Theodore H.
1973 "Foreign Expansion as an 'Institutional Necessity' for U.S. Corpo-

rate Capitalism: The Search for a Radical Model," *World Politics* 25: 369-386.

Morley, Samuel A. and Williamson, Jeffrey G.
1974 "Demand, Distribution, and Employment: The Case of Brazil," *Economic Development and Cultural Change* 23: 33-60.

Nicolaus, Martin
1967 "Proletariat and Middle Class in Marx," *Studies on the Left,* 7: 18-41.

Nunn, Frederick M.
1979 "Chile Since 1973: Historical and Political Perspectives," *Latin American Research Review,* 14: 287-294.

O'Conner, James
1973 *The Fiscal Crisis of the State.* New York: St. Martin's.

Odell, P. R. and Preston, D. A.
1973 *Economies and Societies in Latin America: A Geographical Interpretation.* New York: Wiley.

Pellicer de Brody, Olga
1974 "Mexico in the 1970s and Its Relations with the United States," in *Latin America and the United States: Changing Political Realities.* Stanford, Calif.: Stanford University Press.

Perloff, Harvey and Wingo, Lowden
1961 "Natural Resource Endowment and Regional Economic Growth," reprinted in J. Friedman & W. Alonso (eds.), *Regional Development and Planning.* Cambridge, Mass.: MIT Press, 1964.

Pike, Frederick B.
1963 "Aspects of Class Relations in Chile, 1850-1960," *HAHR* 43: 14-33.

Quijano Obregón, Aníbal
1974 "Imperialism and International Relations in Latin America," in J. Cotter & R. Fagen (eds.), *Latin America and the United States: Changing Political Realities.* Stanford, Calif.: Stanford University Press.

Quintana, Carlos (ed.)
1970 *Development Problems in Latin America.* Austin, Tex.: University of Texas Press.

Ramos, Joseph R.
1970 *Labor and Development in Latin America.* New York: Columbia University Press.

Randall, Laura
1977 "Income Distribution and Investment in Argentina," *Latin American Research Review* 12: 136-153.

Robock, Stefan H.
1970 "Industrialization Through Import Substitution and Export Industries: A False Dichotomy, " in J. W. Markham & G. Papanek (eds.), *Industrial Organization and Economic Development.* Cambridge, Mass.: Harvard University Press.

Roett, Riordan (ed.)
1976 *Brazil in the Seventies.* Washington, D.C.: American Enterprise Institute.

Roxborough, Ian; O'Brian, Phil; Roddick, Jackie
1977

Scherer, F. M.
1970 *Industrial Market Structure and Economic Performance.* Chicago: Rand-McNally.

Seers, Dudley
1963 "Big Companies and Small Countries," *Kyklos* 16: 599-607.

Silverman, Bertram and Yanowitch, Murray (eds.)
1974 *The Workers in "Post-Industrial" Capitalism.* New York: Free Press

Smith, Adam
1776 *An Inquiry into the Nature and Causes of the Wealth of Nations.* Reprint ed., New York: Modern Library, 1937.

Souza, Paulo R.
1978 "Wage Disparities in the Urban Labor Market," *CEPAL Review* First Half: 199-224.

Spence, Jack
1978 "Class Mobilization and Conflict in Allende's Chile," *Politics & Society* 8: 131-164.

Stepan, Alfred (ed.)
1973 *Authoritarian Brazil: Origin, Policies, and Future.* New Haven, Conn.: Yale University Press.

Stewart, Frances
1978 "Inequality, Technology and Payments Systems," *World Development* 6: 275-293.

Street, James H.
1977 "The Internal Frontier and Technological Progress in Latin America," *Latin American Research Review* 12: 25-56.

Tyler, William G.
1976 "Brazilian Industrialization and Industrial Policies: A Survey," *World Development* 4: 863-882.

United Nations Economic Commission for Latin America
1956 *Economic Survey of Latin America, 1955.* New York: United Nations.
1957 *Analyses and Projections of Economic Development, III, The Economic Development of Colombia.* Geneva: United Nations.
1959 *El desarrollo económico de Argentina.* Mexico, D.F.: United Nations.
1966 *The Process of Industrialization in Latin America, Statistical Annex.* New York: United Nations.
1969 *Economic Development and Income Distribution in Argentina.* New York: United Nations.
1972 *Economic Survey of Latin America, 1970.* New York: United Nations.
1977 *Economic Survey of Latin America, 1976.* Santiago, Chile.

U.S. Department of Commerce
1974 "Sales by Majority–Owned Affiliates of U.S. Companies, 1966-

1972," *Survey of Current Business* 54: 25-40.

Vernon, Raymond
1966 "International Investment and International Trade in the Product Cycle," *Quarterly Journal of Economics* 80: 190-207.

Weaver, Frederick Stirton
1970 "Backwash, Spread, and the Chilean State," *Studies in Comparative International Development* 5: 239-251.

Wilkins, Mira
1974 *The Maturing of Multinational Enterprise.* Cambridge, Mass.: Harvard University Press.

White, Lawrence J.
1974 *Industrial Concentration and Economic Power in Pakistan.* Princeton, N.J.: Princeton University Press.

Zeitlin, Maurice, *et al.*
1974 "New Princes for Old? The Large Corporation and the Capitalist Class in Chile," *American Journal of Sociology* 80: 87-123.

CHAPTER 8. CONCLUSIONS

Baer, Werner and Kerstenetzky, Isaac (eds.)
1964 *Inflation and Growth in Latin America.* New Haven, Conn.: Yale University Press.

Brenner, Robert
1977 "The Origin of Capitalist Development: A Critique of Neo-Smithian Marxism," *New Left Review* no. 104: 116-192.

Cassen, Robert H.
1976 "Population and Development: A Survey," *World Development* 4: 785-830.

Crozier, Michel, *et al.*
1975 *The Crisis of Democracy: Report on the Governability of Democracies to the Trilateral Commission.* New York: New York University Press.

Davis, Tom E.
1963 "Eight Decades of Inflation in Chile, 1879-1959, A Political Interpretation," *Journal of Political Economy* 71: 389-397.

Fei, John C. and Ranis, G.
1964 *Development of the Labor Surplus Economy: Theory and Practice.* Homewood, Ill.: Irwin.

Foster-Carter, Aidan
1978 "The Modes of Production Controversy," *New Left Review* 107: 47-78.

Furtado, Celso
1976 *Obstacles to Development in Latin America.* 2d ed. New York: Anchor Books.

Gerschenkron, Alexander
1966 *Economic Backwardness in Historical Perspective.* Cambridge, Mass.: Harvard University Press.

Gonzalez, Alfonso
1974 "Some Effects of Population Growth on Latin America's Economy," in D. B. Heath (ed.), *Contemporary Cultures and Societies of Latin America,* 2d ed. New York: Random House.

Johnston, Bruce F.
1970 "Agriculture and Structural Transformation in Developing Countries: A Survey of Research," *Journal of Economic Literature* 8: 369-404.

Johnston, Bruce F. and Kilby, Peter
1975 *Agriculture and Structural Transformation: Economic Studies in Late Developing Countries.* New York: Oxford University Press.

Kelley, Allen C., *et al.*
1972 *Dualistic Economic Development: Theory and History.* Chicago: University of Chicago Press.

Lambert, Jacques
1967 *Latin America: Social Structures and Political Institutions.* Berkeley, Calif.: University of California Press.

Latin American Perspectives
1977 "Population and Imperialism; Women in Revolution," 4, no. 4.

Lewis, W. Arthur
1954 "Economic Development with Unlimited Supplies of Labor," Reprinted in A. Argawala & S. Singh (eds.), *The Economics of Underdevelopment.* New York: Oxford University Press, 1963.

Malloy, James M.
1970 *Bolivia: The Uncompleted Revolution.* Pittsburgh, Pa.: University of Pittsburgh Press.

Malloy, James M. and Thorn, Richard S. (eds.)
1971 *Beyond the Revolution: Bolivia Since 1952.* Pittsburgh, Pa.: University of Pittsburgh Press.

Marx, Karl
1867 *Capital,* Vol. I. Reprint ed., Moscow: Progress Publishers, 1965.

Mayoraga, Rene Antonio
1978 "National-Popular State, State Capitalism and Military Dictatorship in Bolivia: 1952-1975," *Latin American Perspectives* 5: 89-119.

Moore, Barrington, Jr.
1966 *Social Origins of Dictatorship and Democracy.* Boston: Beacon Press.

Mosely, Hugh
1979 "Monopoly Capitalism and the State: Some Critical Reflections on O'Conner's *Fiscal Crisis of the State,*" *Review of Radical Political Economy* 11: 52-61.

O'Conner, James
1973 *The Fiscal Crisis of the State.* New York: St. Martin's.

Sanchez-Abornoz, Nicolas
1974 *The Population of Latin America.* Berkeley, Calif.: University of California Press.

Stein, Stanley and Stein, Barbara
1970 *The Colonial Heritage of Latin America. Esssys on Economic Dependence in Perspective.* New York: Oxford University Press.
Thorp, Rosemary
1971 "Inflation and the Financing of Economic Development," in *Financing Development in Latin America,* London: Macmillan.
Thorp, Rosemary and Whitehead, Lawrence (eds.)
1979 Inflation and Stabilization in Latin America. New York: Holmes & Meier.
Volk, Steven S.
1975 "Class, Union, Party: The Development of a Revolutionary Union Movement in Bolivia (1905-1952)," *Science and Society* 39: 26-43.
Wachter, Susan M.
1976 *Latin American Inflations.* Lexington, Mass.: D. C. Heath.
Wallerstein, Immanuel
1974 *The Modern World-System: Capitalist Agriculture and the European World-Economy in the Sixteenth Century.* New York: Academic Press.
1979 *The Capitalist World-Economy.* Cambridge: Cambridge University Press.

INDEX